EDI Technical Materials

Energy Investments and the Environment

Selected Topics

A collection of papers prepared for a workshop organized by the Economic Development Institute of the World Bank in October 1990

Edited by

Corazón M. Siddayao

with the assistance of

Lisa A. Griffin

The World Bank
Washington, D. C.

First printing May 1993
Second printing November 1994

The Economic Development Institute (EDI) was established by the World Bank in 1955 to train officials concerned with development planning, policymaking, investment analysis, and project implementation in member developing countries. At present the substance of the EDI's work emphasizes macroeconomic and sectoral economic policy analysis. Through a variety of courses, seminars, and workshops, most of which are given overseas in cooperation with local institutions, the EDI seeks to sharpen analytical skills used in policy analysis and to broaden understanding of the experience of individual countries with economic development. Although the EDI's publications are designed to support its training activities, many are of interest to a much broader audience. EDI materials, including any findings, interpretations, and conclusions, are entirely those of the authors and should not be attributed in any manner to the World Bank, to its affiliated organizations, or to members of its Board of Executive Directors or the countries they represent.

Because of the informality of this series and to make the publication available with the least possible delay, the manuscript has not been edited as fully as would be the case with a more formal document, and the World Bank accepts no responsibility for errors. Some sources cited in this paper may be informal documents that are not readily available.

The complete backlist of publications from the World Bank is shown in the annual *Index of Publications,* which contains an alphabetical title list (with full ordering information) and indexes of subjects, authors, and countries and regions. The latest edition is available free of charge from the Distribution Unit, Office of the Publisher, The World Bank, 1818 H Street, N.W., Washington, D.C. 20433, U.S.A., or from Publications, The World Bank, 66, avenue d'Iéna, 75116 Paris, France.

Corazón M. Siddayao is senior energy economist and Lisa A. Griffin is a consultant in the Finance, Industry, and Energy Division of the World Bank's Economic Development Institute.

Library of Congress Cataloging-in-Publication Data

Energy investments and the environment : a collection of papers
prepared for a workshop organized by the Economic Development
Institute of the World Bank in October 1990 / edited by Corazón M.
Siddayao with the assistance of Lisa A. Griffin.
p. cm. — (EDI technical materials)
Includes bibliographical references (p.).
ISBN 0-8213-2398-9
1. Energy industries—Finance—Congresses. 2. Energy industries—
Environmental aspects—Congresses. 3. Investments—Moral and
ethical aspects—Congresses. I. Siddayao, Corazón M. II. Griffin,
Lisa A., 1962– . III. Economic Development Institute (Washington,
D.C.) IV. Series.
HD9502.A2E5443 1993
333.79'1—dc20 93-9975
CIP

EDI Catalog No. 251/033

Contents

4. Sustainability and the Energy/Environment Connection: Overcoming Institutional Barriers to "Doing the Right Thing"

Morris Miller

5. Indices for a Greenhouse Gas Control Regime: Incorporating Both Efficiency and Equity Goals

Kirk R. Smith, Joel Swisher, Rebekah Kanter, and Dilip R. Ahuja

Foreword

One of the objectives of the Economic Development Institute (EDI) of the World Bank is to enhance the capacity of developing countries to analyze policy alternatives and to design and implement well-conceived development programs.

In keeping with this objective and in the framework of its mandate aimed at increasing its training activities on the subject of the environment, EDI offers seminars addressing the principal questions in the energy sector. These seminars focus on the problems faced by governments (including those related to the environment) and the measures intended to encourage efficiency in consumption, production, and development of energy in a manner that is not detrimental to the environment. These seminars aim to enhance awareness of the analytical tools needed to assist high-level officials in energy ministries and electricity companies. Participants are those who are involved in formulating and recommending demand and supply policies and strategies, and those who provide leadership in requiring or conducting analytical work in energy development and planning enterprises.

The EDI energy program has scheduled several seminars dealing with energy policies and strategies as well as more specific subjects, such as environmental issues associated with energy investments and project evaluation. This volume is a collection of papers commissioned for an English-language workshop on Energy Investments and the Environment held in Washington, D.C. in October 1990. The French version of this collection was used in a French-language workshop with the same title held in Bordeaux, France in June 1991.

Amnon Golan
Director
Economic Development Institute

Preface

This volume contains a collection of papers originally commissioned for an English language Workshop on Energy Investments and the Environment in October 1990 in Washington, D.C.; a French version was used in a French language seminar with the same title held in Bordeaux, France in June 1991.

The basic objective of these one-week seminars, which form an integral part of the Energy Policy and Planning Program of the Economic Development Institute, has been to provide the participants with a basic understanding of the tools and concepts of analysis that would allow them to formulate policy and strategies on the basis of analytical materials provided them by subordinates. The immediate targeted outputs were limited to the following:

(i) to identify and discuss the most important environmental issues relevant to the energy investments developing countries will be making in the foreseeable future;

(ii) to acquire a basic understanding of the analytical skills and methods required to help formulate informed policies that would enhance production and consumption of energy in less environmentally damaging ways; and

(iii) to provide opportunities to the participants to share this understanding with their colleagues in their home countries by providing the appropriate framework and mechanism for doing so.

The longer term targeted output would be (i) the utilization in the participant's home country of the techniques and information introduced in the seminar, and (ii) the provision of extended training activities to fellow nationals or to the region as a result of the exposure and enhanced appreciation gained from the seminar.

These seminars discuss the use of energy and the required investments from a systemic view. Because accounting systems normally include only the direct financial costs of production and consumption of certain goods and services as well as their monetizable benefits, their true social costs and benefits are not reflected in the valuation system. That is, some benefits and costs are "external" to the valuation system in that they accrue to parties other than the immediate buyer and seller, creating a discrepancy ("externalities") between private (immediate) and social (longer term) costs and benefits. By applying basic concepts of choice, scarcity, and value to a longer term view that includes monetary as well as nonmonetary and intertemporal costs and benefits, all recognizable impacts and their implications (i.e. "externalities" in the physical, social, and cultural spheres) can be internalized conceptually and in application. These issues will therefore be so discussed.

The basic approach to protecting the environment in the energy sector is through the efficient use of energy. In making energy investments, the mode of consumption as the objective of the fuel cycle needs to be considered. The environmental implications of certain methods of production and distribution, however, need to be seriously considered as well. Energy efficiency, resource conservation, pollution prevention technologies, and the "polluter pays principle," among others, are management strategies that are among those that are discussed. Also discussed are approaches to correcting incentive and punishment systems to promote efficient environmental management in the energy sector, including "getting the prices right" to improve the basis for making resource efficient and environmentally favorable decisions.

Emphasis is placed on long-term sustainability of resource use and development activity in general, recognizing the interdependence of human activity and ecosphere resilience. By changing the natural environment, energy investments have repercussions on the quantity and quality of human life. Economic growth is still the primary goal of development planning, but the criteria of sustainability will be viewed as ***necessary constraints***. This implies that economic development will be pursued in such a manner that an increase in output and consumption will not seriously impair the availability and quality, including the assimilative capacity, of natural resources over time.

In summary, energy investments imply changes in the physical, social, and economic environment. These changes may affect not only the immediate environment of the investment site, but may extend geographically far beyond national borders, as well as well beyond the lifetimes of the people for whom the investments are intended. In other words, the social costs and benefits of an investment are both short-term and long-term. Furthermore, there are many risks and uncertainties associated with these investments. Proper evaluation and measurement of these costs and benefits as well as an adequate understanding of how risks can be managed are essential first steps to addressing the problem.

It is therefore the purpose of this volume, as it has been of the seminars, to enhance an understanding and awareness of the analytical and policy tools as well as the policy strategies required to address these issues. Such understanding and awareness are especially necessary at the decisionmaking level, because the most intractable environmental problems are those that only political or institutional change can correct.

Organization of the Chapters

The first chapter was prepared as a background paper to design the workshop. All of the other chapters were originally commissioned as papers with one specific purpose: each one was to cover in one major reference material topics which were not readily available in published form elsewhere at the time the seminars were held. Hence, this set of papers is not all-inclusive in its coverage of the major topics on this subject. For example, there is no chapter on the environmental aspects of investments in electricity generation or coal use; these topics were adequately covered in the English workshop in a paper prepared and later published separately by the Office of Energy, United States Agency for International Development.

The "greenhouse gas" issue is touched upon in the chapter by Smith et al. with respect to the equity problem. A chapter focusing on related concerns is not included in this volume, in recognition of the multi-faceted environmental issues requiring the more immediate attention of decisionmakers who must make investments in the energy sector.

In the interest of time and in awareness of the existing commitments of the authors, these chapters have also only been slightly revised from their original versions, with changes basically being in the nature of clarification. Certain sections were deleted to reduce the papers to manageable lengths for this type of publication; the original versions are found in their complete form in the Working Paper Series of the Economic Development Institute. The order of presentation takes into account the contents of each chapter and their logical usefulness to a reader. For this reason, because the chapter by Foell et al. on renewables contains a section on energy planning that serves a preparatory value for the succeeding chapters, it immediately follows the introductory chapter.

Summary of the Chapters

Brief summaries of the chapters are provided in this preface for the convenience of the reader.

Chapter I. "Energy Investments and Environmental Implications: Key Issues in Developing Countries," by Corazón M. Siddayao

Energy investments imply changes in the physical, social, and economic environment. Hence, both the short-term and the long-term costs and benefits of these investments must be taken into account. These changes may affect not only the immediate environment of the investment site but may extend geographically far beyond national borders as well as beyond the lifetimes of the people for whom the investments are intended. This chapter reviews the issues relevant to developing countries. General conceptual and polices issues are discussed. Issues about the measurement of costs and benefits (including issues of "sustainability" and the internalization of externalities resulting from environment changes) as well as the role of opportunity costs in deciding a country's energy investment strategies are raised. The macroeconomic and institutional issues relevant to environmental impacts that might be incorporated in energy planning are suggested.

Chapter II. "Environmental Considerations in Renewable Energy Policy Development and Investment Planning," by Wesley K. Foell, Mark E. Hanson, and Collin W. Green

Both descriptive and prescriptive methods are used in this chapter to consider the environmental impacts of renewable energy systems and their related development and investment planning issues. Part I gives both an historical and current perspective of energy planning for renewable energy sources. Part II provides an overview of renewable energy technologies and systems. It begins with a framework (the reference energy network) for the description of the systems, including selected technical, environmental, and economic parameters. This is followed by a discussion of the major sources or technologies, including biomass, hydropower, geothermal, wind, and solar. Part III provides a prescriptive framework for renewable energy planning and investment analysis. It begins with an overview of the institutional setting within which this framework would be applied. This is followed with an exposition of the conceptual foundation of the framework, namely integrated resource planning. Included in this discussion are the main aspects of the framework; among them are characterizations of resource supply, decision criteria, sustainability criteria, approaches to internalization of impacts, and choices of appropriate investment sequences. This part includes a more detailed discussion of the analytical and operational methods for implementation of the analysis. Part IV presents a small number of historical case studies (including both "successes" and "failures") of recent major programs for implementation of renewable energy systems in developing and industrialized countries. These cases are discussed within the context of the frameworks laid out in Parts II and II. The chapter is completed with brief summary remarks and conclusions in Part V.

Chapter III. "Oil, Gas, and the Environment," by Dennis Anderson

This chapter discusses issues of environmental policy in the production and consumption of oil and gas. It considers exploration and production, the transportation of fuels, refining and end-uses in industry and transport, with special reference to developing countries. The issues are wide-ranging, covering leakages, spillages and accidents, and the treatment and control of emissions and effluents. All countries have a wide range of policy instruments at their disposal -- taxation, subsidy, regulation, and public expenditure -- and the appropriate instrument to use tends to vary with the problem at hand; however, it is suggested that the developing countries would gain more from a policy of taxing pollution rather than regulating it in many situations, or by complementing the regulatory approach by pollution taxes when regulation is indeed necessary. Another general issue is the setting of standards: major environmental improvements can often be achieved at a moderate cost, but costs tend to escalate rapidly if standards are set to higher and higher levels, so there will be real trade-offs here for many countries.

Chapter IV. "Sustainability and the Energy-Environment Connection: Overcoming Institutional Barriers to 'Doing the Right Thing'," by Morris Miller

With few exceptions, in both the industrialized and the developing countries, the legislative record, the policy positions take, and the resources committed with respect to almost all key environmental issues have fallen far short of what might have been expected in light of the public's avowed concern about the seriousness of the environmental problem as a life-threatening issue of global proportion. This raises the question: why is it so difficult to do "the right thing" when there appears to be so much public support and so much appears to be at stake? At both national and international policymaking levels, it is important to understand the reasons behind the barriers to action. This chapter focuses on these institutional barriers, but from the special vantage of the energy and environment relationship and of the relationship of each of these to sustainable development. After considering the barriers of inertia, risk aversion, and vested interests, the author considers the questions: what needs to be done and what could be done about overcoming these barriers at different levels of governance?

Chapter V. "Indices for a Greenhouse Gas Control Regime: Incorporating Both Efficiency and Equity Goals," by Kirk R. Smith, Joel Swisher, Rebekah Kanter, and Dilip Ahuja

Regarding indices for a greenhouse gas control regime, this chapter raises the issue of equity and efficiency in determining indicators. Rather than such indicators as income or energy use, which are open ended, it implies the use of thresholds or indicators that actually have fixed ranges, i.e. have a maximum corresponding to achievement of the level of adequacy. Historical trends and data limitations in emissions are considered in this chapter. The questions of who pays to solve the problem and how much are raised, including issues of responsibility vs. ability to pay. It is argued that repayments to natural debt should be proportional to the amounts "borrowed." The appropriate index for establishing responsibility is the one that measures historic emissions integrated over time divided by population integrated over time. As there are several concerns that need to be addressed in any allocation scheme, the primacy given to such criteria as simplicity, equity, efficiency, the perceived ease of reaching agreements, etc., leads to different indices for allocating carbon budgets. The chapter concludes with discussions of two remaining questions: how should resources be divided between vulnerability reduction and net emission reduction? and how would any allocation scheme actually be implemented?

Background on the Seminars and Acknowledgements

Both the English and French seminars were organized and directed by Dr. Corazón M. Siddayao, Senior Energy Economist, Economic Development Institute of the World Bank. The original workshop was attended by senior government officials at the department head level from Africa, Asia, Latin America, the Middle East, and Eastern Europe. This was followed by a replication in French in Bordeaux, France, organized jointly with the Agence de Coopération Culturelle et Technique (ACCT) in Paris [along with its sub-agencies, the Institut de l'Energie des pays ayant en commun l'usage du français (IEPF) in Quebec and the Ecole Internationale de Bordeaux (EIB)]. It was attended by a similar audience from the francophone countries of Northern and Subsaharan Africa.

We would like to thank all those who in one way or the other contributed to the preparation of this volume. In particular we would like to thank the authors for their contributions and the reviewers for their useful comments, as well as Ms. Lisa A. Griffin for her invaluable contribution in the editing, preparation, and processing of the volume for publication.

Needless to say, any shortcomings remain those of the persons principally responsible for this volume. Furthermore, the views expressed in this volume represent those of the authors and do not represent those of the institutions sponsoring this work.

Corazón M. Siddayao

1

Energy Investments and Environmental Implications: Key Policy Issues in Developing Countries

Corazón M. Siddayao
The World Bank

I. Introduction

Energy systems, like all other economic activities, consume resources, disturb the environment, and create waste. Each activity in an energy system fuel cycle has an associated set of environmental impacts and resultant effect on society. In developing countries, in addition to the environmental impacts associated with modern technological developments in the energy system, there are serious environmental problems associated with heavy dependence on fuelwood and other biomass.

In Africa, for example, understanding the economic and environmental issues associated with the demand and supply of fuels for the household sector is a priority issue. Especially so are the long-term problems of deforestation, soil erosion, and food supply arising from current patterns of traditional fuel consumption, and the problems of financing and appropriately pricing substitute supplies, such as kerosene.

Hence, energy policy and planning issues need to be addressed within the framework of a country's economic development goals. They also need to incorporate the microeconomic foundations of macro policies, the interaction of the energy system with the rest of the economy and the environment, and the role of the institutional framework in implementing energy and environment policies.

The environmental and related policy issues associated with energy investments and end-use are related to coal and other fossil fuels in power generation, transmission, and distribution, petroleum product use, renewables, and the climatic aspects of energy use. Investments in the energy sector are made in different stages of the fuel cycle. There are different ways of describing or classifying these stages. For convenience, one may speak of (i) the resource development stage and (ii) the final product stage. The resource development stage would include exploration and development (surveys, drilling, plant siting, and construction), production (production drilling, mining, tree planting, and harvesting), and transportation of the basic energy resource (crude oil, natural gas, coal, geothermal power, fuelwood) to the processing site (refinery, electric power plant, charcoal processor, or firewood seller). The final product stage would include processing or production of the final product (refining, gas processing, electric power production, charcoal production, firewood preparation, manufacture of solar cells) and distributing or marketing the final product (distribution of petroleum products, natural gas, electricity, charcoal, firewood bundles).

The levels of investments differ according to the type of resource and final energy product. In each of these stages, the environment is affected and additional expenditures may be required to address the resulting issues. Furthermore, environmental concerns may require that more energy efficient technology be installed where available.

This chapter will review the issues relevant to developing countries. In the following parts, general conceptional and policies issues will be discussed, issues about the measurement of costs and benefits and the role of opportunity costs in deciding a country's energy investment strategies will be raised, and macroeconomic and institutional issues to incorporate environmental issues in energy planning will be suggested.

II. General Conceptual and Policy Issues: Growth, Energy, and the Ecosystem

It is now recognized that societies can no longer conduct activities as if economics and ecology were two separate spheres. Economics concerns people's choices, and people make energy choices in the process of transforming their living conditions into more satisfying circumstances. In doing so, their choices entail activities that involve intrusions into the ecosystem. Thus, with increased energy use in the course of economic and social development, people's choices affect their physical, chemical, biological, and social-cultural environment.

The relationship between people and nature, or of "environmental management in development," may be viewed from different perspectives. As Colby [1989] puts it, each paradigm about this relationship is driven by different assumptions about human nature and activity, about nature itself, and the interactions between nature and humans. Each paradigm therefore asks different questions and perceives different evidence, dominant threats or risk, and solutions and management strategies in pursuing development objectives.

A. Sustainability and Development

Still, the use of energy and the required investments cannot be seriously examined other than from a systemic view. The process of producing and consuming energy is an economic activity that is a subset of the ecosystem. Biophysical resources (energy, materials, and ecologically processing cycles) flow from the ecosystem into the economy and degraded (non-useful) energy and other by-products (pollution) flow back into the ecosystem. By changing the natural environment, energy investments have repercussions on the quantity and quality of human life. Current policy discussions draw attention to the necessity of placing emphasis on the long-term sustainability[1] of resource use and development activity in general, recognizing the demands human activity place on the ecosystem and the interdependence of human activity and ecosphere resilience. Economic growth is still the primary goal of development planning, but the criteria of sustainability will be viewed as a ***necessary constraint***. This implies that economic development will be pursued in such a manner that an increase in output and consumption will not seriously impair the availability and quality, including the assimilative capacity, of natural resources over time.

B. Environmental Concerns, Energy, and Development

Environmental concerns may appear to be of low priority in many developing nations, where the obvious priority concerns are those related to meeting the more basic problems for survival -- hunger, malnutrition, etc. While recognizing the importance of these needs, there are at the same time many issues essential to addressing these basic concerns in relation to the near-term and long-term sustainability of energy development programs. Governments may view environmental concerns (e.g., pollution and resource degradation) as the concerns of the rich countries and contrary to their needs and interests, that these are more constraining than helpful. In the final analysis, the poor are harmed more by both pollution and resource degradation than are the rich, because they are less better equipped than the rich, financially or technologically, to respond to these negative impacts from production and consumption [see Smith, 1989a]. Thus developing countries cannot ignore environmental issues while striving for economic change.

The demand for energy in developing countries will increase, whatever the dimensions of their development. The extent of that increase will be based on greater use of fossil fuels [for current patterns, see Table 2 in Siddayao, 1991], and the rate of that increase has raised concerns about the severity of the threat to the environment. The oil consumption of the developing countries (which is one-fourth of that in industrialized countries) may seem small, but this consumption is expected to grow much faster in the next decade. Oil consumption in developing countries, for example, was projected in 1988 to rise from 16 million barrels per day (mmb/d) to 24 mmb/d in the year 2000, or at a rate of 2.4 percent [World Bank, 1988b]. The demand for coal is expected to grow at 2.8 percent per annum; this growth is heavily weighted by expansion of coal capacity in the electric power sector [World Bank, 1988a].

Greenhouse gas issues. -- The potential in developing countries for large percentage increases in emissions of greenhouse gases (GHGs) over the next decades has resulted in suggestions that control over such emissions should be considered as part of near-term development planning. It is unrealistic and unreasonable, however, to expect the developing countries to restrain their energy use for development purposes because of concerns in the international community over the trend toward global warming, especially in light of the many uncertainties that surround the nature of the risks themselves and of the accuracy of projections [see, for example, Cox, 1990]. The rate of increase in fossil fuel use in developing countries may be large but the actual increase for individual countries will, in general, still be small compared to the absolute increases that accompany consumption in highly energized industrialized nations.

---

[1]The notion of sustainabilty is associated with a "process of change in which exploitation of resources, the direction of investments, the reorientation of technology development, and institutional change are all in harmony and enhance both current and future potential to meet human needs and aspirations." [World Commission of Environment and Development (WCED), 1987].

The potential damage to the environment may not be comparable to those arising from the accumulated energy-using capital stock in these advanced countries, given the already existing sources of emissions and patterns of industrial emissions of carbon dioxide [see, for example, the patterns for the period 1955-1985 in Figure 1 in Siddayao, 1991]. As Smith [1989a] puts it, just as economies take on a financial debt in order to grow faster, they take on a "natural debt" as they borrow the assimilative capacity of the environment by releasing waste gases faster than they can be removed naturally. In this respect, developed countries are at this point holders of the largest "natural debt."

Developing countries receive advice from many quarters not to replicate the environmentally unsound policies and practices of the industrialized countries. But unless such advice is accompanied by viable alternatives it is not acceptable, if it implies that developing countries should stagnate in the interests of overall environmental protection [see Conable, 1989; Saunders, 1989; and World Bank, 1989b]. In the immediate future they may not have access to the technology that will allow them to shift to processes in the power and transport sector as well as in industries that are less energy intensive or that are relatively more environmentally benign.

Although accepting, for example, that the threat of large percentage increases from developing countries in the emission of GHGs is important enough to warrant changes in present development pathways, Smith [1989a] notes that, on the contrary: (i) the best way to protect the poorest groups is to bring them as soon as possible to a minimum level of development at which they can be expected to adequately handle environmental stress, and (ii) the extra GHG emissions necessary to accomplish this task are minuscule in the global GHG picture and thus will not be critical in determining climate change. Smith further recommends that the best approach for a developing country planner worried about climate change may be to accelerate those aspects of development that will assist their poorest and most vulnerable populations in attaining the levels of health, flexibility, education, and resilience that will allow them to cope with environmental stress of all sorts, including climate change. This may offer a much more effective least-risk development pathway than would one attempting to rank development projects on the basis of greenhouse gases.

In the meantime, developing countries are already being encouraged and are attempting to practice conservation and to use energy more efficiently [see, for example, World Bank, 1989a,b]. This approach is both economically efficient and would help reduce the generation of environmental "bads" into the atmosphere. At the same time, by reducing the demand for fossil fuels, efficient energy use would, in the process, reduce the risks associated with environmentally harmful accidents, such as those that result from the demand for oil, for example. Most lending agencies support the move toward higher generation of energy in developing countries as a corollary of development, accompanied by greater end-use efficiencies. For example, the World Bank has lending programs for conservation and for increased use of renewables. Over the long term, technology would need to be developed and adopted in developing and industrialized countries that would use forms of energy which are less harmful to the environment. [See Conable, 1989.]

Until that goal is met, however, the energy requirements of developing countries will have to be met largely by the use of existing fossil fuels. The choice of fuels then becomes crucial. Expanded use of natural gas, which substantially less carbon dioxide than oil or coal into the atmosphere, will significantly reduce harmful emissions.

C. Internalizing Externalities, Conservation, and Opportunity Costs

The basic approach to protecting the environment in the energy sector is through the efficient use of energy. In making energy investments, the mode of consumption as the objective of the fuel cycle needs to be considered. The environmental implications of certain methods of production and distribution need to be seriously considered as well, however. Energy efficiency, resource conservation, pollution prevention technologies, and the "polluter pays" principle are among the management strategies that are now often discussed in considering environmental issues. So are approaches to correcting incentive and penalty systems (or "carrot and stick" measures) in order to promote efficient environmental management in the energy sector, including "getting the prices right" to improve the basis for making resource efficient and environmentally favorable decisions.

Because accounting systems normally include only the direct financial costs of production and consumption of goods and services as well as their monetizable benefits, their true social costs and benefits are not reflected in the valuation system. That is, some benefits and costs are "external" to the valuation system in that they accrue to parties other than the immediate buyer and seller, creating a discrepancy ("externalities") between private (immediate) and social (longer term) costs and benefits. By applying basic concepts of choice, scarcity, and value to a longer term view that includes monetary as well as nonmonetary and intertemporal costs and benefits, all recognizable impacts and their implications (i.e. "externalities" in the physical, social, cultural, and other spheres) can be internalized conceptually and in application.

Ecosystem processes, rather than just stocks of physical resources, will be considered as resources and capital which should be efficiently used, employing the appropriate technology to ensure effective use and conservation. This notion recognizes the existence of a relationship between man and nature that involves "trade-offs," but it also recognizes that a better accounting of the true values of functioning natural systems to economies is necessary. Essential to this is the application of the concept of marginal opportunity costs, which combines the direct costs of resource use, the externalities arising from ecological linkages, and a user cost component associated with nonsustainable resource use. Formulated in this way, implications arise for shadow pricing exercises, national accounting of externalities, and the choice of sector and geographical areas for project appraisal [see Pearce and Markandaya, 1989].

Corrective measures to internalize externalities are not always easily implemented, nor are they universally effective. Whatever the level of adjustments developing countries adopt, none will be cost-free. The various actions they will have to take in their own interests and in the interest of the international community involve substantial costs. It is not a matter of funds being redirected from one set of development objectives to another but of genuine additional costs. For example, inclusion of the environmental aspect in project and other lending would require additional staff time and increase the costs associated with each project loan, both on the part of the lender and on the part of the borrower responsible for preparing environmental assessments.

Hence, the questions related to the opportunity costs of energy investments are of three forms: (i) short-term, (ii) medium-term, and (iii) long-term. At each stage the social costs of addressing the environmental impacts of energy investments need to be addressed, but the nature of the opportunity costs vary according to the life of the impacts.

III. Evaluating the Economic and Social Opportunity Costs of Environmental Degradation from Energy Investments

Some environmental impacts of the principal energy sources are briefly summarized in the Appendix. A more detailed discussion of some of these impacts is found in Vukina [1989].

Damage to the environment does not happen suddenly. Occasionally one accident will hold the public's sustained attention (e.g., the Exxon Valdez accident), but many environmental insults take a long time to develop. Some of these are known and may be anticipated, but for many others current knowledge may still be inadequate. Little is known overall about the ways in which humanity affects the environment.

Furthermore, environmental issues deal with consequences that are long-term in nature. Benefits may not show up immediately, nor may damages. Undoubtedly the earth is extraordinarily resilient. Undoubtedly, too, the primitive state of understanding of the environment means that some surprises lie in wait. Not all surprises will be beneficial nor will these changes happen gradually, so that there would be plenty of time to adjust.

Notwithstanding these uncertainties, the risk of damage -- especially when assessable -- cannot be ignored in policy and investment planning. But how does one deal with them? Some basic questions need to be asked. What are the risks associated with making a specific energy investment? What approach should be used in evaluating the issues? How does one evaluate the merits of these issues? What is the time frame to be considered? Who benefits and who gets hurt?

For example, some may argue that technological progress will tend to reduce the benefits from energy development projects, such as a hydropower dam, because of the possible emergence of superior electricity generating techniques over time. This assumes a constant rate of progress in hydropower technology. The questions really are: When will the type of technological change occur that will not justify the project? Over what time frame must the evaluation be made?

A. Measuring Benefits and Costs

Evaluation measures of the environmental impacts arising from energy investments and of the economic and social consequences, both short-term and long-term, may take various names and different steps. In the final analysis, however, each rational decisionmaking procedure is a careful consideration of the advantages and disadvantages of an action, whether this be a policy action or an investment. This applies whether this be cost-benefit analysis, cost-effectiveness analysis, risk-benefit analysis, environmental impact assessment, or economic models incorporating environmental parameters. Coverage may differ in scope and specifics, but a comprehensive evaluative analysis would include variables such as political acceptability, legality, income distribution, macroeconomics, socioeconomic effects, in addition to the purely technical aspects of environmental damage or benefit.

On the whole, all decision rules contain the following basic features: (i) they define gains and losses according to some objectives and (ii) they measure the gains and losses. Measurement of such gains and losses involve judgmental weighting and ordering according to some scale of social and political criteria.

Formal cost-benefit analysis essentially asks: If a particular policy option is pursued, what good will come of it, and what will have to be sacrificed to get it? It is a simple extension to ask whether the former is worth the latter. It is basically a question of opportunity costs.

The basic approach to cost-benefit analysis may be summarized as follows [Maler, 1984, pp. 3-4, as summarized in Vukina, 1989]:

(i) The value to an individual of a consequence from a project is the amount he or she is willing to pay for having that consequence in the case of a benefit, or the amount he or she is willing to pay to avoid that consequence in the case of a cost. (This is the concept of opportunity cost.)

(ii) Whenever consequences from a project consist of goods and services bought and sold by consumers at certain prices, these services represent the values that should be used in aggregating those consequences.

(iii) If consumption is rationed, either by disequilibrium in markets (e.g., unemployment) or by government regulations (e.g., foreign exchange controls), the willingness to pay may not be equal to the current market price, and the market prices must be corrected for the disequilibrium (shadow prices).

(iv) If some of the consequences from a project are not valued at all on the market, then special methods have to be developed in order to mimic the market when such consequences are to be measured.

Cost-benefit analysis goes beyond project analysis. It is a useful tool in policy analysis. For example, it can be applied in cases where a target level of environmental quality has to be determined. The problem is defined in terms of determining the optimal environmental quality by maximizing net social benefits. The social value (or stream of social benefits flowing from the project) and costs of the project are identified and estimated over time. With the data determined, the social rate of return must be estimated to determine the present value of the net benefits for each of the alternatives under consideration, and the decision taken that would maximize the present value of net social benefits.

The method for applying cost-benefit analysis to government decisionmaking relative to energy investments is similar to that for private decisions. The social opportunity cost of an energy investment is the value to society of the next best alternative use to which resources that would be employed in that investment would be put. For example, one of the opportunity costs to a nation settling the environmental dispute associated with an offshore petroleum investment may be measured in terms of the next best alternative use of the resources employed in settling the dispute, the cost of consuming an alternative fuel in the short-term or medium-term because of the inaccessibility of the disputed resources, and the costs of arriving at an agreement [see Siddayao, 1978].

Cost-effectiveness analysis is an ex-post type of analysis, i.e. after a decision has already been made to invest, this measure is used to determine the most cost-effective approach to ensuring the rational use of scarce resources. It says nothing about whether the original decision was good or not. ***Multi-criteria analysis*** is an application of cost-benefit analysis to include social and political criteria in the evaluation procedure in addition to economic analysis.

Risk-benefit analysis is really cost-benefit analysis in the context of risky events. Government officials making decisions about risk issues face a difficult problem. The public wants to reduce risks inherent in modern life, but there is a cost to reducing such risks. Risk management refers to the process through which a variety of considerations -- scientific, legal, political, economic (benefits and costs), and even philosophical -- are taken into account, and a decision is reached concerning an environmental issue. This includes provision for human error in performance (e.g., Chernobyl, Three Mile Island). If society is to make the most of its endowments of scarce resources, it should compare what it gains from a risk management policy (that is, benefits) from what it gives up by taking resources from other uses (costs). When society undertakes risk management activities, one assumes that the results are worth more in this sense than what society would forego by diverting resources from other uses.

Environmental impact assessment pays particular attention to the environmental consequences of a policy or action. This type of evaluation may incorporate a cost-benefit analysis within a broader set of terms of reference. This type of assessment allows for objectives other than economic efficiency to be explicitly recognized.

B. Managing Risk

Many of the environmental consequences and the costs of development projects may be either completely irreversible, or reversible only over a very long time scale by human standards. For example, a valley which is flooded for a hydroelectric dam cannot be restored to its original state (assuming, of course, that the original state was desirable). A decision not to construct a hydroelectric plant involves a foregone benefit. The damage avoided by not undertaking its development must be weighed against the benefits which would result from having the project in operation. A "no development" strategy allows for the option to develop it at a later stage, whereas the "development strategy" leaves no option to reverse a damage if one results. This implies that a development strategy should take very careful consideration of all possible consequences from a decision to invest in a project. There may be a point in project planning where the sacrifice of short-term gain is desirable in order to prevent elimination of future options.

Environmental risks cannot be completely avoided. Difficult choices must be made about how best to control particular risks using the limited resources available. These choices involve trade-offs. Economics can help with these decisions by providing information on the pros and cons of particular courses of action. Although some may reduce economics to the science of scarcity, it is in fact the science of choice, given scarcity.

Society is limited in the resources it can allocate to the control of environmental risks. Thus, it is important to think analytically about which risks to control first and how much control to pursue. Trade-offs will be made when these risks are addressed. For example, since the cost of abolishing pollution may rise steeply as it diminishes, one may ask if it may be wiser to get rid only of pollution that clearly does harm. Sometimes it may be worth acting in spite of uncertainty (as with global warming), but the greater the uncertainty, the greater the need to be cost-effective.

At some point, decisionmakers will have to say to themselves that additional risk reductions will be so expensive that they are probably not worth the additional effort and costs, given the other demands on society's limited resources at any given time. Environmental economics makes these decisions explicit. In other words, it forces decisionmakers to say that society can afford or cannot afford to pursue a certain strategy.

Furthermore, the issue of the distributional effects of any decision that is made is important. Cost-benefit analysis is in one sense distributionally neutral. Application of the "polluter pays" principle in the case of acid rain may result in one group of people bearing a heavier share of the total costs of emission control. The project may appear to be sensible economically, but it may not be distributionally or politically acceptable.

There are also qualitative dimensions to risk management. What may appear to be a quantitatively small risk may be perceived to be significant by the public so that decisionmakers may attach a larger weight to it. Where monetary values with respect to a socially sensitive risks are not clear, decisionmakers have to provide a nonmonetary premium to either the costs or the benefit.

IV. Other Issues

A. Macroeconomic Policies, Investments, and the Environment

What implications do energy demand and supply policies, tied to economic development policies, have for investments and, hence, for the environment? For example, taxes and pricing of petroleum products in many developing countries are tied to national revenue and income distribution objectives. In the case of policies promoting the use of diesel fuel, the engineering concept of energy efficiency is a factor in favorably pricing diesel relative to gasoline. These policies -- which result in increased investment in diesel-run vehicles and machinery -- have not, however, incorporated the air pollution impacts and health risks arising from increased diesel fuel use in the measurement of costs and benefits, not to mention the resulting social costs arising from refinery imbalances. [See, for example, the cases in Asia discussed in Siddayao, 1988.]

B. Institutional Policy Issues

Governments in all developing countries recognize the need for informed policy decisions in the energy sector and for developing in-house expertise to provide the framework for arriving at such decisions. The need levels for assistance in achieving this goal vary among regions. How can the policy implications of the environmental impacts of energy investments, be brought to the attention of leaders in developing countries so that these can be incorporated in the policy and institutional framework? How can adequate expertise be developed and sustained to bring about changes in the analytical and planning stages that would lead to incorporation of environmental considerations at the policy formulation level? How can institutional changes be made to deal with this additional input in the development policy process?

Each country faces different socio-economic conditions and must make different trade-offs in balancing environmental concerns and development goals.

V. Summary and Conclusions

In summary, economic development will remain the primary goal of developing countries. This development will require increased energy consumption. Energy investments will need to be made, and these imply changes in the physical, social, and economic environment. These changes may affect not only the immediate environment of the investment site but may extend geographically far beyond national borders as well as well beyond the lifetimes of the people for whom the investments are intended. In other words, the social costs and benefits of an investment are both short-term and long-term. Furthermore, there are many risks and uncertainties associated with these investments. Proper evaluation and measurement of these costs and benefits at different stages of the production and consumption cycle of specific fuels, as well as an adequate understanding of how risks can be managed are essential first steps to addressing the problem. At some point, decisionmakers will have to say to themselves that additional risk reductions will be so expensive that they are probably not worth the additional effort and costs. Decisionmakers must decide whether or not society can or cannot afford to pursue a certain strategy.

The environmental relevance of efficiently producing and consuming energy cannot be overemphasized. Basic understanding and awareness of the analytical and policy tools and strategies required to address these issues are especially necessary at the decisionmaking level, because the most intractable environmental problems are those that only political or institutional change can correct.

References

Colby, Michael E. [1989]. *The Evolution of Paradigms of Environmental Management in Development.* Policy, Planning and Research Working Papers, WPS 313. Washington, D.C.: World Bank.

Conable, Barber [1989]. "Development and the Environment: A Global Balance." *Finance and Development*, vol. 26, no. 4 (December).

Cox, Loren [1990]. "Energy Policy and Global Warming: Using the Imprecise to Deal with the Uncertain." Paper presented at the International Conference of the International Association for Energy Economics, January 4-6, 1990, held in New Delhi, India.

Maler, K. G. [1984]. "Cost-benefit Analysis: The Basic Facts." In Y. J. Ahmad, P. Dasgupta and K. G. Maler (editors), *Environmental Decision-Making, Vol. Two.* London: Hodder and Stoughton.

Pearce, David and Anil Markandya [1989]. "Marginal Opportunity Cost as a Planning Concept in Natural Resource Management." In Gunter Schramm and Jeremy J. Warford (editors), *Environmental Management and Economic Development.* Baltimore, Maryland: The Johns Hopkins University Press (for the World Bank).

Saunders, Robert J. [1989]. "Bank Policy and Operational Options with Regard to Greenhouse Gases and Global Warming." Manuscript (July 19, 1989). Washington, D.C.: World Bank.

Siddayao, Corazón M. [1978, 1980]. *The Offshore Petroleum Resources of Southeast Asia: Some Potential Conflicts and Related Economic Factors.* Kuala Lumpur, Malaysia: Oxford University Press.

Siddayao, Corazón M. [1988]. "Policy and energy use: Asia's adjustment to the changing energy picture." Invited paper for a special developing country issue of *The Energy Journal*, vol. 9. (World Bank Reprint Series No. 444, Washington, D.C.: World Bank, 1989.)

Siddiqi, Toufiq [1989]. "Implications of Climate Change for Energy Policies in Asia." Paper prepared for the Workshop on "Responding to the Threat of Global Warming: Options for the Pacific and Asia," sponsored by the Argonne National Laboratory and the East-West Center, June 17-27, 1989, held in Honolulu, Hawaii.

Smith, Kirk R. [1989a]. "Developing Countries and Climate Change: Implications for Risk Management." Paper presented at the Workshop on "Responding to the Threat of Global Warming: Options for the Pacific and Asia," sponsored by the Argonne National Laboratory and the East-West Center in June 1989. Honolulu, Hawaii: East-West Center.

Smith, Kirk R. [1989b]. "Village Stoves and Climate Change: How Close the Connection?" Draft. Honolulu, Hawaii: East-West Center.

Spiewak, Irving and Alvin M. Weinberg [1985]. "Inherently Safe Reactors." In J. M. Hollander, H. Brooks, and D. Steinlight (editors), *Annual Review of Energy*, vol. 10: 431-462.

Vukina, Tomislav [1989]. "Energy and Environment: Some Key Issues." Draft paper prepared for the Finance, Industry, and Energy Division of the Economic Development Institute. Washington, D.C.: World Bank.

Warford, Jeremy and Zeinab Partow [1989]. "Evolution of the World Bank's Environmental Policy." *Finance and Development*, vol. 26, no. 4 (December): 5-8.

World Bank [1988a]. *Price Prospects for Major Primary Commodities*. Report No. 814/88. Vol. III: Energy, and Metals and Minerals. Washington, D.C.: World Bank.

World Bank [1988b]. *A Visual Overview of the World Oil Markets*. Industry and Energy Department Working Paper, Energy Series Paper No. 8. Washington, D.C.: World Bank.

World Bank [1989a]. *Energy Efficiency Strategy for Developing Countries: The Role of ESMAP*. A Background Paper for Discussion at ESMAP's Annual Meeting, November 27-29, 1989 held in Paris. Washington, D.C.: World Bank.

World Bank [1989b]. *Greenhouse Gases and the Potential for Global Warming: Energy Options for the Developing World and ESMAP's Role*. A Background Paper for Discussion at ESMAP's Annual Meeting, November 27-29, 1989 held in Paris. Washington, D.C.: World Bank.

World Bank [1989c]. *Household/Rural Energy and the Environment: Recent Experience and Prospects*. A Background Paper for Discussion at ESMAP's Annual Meeting, November 27-29, 1989 held in Paris. Washington, D.C.: World Bank.

World Commission of Environment and Development [1987]. *Our Common Future*. Oxford and New York: Oxford University Press.

Appendix

Summary of Environmental Impacts by Energy Source

Some environmental impacts of the principal energy sources are briefly summarized below. A more detailed discussion of some of these impacts are found in a background paper prepared for the Energy Investments and the Environment Workshop by Vukina [1989].

A. Fossil Fuels

Air pollution. -- The combustion of fossil fuels gives rise to a number of airborne effluents, the most important of which are sulfur oxides, nitrogen oxides, carbon monoxide, and carbon dioxide. The quantities of these emissions vary according to the fuel used, its composition, and the measures adopted to reduce emissions.

Air pollution comes in the form of smog, acid pollution, and particulate pollution. By far the most common cause of smog (also called photochemical smog) is automobile emissions (at least 90%). The interaction of the hydrocarbons and nitrogen oxides emitted by automobile exhausts interact in various ways in the presence of ultraviolet radiation, and produce toxic products that affect human health and plant life.

Greenhouse effect. -- Global climate warming is the result of the capacity of certain long-lived atmospheric trace gases [carbon dioxide, chlorofluorocarbons (CFCs), halons, methane, tropospheric zone, and nitrous oxide] to trap some of the radiant heat which the earth emits after receiving solar energy. Because this phenomenon is similar to the capacity of a greenhouse to trap heat, it is commonly referred to as the "greenhouse effect." In particular, carbon dioxide in the atmosphere allows ultraviolet radiation from the sun to pass on to the surface of the earth. It, however, also blocks the infrared radiation from the warmed earth from escaping out of the atmosphere. The earth is habitable because of this radiation differential at some "natural" range. If infrared-induced heating were not present, the atmosphere of the earth would not sustain life as it is known [see Cox, 1989].

Particulate pollution and cooling effect. -- Dust and other light particles (including those emitted from power plants and cars) which remain suspended in the air for prolonged periods can, by reflecting incoming light, reduce the amount of solar radiation reaching the earth, thereby producing a cooling effect. It has thus been suggested that the opposing effects from carbon dioxide and particulate pollution will cancel each other out, resulting in zero net climatic change. There may be some mitigation of climatic effects, but it is unclear if this is really the case.

The more specific impacts are summarized below.

1. <u>Coal</u>

With the dramatic increases in the price of oil in the 1970s, efforts have been made to expand the production and use of coal, to reduce dependence on oil. The environmental impacts of coal use as an energy source are present in mining, processing, transport and storage, and utilization.

Production. -- In underground mining, the most prominent occupational hazard is the black-lung disease. Underground accidents are other risks. Mining by itself implies changes to the underground structure of the area. Surface mining gives rise to other impacts: i.e. potential impact on land use, including aesthetics, direct effects on human settlements, and impacts on the total infrastructure of an area. Both types of mining have long-term impacts on the water resources in the mining area, e.g., acid mine drainage.

The process of cleaning coal implies pollution from liquid effluents and the amount of pollution depends on the physical properties of coal.

Utilization. -- Coal combustion has effects on health and contributes to the "greenhouse effect." It results in the emission of air pollutants (sulfur oxides, nitrogen oxides, carbon monoxide, particulates, organic compounds, etc.) and the creation of ash wastes which require disposal. Coal conversion processes (i.e. conversion of coal to different grades of liquid and gaseous fuels) are identified with wastes and emissions but there are now known control measures that make these processes environmentally acceptable.

Coal-burning power plants are the main producer of sulfur oxides; other sources of this gas are coal burned for residential heating.

Coal utilization has other effects. These include discoloration of building surfaces, acidification of freshwater lakes, and acidification of precipitation ("acid rain"). These negative effects unfortunately are, by their nature, not confined to an area but travel across political boundaries.

2. Oil

The environmental impacts of oil and natural gas arise in the various stages of the oil industry: exploration, production, transportation, refining, and utilization. In addition to occupational hazards, accidents and natural hazards during the exploration, production, and transportation of oil are the main causes of oil spills both on land and on sea. Brine used in oil production also need to be disposed of properly. Sulfur emissions at the production site are also a concern, and the severity of their impact depend on the sulfur content of oil the produced. The impact of support facilities on traditional activities and quality of life (farming, fishing, tourism, recreation, etc.) also need to be assessed [see, for example, the discussion in Siddayao, 1978].

Oil refineries. -- Among the environmental impacts identified with refineries are the large water requirements for processing and cooling and the safety problems associated with risks of fire and explosions. Refineries also emit airborne effluents (sulfur, nitrous oxides, carbon dioxide) as well as liquid waste pollutants from chemicals used in or resulting from processing (oil, grease, phenols, ammonia). Today's technology, however, makes it possible for refineries to discharge low concentrations of these pollutants.

End-use. -- Vehicles contribute more to the total emission of carbon monoxide and hydrocarbons than stationery sources.

3. Natural Gas

The impacts associated with natural gas will be similar to that for oil in exploration, production, and transportation. But natural gas is identified with lower pollution in use.

B. Renewables

1. Hydropower

The environmental effects of hydropower development are associated with dam and reservoir construction as well as power transmission. Conventional hydroelectric developments use dams and waterways to harness the energy of falling water in streams to produce electric power. Dam construction sets in motion a series of impacts on physical, biological, and socio-cultural systems. Changes in the hydrological regime affect plant and animal life, flooding patterns, the suitability of water for drinking, irrigation, etc., and the socio-economic patterns in the general area of the development.

2. Energy from Biomass

Biomass is defined as renewable organic matter produced by photosynthesis, directly in the case of plants and indirectly in animals whose ultimate food source is plant material. Biomass is perhaps the most important source of energy in terms of actual users, because it is the principal fuel for the majority of people in most developing countries.

Biomass as an energy source has positive and negative effects on the environment. Among others, the conversion of organic waste into fuel reduces the environmental hazards associated with this waste. On the other hand, if biomass use is not properly managed (excessive cutting of trees, slash and burn practices, etc.), various detrimental environmental consequences may result, e.g., soil erosion, desertification, climatic change, air quality, etc. Furthermore, there is evidence that woodfuel combustion in households has negative effects on indoor air quality [see, for example, the study of Smith, 1989b].

Biogas. -- Although there are many benefits to biogas use, there are also negative effects associated with large-scale biogas developments. Among these are land requirements, storage and handling of wastes, and handling of large quantities of waste water products.

Ethanol. -- The production of alcohol from fuel crops raises a number of important environmental and socio-economic issues related to land requirements, fertilizer and pesticide use, possible competition with food production, and the management of large amounts of effluents.

3. Nuclear Energy

The environmental aspects of the production and use of nuclear power has been a cause for public concern for many years. Most of these concerns are related to radiation which may be associated with some stages in the nuclear fuel cycle, including accidents, decommissioning of nuclear facilities, theft, and misuse of plutonium.

Nuclear power and renewable energy sources are considered highly desirable from the perspective of reducing carbon dioxide emissions [see Siddiqi, 1989]. The type of nuclear power plants that are in widespread use today do not enjoy a great deal of confidence in many countries, particularly in light of the Three Mile Island and Chernobyl accidents. Several potentially safer designs have been suggested in recent years and it is believed by some analysts that a number of these may become commercially viable in the next 20 years [see Spiewak and Weinberg, 1985].

The problems associated with long-term storage of highly radioactive wastes from the nuclear industry are well known; the risks can be reduced but not completely eliminated. Thus societies would have to decide, for the present generation and for future generations, how such risks compare with the risks from global climatic change.

4. Geothermal Energy

Geothermal energy has been used for the production of electricity for decades. Geothermal energy is also used for space heating and in agriculture (e.g., fish drying, timber and pulp processing). Negative environmental effects may be site specific and the extent depends highly on the geochemical characteristics of the reservoir. Hydrogen sulfide is the main airborne effluent of real concern in geothermal fields. Thermal pollution from geothermal power plants, as well as groundwater contamination and subsidence in the course of field development are other environmental risks.

5. Solar Energy

Utilization of solar energy is generally environmentally benign, but there are environmental risks associated with potential chemical pollution from the manufacture of photovoltaic cells. ***Indirect solar*** energy comes in the form of wind, sea, and tidal power. The risks associated with these energy sources are noise and interference with the normal environment.

2

Environmental Considerations in Renewable Energy Policy Development and Investment Planning

Wesley K. Foell, Mark E. Hanson, and Collin W. Green
Resource Management Associates of Madison, Inc.

I. Context of Energy Planning for Renewable Energy Sources

A. Historical Perspective

Historically, environmental considerations have played at most a minor role in the energy planning process in developing countries. The demand for economic development and the particular economic, political, and social factors characteristic of many developing countries has created a tremendous pressure on energy resources. This pressure has often led to resource exploitation at the expense of longer-term environmental consequences and development goals. Before the late 1960s, industrialized and developing countries alike generally designed their energy systems, chose their energy technologies, and located their energy facilities on the basis of ready availability of fuels, conventional costs of fuels and capital equipment, and physical access to appropriate infrastructure and facilities.

Since the early 1970s, industrialized countries have demonstrated an increasing tendency to incorporate environmental considerations into their energy planning and management, although this has varied considerably among the countries and even among various regions and sectors of individual countries. Until the past few years, this tendency has been much less pronounced in the developing countries. What has recently become evident however is an increasing awareness among some developing countries of the overarching issue of sustainable economic development, based on the efficient management and use of natural resources, coupled with the conservation and restoration of basic ecological systems. One can speculate on the reasons for this growing awareness. Among the prime factors which have been identified here are:

- A rapidly growing information base about the environmental impacts of energy systems, including a number of documented and publicized cases of poor planning or management which have led to severe problems affecting development;

- A small but nevertheless increasing public participation by individuals and various public/private institutions in national development and implementation of policy on these environmental matters; and

- An increasing *global* attention devoted to energy/environmental matters by technical assistance institutions, international donors, other international organizations, and the scientific community.

Despite these indications of modest progress, energy-related environmental deterioration appears to be quite serious in many developing (and industrialized) countries, as well as in particular regions of the world, and at the global level. The driving force behind this worsening situation is the continued rapid growth of energy resource extraction and consumption. Coupled with this growth, energy policy has developed primarily in response to immediate or short-term economic and political pressures, rather than on the basis of an understanding of the functions and roles of ecosystems, and the full costs and benefits of alternative policies, including those based on a sustainable growth pattern. This problem manifests itself in a wide variety of forms, e.g., the inadequate management of rural demand for fuelwood and other biomass sources, or at another extreme, urban growth policies (or lack thereof) which foster tremendously energy-intensive urban transport systems, likely unsustainable in the long run from both an energy resource and environmental perspective.

Renewable energy resources in particular have not been accorded adequate attention in the planning and management process. There are a number of reasons for this, but perhaps the most significant of these has an institutional basis. In general many of the most important renewable energy resources fall outside the customary boundaries of the institutions frequently responsible for planning and implementing energy systems, e.g., oil and gas companies or authorities, electric utilities, coal suppliers, etc. Further complicating the matter is the multiple purpose or multiple use to which many renewable energy resources are subjected, e.g., multiple-purpose forests, rivers, agro-industry plantations, and sources of agricultural wastes. This not only exacerbates the difficulties of analysis and assessment but also may blur the basis of environmental protection responsibility and jurisdiction.

The multi-purpose nature of many renewable energy resources may place a greater burden of complexity on both analysis and decisionmaking, often extending their domains significantly beyond the energy sector. For example, agriculturally-based biomass for alcohol production involves significant trade-offs between the energy and agriculture sectors, including environmental impacts in the supply as well as the consumption components of the systems. The costs of these impacts may also be distributed widely across the system.

B. The Role of Renewable Energy Resources Today

Renewable resources have experienced what might be termed roller-coaster behavior in energy resource planning over the past few decades. In response to the dramatic oil price increases of the 1970s, there was a surge of optimism about their future role and economic viability in supplying a significant portion of the energy in many countries. Renewable systems based on solar energy, wind, and biomass fuels received great attention during the period when conventional wisdom forecast the coming end of plentiful and low-cost fossil fuels. Some energy planners visualized that renewable energy systems would come on-line in the near future at costs lower than those based on conventional fuels, although such perceptions waxed and waned with the rise and fall of oil prices.

As a result of this, one can look back on valuable experiences in several countries with policies and major implemented programs for renewable energy during the one and one-half decades following the initial oil price run-up. In general, one finds from retrospective a review of these programs that the approaches taken often had some technical successes, but frequently have not proven economically viable, at least in the short run, in comparison with direct private costs of fossil fuels. Viewed from the resource economist's perspective of the supply curve, the incremental supply cost of the renewable resources was higher than that of the competing conventional sources. In some situations where renewable (or conservation) sources were implemented by the end-user, renewable energy options were unfairly disadvantaged because the end-user was faced with the ***marginal*** cost of renewable energy sources, compared to the ***average*** cost of conventional energy sources. In any event, from this particular perspective of marginal conventional costs, there was a compelling logic in these cases to continue to first bring conventional sources on-line.

It is nevertheless important to note that despite the economic difficulties with some recent programs, renewable resources continue to play a significant role in supplying energy to many regions and countries. For example, in Wisconsin biomass-based fuel provides approximately five percent of the total end-use energy consumed [Wisconsin Department of Administration, 1989]. This amount exceeds the total end-use energy supplied by the state's three commercial nuclear power plants. On a global basis, biomass is a significant global energy source, accounting for an estimated 48 exajoules/year (EJ/yr) in developing countries and 7 EJ/yr in industrialized countries. Unfortunately in most developing countries, it is typically used in inefficient cooking devices.

Today, many energy policymakers and decisionmakers once again find themselves in the situation where they are questioning the future role of oil and indeed, the role of all fossil fuels. The uncertainty rests not only on fossil fuel availability or price but also on the growing awareness of the potential of global climate change due to greenhouse gas emissions, primarily from combustion of fossil fuels. One of the emerging consequences of this awareness is an increasing attention devoted once again to renewable resources and their possible role in addressing global climate change.

In addition, the particular role of biomass in carbon fixation has contributed another dimension of complexity to the evaluation of its role in future energy systems. Because this role is ***global*** in extent, it particularly complicates both the analysis and the decisionmaking/implementation process. Indeed, the addition of this truly global impact to the decisionmaking and planning process may do more to transform (perhaps revolutionize) the energy policy and implementation process than any single consideration heretofore made.

C. Objectives and Organization

The primary objective in this chapter is three-fold. ***First***, to lay out an appropriate framework for describing the quantifiable and unquantifiable environmental impacts of a broad range of renewable energy systems in a manner that is compatible with those used for conventional energy systems. ***Second***, to provide a prescriptive planning and investment framework, based on integrated resource planning, which permits the incorporation of environmental considerations for renewable energy resources and the comparison of renewables, conventional energy sources, and conservation on a consistent basis. ***Thirdly***, to use a small number of selected case studies of renewable energy systems in developing and industrialized countries to illustrate some of the salient points of this chapter.

As with other types of energy resources, there exists a broad array of both needs and options for approaching the planning and investment strategies for renewable energy resources. The institutional structures within which supply options are formulated, evaluated, and implemented, range from large government agencies or multinational energy firms down to individual suppliers. The demand options, on the other hand, are usually more diverse and dispersed, although government can, of course, play an important role in the process through its economic and non-economic instruments of pricing, incentives, standards, etc. In this chapter, descriptive and prescriptive approaches are combined to consider energy planning and investment analysis. The emphasis will be on the process of resource and technology evaluation and selection, including the issues of environmental controls. Although some mention will be made of other issues such as pricing policy, the scope of these topics is beyond the space available here.

The descriptive analysis here provides a representation of system components and selected estimated emissions rates and material requirements under specified configurations. The prescriptive analysis provides a framework for planning and investment analysis, designed primarily from the perspective of a government agency or firm with responsibility for energy strategies and investment planning.

The organization of the remainder of this chapter is as follows. Part II provides an overview of renewable energy technologies and systems. It begins with a framework (the reference energy network) for description of the systems, including systems at various levels of spatial extent, as well as selected technical, environmental, and economic parameters. This is followed by a discussion of the major sources or technologies, including biomass, hydropower, geothermal, wind, and solar.

Part III provides a prescriptive framework for renewable energy planning and investment analysis. It begins with an overview of the institutional setting within which it is envisioned this framework would be applied. This is followed with an exposition of the conceptual foundation of the framework, namely, integrated resource planning. Included in this discussion are the main aspects of the framework; among them are characterization of resource supply, decision criteria, sustainability criteria, approaches to internalization of impacts, and choice of appropriate investment sequences. This part includes a more detailed discussion of the analytical and operational methods for implementation of the analysis.

Part IV presents a small number of historical case studies (including both "successes" and "failures") of recent major programs for implementation of renewable energy systems in developing and industrialized countries. These cases are discussed within the context of the frameworks laid out in Parts II and III. The chapter is completed with brief summary remarks and conclusions in Part V.[1]

II. Overview of Renewable Energy Technologies and Systems

The prescriptive planning framework for renewable energy resources, as introduced above and described in more detail in Part III, is based in part upon an analysis of physical environmental impacts associated with specific energy systems. It requires a method and an information base for providing the environmental analysis. This part of the chapter describes the method, including concepts and procedure for the analysis. It also lays out, in summary form, an information base for twelve of the main renewable energy technologies and systems.

A. Framework for Description of the Systems

The incorporation of environmental considerations into the energy planning and investment analysis raises a number of important questions. Perhaps one of the most crucial of these addresses the stage or point in the planning and implementation process at which such considerations are explicitly introduced. In industrialized countries in recent years, there has been an increasing tendency toward conducting generic environmental assessments of energy options at the national level to determine overall policy on a particular energy related program or objective. The advantage of this approach is that it brings environmental concerns into the process at an early stage, avoiding the inflexibility which often occurs if these issues are not addressed until they arise in the context of a specific site or energy facility. At this late stage of project implementation, it is often difficult, or at least very expensive, to incorporate environmental concerns.

Therefore, in applying impact analysis of the type to be described below, it is important to make a distinction between environmental assessment at different system levels or scales. The scale chosen influences the geographical region and the aggregation of energy systems considered. It has proven useful to distinguish between the national level, the local or regional level, and the site-specific or facility level. Although there may in some cases be a blurring of this distinction depending upon the size of the country, nature of the technology, etc., it is important to establish the basis early in the analysis process.

Site-specific analyses are generally straightforward to carry out because they are based on technical, economic, and environmental parameters which are often reasonably well understood. In contrast, regional, national, and global assessments are often considerably more complex and usually require considerable judgment in the aggregation of system characteristics and parameters. Regional (sub-national) analyses are conducted either because a specific regional institutional entity has responsibility for energy planning or because a

[1]Appendices found in Foell et al. [1992] contain more detailed information and literature sources on environmental impacts of renewable energy systems, as well as a more detailed description of the formalism of multi-attribute decision analysis as it is applicable to the energy investment planning problem addressed in this chapter.

specific regional spatial scale of analysis is necessary. National analyses have most commonly been used to address strategies involving the choice of a set of energy technologies on a national basis, e.g., a biomass fuels program or a synthetic fuels program. They are often targeted to address questions such as resource development needs and timing, research and development programs, investment strategies, and of course, the degree and magnitude of economic, environmental, and social effects of major energy programs.

The descriptive analysis, particularly for ***regional and national analyses***, is based upon a system-wide perspective. The energy system for which the environmental impacts are calculated should encompass the complete fuel chain for each type of energy considered. The fuel chain consists of such steps as resource extraction, transportation, refining, conversion, and consumption at the point of end use. This fuel chain is defined in terms of the "reference energy network" (REN) [Foell, 1981].

Impacts are tabulated at each point in the fuel chain, as indicated in Figure 1. These impacts may represent both "intermediate" and "final" effects of impact pathways. The use of intermediate impacts is common in policy discussions. For example, excess risk of emphysema is considered to be the end result of a number of causal events, including pollution emissions, pollution transport, human exposure to the pollutants, and potential damage to health. Figure 2 shows several impact pathways associated with electricity generation, one type of conversion process included in the fuel chain. It should be noted that the impacts are expressed in a wide variety of units, such as fatalities, hectares of land use, and volumes or weights of solid waste.

Determining what in fact is the "end-result" of a given environmentally damaging process is not a simple matter and requires considerable judgment in actual application. Some analysts have chosen to use a hierarchical or "layered" approach [Cirillo, 1989] to this type of assessment, with each layer providing more information on the environmental effects of an energy system. The impact analysis layers are: (i) Environmental Burdens Analysis, (ii) Pollutant Transport Analysis, and (iii) Effects Analysis. Table 1 gives a typical set of impacts calculated under that procedure.

It is clear that impacts calculated according to these types of Reference Energy Networks are ***quantified*** impacts only. Quantified environmental impacts are those for which an adequate scientific basis exists for evaluation and characterization in mathematical terms, including ranges of values to convey uncertainty or varying conditions. Quantification does allow a detailed examination of assumptions and results and permits a direct association to be made between the energy system and environmental impacts, providing one basis for policy analysis and planning. However, they obviously do not represent all of the impacts known to occur -- both the quantified and the unquantified -- and care must be taken to incorporate in some other manner the unquantified impacts, even including those which are as yet unrecognized. These latter impacts are often included in the category of "surprises," and have been the subject of much discussion in the widely developed literature of "resilience" and "adaptive environmental management" [Holling, 1978; Clark, 1986].

Environmental information data bases based on RENs are a complex but necessary and useful framework for representing and comparing renewable and conventional energy systems. Judgments are required in deciding how much information should be collected and in which forms it should be presented in terms of intermediate and final effects for both quantified and unquantified impacts.

Figure 1: Typical environmental impacts associated with each point in the fuel chain

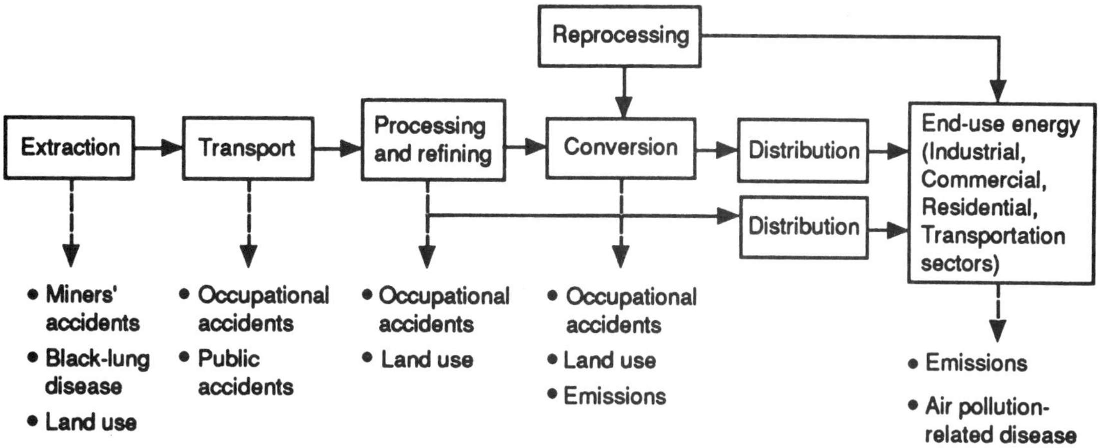

Source: Foell et al. [1981].

Figure 2: Impact pathways for electricity generation

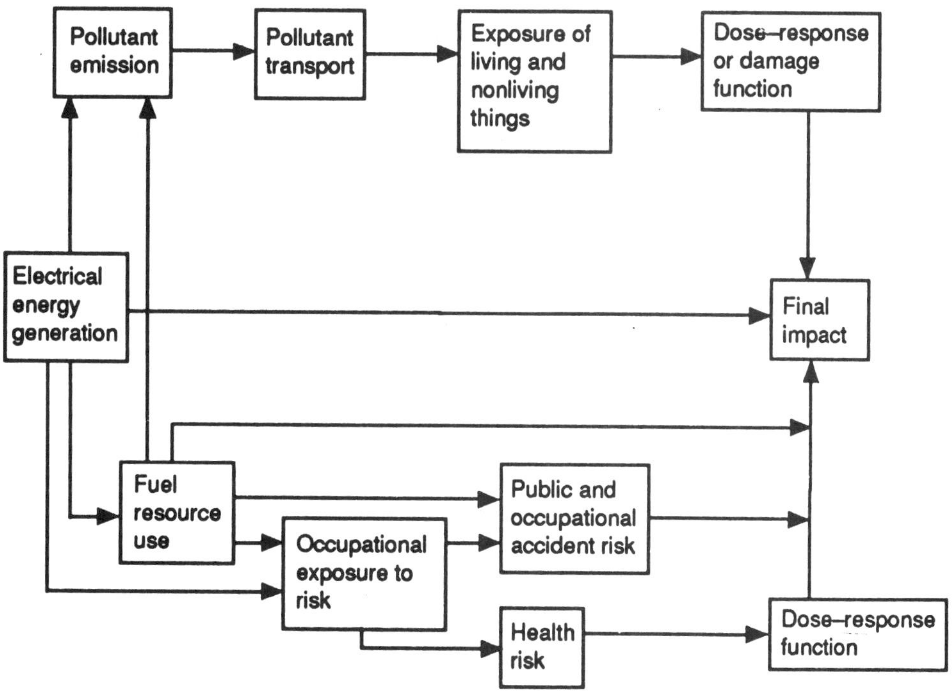

Source: Foell et al. [1981].

Table 1: Hierarchical Approach to Environmental Assessment

Environmental Burdens Evaluation

- Emissions
- Effluents
- Resource Use
- etc.

Pollutant Transport Analysis

- Air pollutant dispersion
- Water pollutant movement
- Solid waste disposal
- etc.

Effects Analysis

- Exposure rates
- Health effects
- Ecosystem impacts
- Materials damage
- etc.

Source: Cirillo [1989].

B. Summary Description of Selected Renewable Energy Systems

The remainder of this part presents a summary description and discussion of the environmental impacts (both intermediate and final) of twelve renewable energy systems which have been selected as representative of those under consideration or of potential interest in developing countries. There are numerous other systems or permutations of these systems. The systems summarized are:

- Residential Wind Energy Conversion System
- Wind Farm Electric
- Mini/Micro Hydro
- Central Geothermal Hydrothermal Plant
- Direct Combustion Wood Electric (power only)
- Wood Methanol
- Sugar Ethanol and Corn Ethanol
- Urban Waste (power only)
- Central Station Solar-Thermal Electric
- Central Photovoltaic Electric
- Dispersed Residential Photovoltaic System
- Residential Solar Thermal Hot Water Heating System

For the purpose of providing a comparative framework including conventional energy sources and technologies, quantitative information for two conventional systems have also been included:

- 500 megawatt (MW) Conventional Coal Electric Plant
- 1000 MW Boiling Water Reactor Nuclear Electric Plant

Figures 5 and 7 show schematic examples of the Reference Energy Networks for two systems, the Direct Combustion Wood Electric System and the Central Station Solar Thermal Electric System, respectively. The contrast in the degree of precision and quantification in the two figures is meant to illustrate different stages in the process of systems description and of the development of impact descriptions. It also implicitly raises the point that some impacts are strongly dependent on the details of a specific system, and that their analysis may require that the system be precisely defined. ***Thus a word of caution is inserted here to warn against indiscriminate use of literature-based impact parameters, including those in this chapter, without ascertaining that they are based on the appropriate system and technology.***

In general, to be useful in the planning framework described in Part III, the Reference Energy Network for the various energy systems should contain technical, economic, and environmental parameters. During the past fifteen years, there have been a large number of studies in the United States and elsewhere to develop data bases for a great variety of reference energy networks. In general, much of this work has focused on conventional energy systems rather than renewable systems, partially due to the relatively lower penetration of the latter technologies.[2]

---

[2]Appendix D in Foell et al. [1992] provides a list of several sources of information useful for developing reference energy networks.

As an example for assembling an information base in descriptive impact analysis, a set of qualitative and quantitative tables was developed for selected categories of impacts of the twelve renewable energy technologies based on secondary published data. The impact categories have been chosen to encompass what was judged to be a reasonable spectrum of the effects of primary concern. The qualitative tables are very useful for screening purposes in the initial or preliminary stages of the integrated resource planning process. Tables 2-a and 2-b provide an example of this type of table for four of the selected renewable energy systems.

Quantitative tables with numerical coefficients have been developed from the literature for four impact categories:

- Airborne Emissions (carbon, sulfur oxides, particulates, heavy metals, and other).

- Waterborne Emissions (nitrates, dissolved solids, sulfates, aqueous, and other).

- Solid Wastes Generated (dust or sludge, mining overburden, fly or bottom ash, iron oxides, and other).

- Land and Material Requirements (land use, consumptive water use, steel, aluminum, concrete, and other).

The first and last of the above four quantitative tables are shown in Tables 3 (3-a and 3-b) and 4 (4-a and 4-b), respectively.[3] The values in the tables are expressed as "lifecycle" coefficients, i.e. in terms of the quotient of a quantity (e.g., tons) used or produced over the entire useful life of the plant and the total energy [e.g., gigawatt-hours (GWh)] produced by the plant during its life. "Lifecycle" units are useful in comparing energy sources which have a large, one-time input of resources with sources that have a continuous input throughout their operational life.

In order to help distinguish among impacts along the fuel chain, they are disaggregated according to whether they originate from "resource development" or from the "final product" stage, respectively [Siddayao, in this volume]. To recapitulate, the resource development stage includes exploration and development (surveys, drilling, plant siting, and construction), production (production drilling, mining, tree planting, and harvesting), and transportation of the basic energy resource (crude oil, natural gas, fuelwood, etc.) to the processing site (refinery, electric power plant, charcoal processor, firewood seller, etc.). The final product stage includes processing or production of the final product (e.g., refining, electric power production, charcoal production, firewood preparation, manufacture of solar cells) and distributing or marketing the final product (distribution of petroleum products, electricity, charcoal, firewood bundles, etc.).

Quantitative and qualitative information of the impacts in the different stages is an important first step in the analysis. It must then be supplemented with further analysis, often related to environmental impact abatement strategies. For example, the airborne emission in Table 3 could be modified by the addition of a small number of air pollution abatement strategies. The technology parameters for the appropriate control equipment are generally available in the aforementioned data bases, but need to be periodically updated.

---

[3] All four quantitative tables are contained in Appendix B in Foell et al. [1992] along with tables for thirteen qualitative impacts.

Figure 3: System Descriptions

Coal Plant:
500 MWe
3500 GWh of electricity generated annually
Lifetime of 30 years.
1.9 million tons of Eastern Bituminous coal annually.
Wet lime/limestone scrubber used to control SO_x emissions.

Nuclear Plant:
1000 MWe Boiling Water Reactor design.
6130 GWh of electricity generated annually.
34 tons of Uranium fuel used annually.

Central Photovoltaic Electric:
100 MWe facility located in Barstow, California (hypothetical).
15% cell efficiency.
209 GWh of electricity generated annually.
Lifetime of 30 years.
Provides peak power to electricity grid.

Residential Solar Thermal Hot Water:
Site: Denver, Colorado.
System: Flat plate collectors
Heat transferred to a water/glycol storage tank.
Lifetime: 30 years.
Size: 50 ft^2 collector with 90 gallons of storage.
Efficiency: 22%.
Annual energy production: 7.0 X 10^6 BTU
System provides 75% of reference load
Capacity factor: Not determined.

Residential De-centralized PV:
Site: Phoenix, Arizona
System: PV cells contained within roofing shingles.
Utility provides backup power. Excess power enters utility grid.
No onsite storage.
Size: 904 ft^2 collector area
8.5 kWp power.
Capacity factor: 30%
Annual energy production: 69.4 X 10^6 BTU
Efficiency: 10%
Lifetime: 30 years.

Solar Thermal Electric Central Station:
Site: Southwest United States
Size: 100 MWe
7.45 x 10^6 BTU
Annual capacity factor: 50%
Annual energy production: 1.5 x 10^{12} BTU
Efficiency: 23.4%
Lifetime: 30 years.

Residential WECS:
System: 3 blades on a horizontal axis
25 ft. in diameter
Low wind scenario at 30 ft. 12-15 mph
System operates in winds 8-50 mph

Residential WECS: (continued)
Size: 15 kWe capacity
Annual capacity factor: 22%
Annual energy production: 98.7 X 10^6 BTU
Efficiency: Varies with wind speed, up to 45%
Lifetime: 30 years

WECS electric application:
System: Horizontal axis rotor that turns at constant speed by varying pitch of blades.
Size: 1.5 MWe
219 ft. diameter rotor.
Annual capacity factor: 33%
Annual energy production: 4.33 X 10^6 kWh
Efficiency: Varies with wind speed, up to 45%
Lifetime: 30 years

Wood combustion Electric Plant:
System: Steam turbines, Spreader stoker furnace.
Size: 62 MWe
Annual capacity factor: 80%
Annual energy production: not available
Efficiency: 19.3%
Lifetime: 20 years

Wood to methanol plant:
Size: Will support space heating and hot water needs for about 8100 homes.
Annual capacity factor: 90%
Annual energy production: 3.62 X 10^{12} BTU
Efficiency: 57% Net
Lifetime: 20 years

Corn to Ethanol Plant:
System: 50 million gallon 99.5% ethanol per year
By products: distillers dry grain and animal feed.
Boiler burns #6 II high sulfur coal
Size: 50 X 10^6 gal per year
Annual capacity factor: 90%
Annual energy production: 3.78 x 10^{12} BTU
Efficiency: 68.9%
Lifetime: 20 years

Municipal Sludge to Biogas Plant:
System: 200 x 10^6 gal of sludge digested per day.
2 million people
Capacity factor: 100%
Annual energy production: .52 x 10^{12} BTU Net
Efficiency: 39%
Lifetime: 20 years

Central Geothermal Electric Plant:
System: Vapor dominated at PG & E, Geisers, California
Size: 110 MWe
Annual capacity factor: 80%
Annual energy production: 2.63 X 10^{12} BTU
Efficiency: 16%
Lifetime: 30-35 years

Source: Authors.

Table 2-a: Qualitative Description Of Environmental Impacts Of Selected Renewable Energy Systems (Central Systems)

	Central Station Solar Thermal Electric	Central Photovoltaic Electric
Location of Impacts	Localized to station site and fabrication facilities.	Localized to station site and fabrication facilities.
Land Requirements	Permanent use of large land area, no reclamation until plant is decommissioned.	Permanent use of large land area, no reclamation until plant is decommissioned.
Water Requirements	Heliostat washing but little water throughput.	Minimum requirements for cell cleaning.
Material Requirements	Larger inputs than fossil fuel plants per unit energy. Glass, copper, aluminum, steel, insulation. Relatively little maintenance.	Requires exotic inputs. Some toxic (cadmium sulfide, and explosive (saline). Proper disposal is a factor. Relatively little maintenance.
Airborne Pollution	None under normal conditions. Other releases, from fire/accidents: sodium hydroxide, nitrogen oxide, sodium oxides, dust, and mist.	Fabrication emissions are small. Thin film fabrication requires large quantities of gases. Toxic: arsine, diborane, hydrochloric acid. Explosive: hydrogen, methane, saline residue.
Liquid Wastes	Antifreeze, rust inhibitors, biological inhibitors, boiler blowdown and heavy metals leached from system during use must be contained. Herbicide use on land to deter vegetation growth. Detergents in cleaning.	No liquid wastes in cell fabrication deposition process. Herbicides used on land to prevent vegetation growth. Detergents in cell washing fluid.
Solid Wastes	Upon decommissioning, non-recyclables: fiberglass, glass, coolant, and insulation, must be disposed of. No animal wastes, yet coolant requires periodic changes.	Byproducts of deposition process: cadmium, arsenic. Some wastes will require hazardous classification. Decommissioning requires proper disposal of non-recyclables.
Visual Intrusion	Aesthetic impact similar to fossil plants including steam but excluding air emissions.	Impact includes large land use without stacks or cooling towers.
Thermal Impacts	Similar to fossil fuel plant discharges.	None
Public and Occupation Health and Safety	Hazard to eyesight from reflectors. Hazard from toxins in coolant fluids.	Electric shock, fire hazards and spontaneous combustion in fabrication. Hazard from toxic gas exposure.
Noise	Shares some characteristics of steam generating plants.	Negligible
Changes to Natural Ecosystem	Soil erosion and compaction. Wind diversion. Potential decrease in evaporation rate from soil.	Soil erosion and compaction. Wind diversion. Potential decrease in evaporation rate from soil.
Other Effects	Use of herbicides may effect ground water.	Use of herbicides may effect ground water.

Source: Authors.
Note: See Figure 3 for system descriptions.

Table 2-b: Qualitative Description Of Environmental Impacts of Selected Renewable Energy Systems (Decentralized Systems)

	Dispersed Residential Photovoltaic System	Residential Solar Thermal Hot Water Heating System
Location of Impacts	Localized to station site and fabrication facilities.	Localized to station site and fabrication facilities.
Land Requirements	Minimal: Typically uses roof top.	Minimal: Typically uses roof top.
Water Requirements	Minimum requirements for cell cleaning.	Negligible
Material Requirements	Requires exotic inputs. Some toxic (cadmium sulfide), and explosive (saline). Proper disposal is a factor. Relatively little maintenance.	Large material requirements: fiberglass, steel, glass, copper, aluminum. Relatively little maintenance.
Airborne Pollution	Fabrication emissions are small. Thin film fabrication requires large quantities of gases. Toxic: arsine, diborane, hydrochloric acid. Explosive: hydrogen, methane, saline residue.	Fabrication emissions are small.
Liquid Wastes	No liquid wastes in cell fabrication deposition process. Detergents in cell washing fluid.	Antifreeze, rust inhibitors, biological inhibitors and heavy metals leached from system during use must be contained.
Solid Wastes	Byproducts of deposition process: cadmium, arsenic. Some wastes will require hazardous classification. Decommissioning requires proper disposal of non-recyclables.	Upon decommissioning, non-recyclables: fiberglass, glass, coolant and, insulation; must be disposed of. No animal wastes.
Visual Intrusion	Minimal impact of building design and appearance. May eliminate need for transmission facilities.	Minimal impact of building design and appearance. May eliminate need for transmission facilities.
Thermal Impacts	None	None
Public and Occupation Health and Safety	Similar to home construction risks. Electric shock and fire hazards. Hazard from toxic gas exposure.	Similar to home construction risks. Hazard from exposure to toxins in coolant. Fire hazard.
Noise	None	None
Changes to Natural Ecosystem	None	None
Other Effects	None	Most risks incurred at the place of benefits. Internalized costs and benefits.

Source: Authors.
Note: See Figure 3 for system descriptions.

Table 3-a: Estimated Airborne Emissions for Selected Renewable Energy Systems (Excluding Biomass) (Tons per GWh)

	Conventional		Hydro	Wind		Solar				Geothermal
	500MW Conventional Coal	1000MW Nuclear BWR	Mini/ Micro Hydro	1.5MWe Electric WECS	15kWe Residential WECS	Solar Thermal Electric	100MW Photovoltaic Electric	Residential Decentralized Photovoltaic	Residential Thermal Hot Water	110MWe Central Geothermal
Carbon										
Resource Development	0.037	0.705	NA	NA	NA	NA	NA	NA	NA	--
Final Product	453.635	2.988	--	--	--	--	2.526	--	--	12.130
Total	453.672	3.693	--	--	--	--	2.526	--	--	--
Sulfur-Oxides										
Resource Development	0.057	0.025	NA	NA	NA	NA	NA	NA	NA	NA
Final Product	2.914	0.003	--	--	--	--	0.023	--	--	NA
Total	2.971	0.029	--	--	--	--	0.023	--	--	NA
Particulates										
Resource Development	1.483	0.003	NA	NA	NA	NA	NA	NA	NA	--
Final Product	0.143	neg	--	--	--	--	0.017	--	--	0.024
Total	1.626	0.003	--	--	--	--	0.017	--	--	--
Heavy Metals (Lead)										
Resource Development	--	--	NA	NA	NA	NA	NA	NA	NA	--
Final Product	0.030	NA	--	--	--	--	--	--	--	--
Total	0.030	--	--	--	--	--	--	--	--	--

Source: Authors.
Note: See Figure 3 for system descriptions.
Legend: neg = negligible; NA = not applicable; -- = information not available; TR = Trace; GWh = gigawatts per hour; MW = megawatts; MWe = megawatts electric; kWe = kilowatts electric; BWR = Boiling water reactor; WECS = Wind energy conversion system

Table 3-b: Estimated Airborne Emissions for Selected Renewable Energy Systems (Biomass) (Tons per GWh)

	Biomass				
	62 MWe Combustion Wood Electric	Wood Methanol	Corn Ethanol	Municipal Sludge Biogas	25MW RDF Incinerator
Carbon					
Resource Development	--	--	--	--	neg
Final Product	--	--	65.610	147.000	--
Total	--	--	--	--	--
Sulfur-Oxides					
Resource Development	NA	NA	NA	--	neg
Final Product	1.841	TR	0.846	0.980	--
Total	1.841	TR	0.846	--	--
Particulates					
Resource Development	--	--	--	--	neg
Final Product	TR	TR	0.094	--	--
Total	TR	TR	0.094	--	--
Heavy Metals (Lead)					
Resource Development	--	--	--	--	neg
Final Product	--	--	--	0.580	--
Total	--	--	--	--	--

Source: Authors.
Note: See Figure 3 for system descriptions.
Legend: neg = negligible; NA = not applicable; -- = information not available; TR = Trace
GWh = gigawatts per hour; MW = megawatts; MWe = megawatts electric; kWe = kilowatts electric; RDF = refuse derived fuel

Table 4-a: Estimated Land and Material Requirements for Selected Renewable Energy Systems (Excluding Biomass) (Tons per GWh)

	Conventional		Hydro	Wind		Solar				Geothermal
	500MW Conventional Coal	1000MW Nuclear BWR	Mini/ Micro Hydro	1.5MWe Electric WECS	15kWe Residential WECS	Solar Thermal Electric	100MW Photovoltaic Electric	Residential Decentralized Photovoltaic	Residential Thermal Hot Water	110MWe Central Geothermal
Land Use (Acres)										
Resource Development	0.082	0.015	--	NA	NA	NA	NA	NA	NA	0.0341[a]
Final Product	0.008	0.012	--	0.006[b]	0.006[c]	0.076	0.080	neg	neg	0.001
Total	0.090	0.027	--	0.006	0.006	0.076	0.080	neg	neg	0.035
Consumptive Water Use (Acre-Ft)										
Resource Development	0.023	0.046	NA	NA	NA	NA[d]	NA	NA	NA	--
Final Product	3.097	4.078	NA	NA	NA	0.069[e]	0.102	neg[a]	0.006[f]	0.073
Total	3.120	4.124	NA	NA	NA	0.069	0.102	neg	0.006	--
Steel										
Resource Development	0.202	0.199	NA	NA	NA	NA	NA	NA	NA	--
Final Product	NA	NA	--	1.068	0.250	5.342[e]	1.838	0.409	1.705	--
Total	0.202	0.199	--	1.068	0.250	5.342	1.838	0.409	1.705	--
Aluminum										
Resource Development	0.039	0.001	NA	NA	NA	NA	NA	NA	NA	--
Final Product	NA	NA	--	NA	NA	0.387[e]	0.019	0.003	1.347	--
Total	0.039	0.001	--	NA	NA	0.387	0.019	0.003	1.347	--
Concrete										
Resource Development	0.876	1.816	NA	NA	NA	NA	NA	NA	NA	--
Final Product	NA	NA	--	3.581	0.693	19.32[e]	1.384	NA	NA	--
Total	0.876	1.816	--	3.581	0.693	19.320	1.384	NA	NA	--

Source: Authors.

Notes: See Figure 3 for system descriptions.

[a] Water for washing is estimated at 500 gallons/year or 75.17 Acre-foot/GWh.

[b] Do not know if wake is considered.

[c] Does not consider wake.

[d] Water is used as working fluid. Boiler water and heliostat washing.

[e] Maximum value taken from a range of values.

[f] Includes initial coolant water and replacement coolant water every third year. Does not include water for cell washing which is deemed necessary.

Legend: neg = negligible; NA = not applicable; -- = information not available; TR = Trace; GWh = gigawatts per hour; MW = megawatts; MWe = megawatts electric; kWe = kilowatts electric; BWR = Boiling water reactor; WECS = Wind energy conversion system

Table 4-b: Estimated Land and Material Requirements for Selected Renewable Energy Systems (Biomass) (Tons per GWh)

	Biomass				
	62 MWe Combustion Wood Electric	Wood Methanol	Corn Ethanol	Municipal Sludge Biogas	25MW RDF Incinerator
Land Use (Acres)					
Resource Development	910.0[a]	2523.0[b]	--	NA	NA
Final Product	0.0137	0.001	0.002	0.002	.013[c]
Total	--	252.301	--	0.002	--
Consumptive Water Use (Acre-Ft)					
Resource Development	--	--	--	NA	NA
Final Product	8.389	2124	1.144	0.000[d]	--
Total	8.389	2124	--	0.000	--
Steel					
Resource Development	--	--	--	NA	NA
Final Product	--	11.2	0.525	0.358	--
Total	--	--	--	0.358	--
Aluminum					
Resource Development	--	--	--	NA	NA
Final Product	--	--	1.240	NA	--
Total	--	--	--	NA	--
Concrete					
Resource Development	--	NA	NA	NA	NA
Final Product	--	2.893	1.050	5.183	--
Total	--	2.893	1.050	5.183	--

Source: Authors.

Notes: See Figure 3 for system descriptions.

[a] Assume temperate forest yields 1 cord/acre/year dry wood.
50% moisture content. 2 tons (dry) per cord.
Plant needs are 356×10^3 tons per year.

[b] Assumes total of 5.36×10^6 acres total feedstock supply land.

[c] Assume plant needs for land are the same as for wood combustion.

[d] Water recycled.

Legend: neg = negligible; NA = not applicable; -- = information not available; TR = Trace
GWh = gigawatts per hour; MW = megawatts; MWe = megawatts electric; RDF = refuse derived fuel

C. Summary Discussion of Major Systems

In addition to the REN diagrams and the tables of quantitative and qualitative environmental impacts, the summary discussions of renewable energy sources in this part provide a brief status report on these systems. These summary discussions provide a synopsis of not only the environmental status of the systems, but commentary on the technical and economic status of the systems. Attempting to provide a summary discussion is difficult due to the variability within each of the systems as well as variability in the success in the use of the systems in different settings, even when the technologies involved have been quite similar. For example, wood-fired power production has been largely a failure to date in the Philippines, while it has been partially successful in areas of northern Europe, the United States, Canada, and Indonesia. Similarly, solar hot water systems for domestic use have been very successful in Cyprus and Israel, while they have hardly made any inroads in Tunisia, a country in the same region with similar climatic conditions.

1. Biomass

a. Wood and Other Biomass Direct Combustion. The energy system for the direct combustion of biomass for power, process heat, or combined heat and power (cogeneration) is quite similar to that for conventional fossil fuel combustion except that the primary resource is biomass rather than a fossil fuel. Figure 4 represents the main features of this system in the case of wood combustion for cogeneration. As Figure 4 shows, specialized harvesting and transportation equipment are utilized in harvesting the fuel and transporting it to the power plant. Because of the high water content and low energy density of biomass, transportation haul lengths will usually be limited. The feed systems, boilers, and generators are fairly standard, although fluidized bed boilers have proven to be particularly appropriate for wood and wood wastes.

The economics of the system are dependent on the cost of the primary energy source. Wood boilers, for example, are common throughout much of the world in the forest products industry because of the availability of wood or waste and scrap wood. The use of wood cut exclusively for direct combustion appears to be limited due to the difficulty in competing with coal, oil, and natural gas at current prices.

b. Liquid and Gaseous Fuels. Liquid and gaseous fuels can be produced from virtually all forms of biomass by a number of processes. The two most common liquid fuels are alcohol-based products ethanol and methanol, while the most important gaseous fuels are syngas and biogas. The type of fuel ultimately produced depends on the type of conversion process as described in Figure 5. The two main types of biomass transformation processes are biochemical and thermal conversion.

The fermentation of grains, sugar cane, and other woody or herbaceous crops rich in sugar or starch produces grain alcohol or ethanol. Ethanol is a relatively clean burning fuel that can be used as a substitute for gasoline in modified internal combustion engines or as a non-lead, octane-enhancing gasoline additive. The major producers of ethanol include Brazil, the United States, and France.

Biogas is produced by the biochemical process of anaerobic digestion, the same process used to treat sewage wastes and sludge. Biogas is a medium British thermal unit

Figure 4: Reference Energy Network for Direct Combustion Wood Electric System

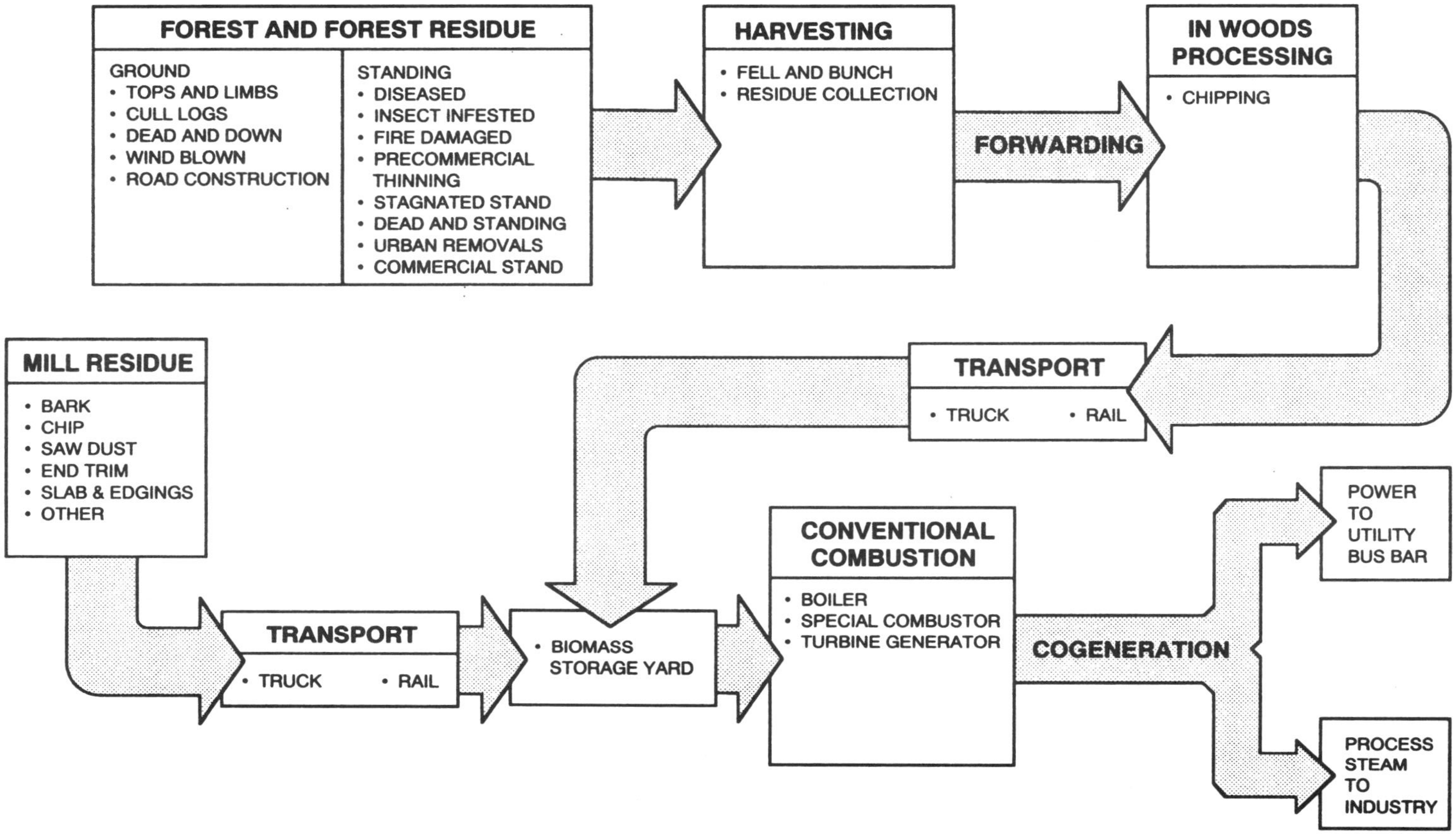

Source: Resource Policy Center [1980].

Figure 5: Options for Biofuels Production

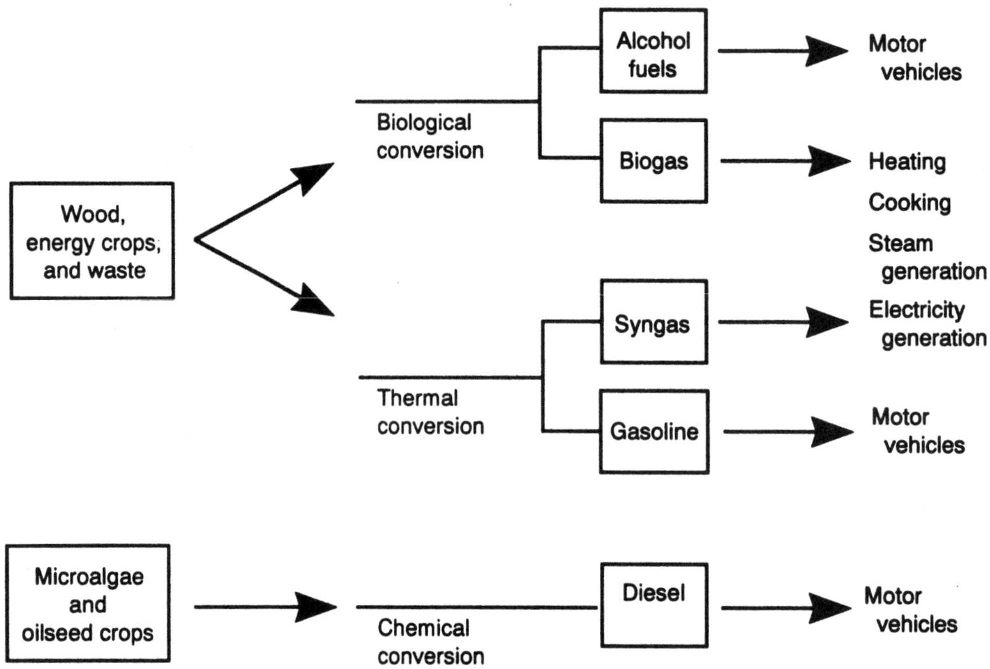

Source: Adapted from Brower [1990].

(medium-BTU) mixture of methane and carbon dioxide which can be purified to yield high-BTU methane, the principal component of natural gas. Biogas may also be produced from animal wastes, crop residues, and sewage. Small anaerobic digesters have been relatively successful in developing countries. For example, in China over seven million small digestion systems have been installed to partially meet the cooking, space heating, and lighting demands of a number of small rural communities [Brower, 1990]. In the United States, the majority of biogas plants have been constructed to collect the gaseous emissions produced from decomposition in landfills. As of 1988, 50 plants were in operation and another 40 plants were either in construction or being planned [Brower, 1990].

Methanol can be produced through catalytic reactions from the medium-BTU gaseous products of either gasification or pyrolysis. Methanol is a high-octane fuel that, like ethanol, can be used in automobiles fitted with special combustion engines or as an additive in gasoline. Currently there is little industrial interest in converting biomass to methanol because it is less costly to derive methanol from natural gas.

c. Environmental Aspects. The environmental effects of wide-spread use of biomass resources for energy can be broken down into three categories: biomass resource production, conversion, and end-use. Environmentally, biomass production has some distinct advantages and disadvantages. The advantages are that if the feedstock is grown on a renewable basis (in a plantation or in a less intensively managed production system such as natural forest), carbon release and carbon uptake balance each other. Some marginal lands may be found to be more economical when supporting energy crops than other agricultural crops, and a greater portion of harvested plant material may be used, increasing the economic value of the harvest.

In the conversion process, solid and liquid wastes can be utilized to reduce water pollution and waste products can provide a benefit as organic fertilizer if they are collected and applied to the land. In the case of biogas production, sanitary conversion of manure and human sewage into energy and slurry fertilizer will reduce the incidence of schistosomiasis. Finally, biomass combustion produces little sulfur and ash, and particulates are readily controlled.

The environmental disadvantages of biomass are generally associated with production and harvesting practices. Careful wood harvesting and avoidance of steep slopes can minimize erosion. Intensive biomass production, on the other hand, often requires the application of fertilizers and other chemicals which are a threat to water bodies. On a broader scale, an important biomass issue is the type of land used for production. For example, reforesting marginal and damaged lands has a very different consequence than harvesting old growth forest (tropical or temperate) or displacing agricultural land. Some crops, such as corn as it is currently produced in the United States, require large inputs of energy in the form of fertilizers, operation of equipment, herbicides etc. After accounting for these energy inputs and others for transportation and distillation of ethanol, the energy balance on premium fuels has been shown to be poor. In other words, the premium energy inputs approximately equal the premium energy produced. The profit derived from corn-based ethanol relies upon subsidies, including the exclusion of gasoline and ethanol mix fuels from some or all motor vehicle fuel taxes. Under these circumstances, biomass fuels are not an economically advantageous option.

Burning methanol and ethanol instead of gasoline would substantially reduce major pollutant emissions in motor vehicle exhaust. This is a particularly important advantage in large cities. There would be an increase in aldehydes yet there is debate over what levels are harmful and how much of the pollutant can be removed with a catalytic converter [Brower, 1990].

2. Geothermal

There are three types of geothermal resources: hydrothermal, dry hot rock, and geo-pressured. The ultimate use of geothermal resources will depend on the type of resource developed. Currently, only hydrothermal resources have been exploited. Geo-pressured and hot dry rock resources are still in the resource definition and experimental stages in the United States. The main producers of power from geothermal energy are the Philippines, New Zealand, Iceland, and the United States. Global installed capacity is more than 4700 megawatts electric (MWe) [World Resources Institute, 1988].

The main features of a geothermal energy system are: geothermal wells, a well head, pipes for transporting energy in liquid or vapor form, a central conversion plant, and wells for reinjecting the spent geothermal fluid or abatement facilities.[4] Energy conversion and use processes depend strongly on whether the geothermal fluid is liquid or vapor-dominated. Steam-turbine technology is in an advanced state of development and equipment used in exploiting hydrothermal geothermal resources is adapted directly from the conventional power industry.

The environmental effects of geothermal energy sources are highly site-dependant and technology-dependant (open system or closed system) as geothermal reservoirs have a wide range of geothermal and chemical properties. For this reason it is not possible to describe a "typical" geothermal energy system. Thus, it is important to note that environmental impacts and the use and effectiveness of mitigation techniques can be constructively considered only on a site-by-site basis.

The major environmental impacts of geothermal resource development are associated with the release of geothermal fluids and their dissolved gases and solids into the environment. Impacts connected with geothermal fluids can be partially ameliorated with the treatment or reinjection of the waste geothermal fluids. In addition, while CO_2 emissions dominate the gaseous emissions from most geothermal wells, overall emissions of CO_2 per unit of energy are still less than levels associated with fossil fuel plants [Organization for Economic Cooperation and Development (OECD), 1988]. Land subsidence and induced seismicity from the removal or forced injection of geothermal fluids are other environmental factors that must be considered.

3. Wind Power

Wind Energy Conversion Systems (WECS) capture solar energy stored in air movements caused by the uneven heating of the earth's surface. Most modern systems use lift across an airfoil surface (a concept similar to that of an airplane propeller) while some systems employ drag forces to turn the blades of the rotor. The rotor is commonly connected to an electric generator to produce direct current, although mechanical pumps are used in some countries. The main features of a Wind Energy Conversion System using three airfoil

---

[4]Energy systems for three different geothermal sources are represented in Appendix Figure A-5 in Foell et al. [1992].

blades are a rotor, transmission, electrical generator, and control system, all mounted on a tower.

The power output of WECS are determined by wind speed and rotor size. Wind speed is the principal factor governing the power output from WECS and represents a major constraint on their siting requirements. Typical systems will not operate in winds of less than 10 kilometers/hour (km/h). The power output and size of WECS vary significantly. The majority of wind turbines now in operation are intermediate in size, generating approximately 50 to 300 kilowatts (kW) peak capacity. Most WECS are located in industrialized countries such as Denmark, the Netherlands, and the United States.

The levelized cost of electricity generated from WECS can be competitive with intermediate and peak conventional generating costs in regions with favorable wind regimes, generating power for about 7-9 kilowatt-hours (kWh).[5] Since winds are variable over time, extensive use of wind power requires back up or energy storage. The need for storage is reduced somewhat due to the fact that wind speeds often follow consistent daily patterns (see discussion of storage in Section C.4 on direct solar energy).

Environmentally, WECS have some very clear advantages and some unique drawbacks. Once in place, these energy systems are essentially benign, producing no air emissions, water emissions, or wastes. The physical land required by a single machine is quite small comprising only the size of the base.

The negative impacts of WECS appear to be local in scale. Wind farms comprised of hundreds of WECS will require relatively large land areas allowing for a moderate distance between individual machines to account for the wake produced by the rotors. Noise generated from the rotors will create siting constraints. Comparatively large distances may be needed between WECS and residential communities [800 to 2500 meters (*m*)], although it may be possible to reduce this distance to between 300 to 500 *m* through suitable amelioration techniques. Finally, there is the combined visual impact of large clusters of WECS and their associated power transmission lines. The degree of impact will be largely subjective on the part of local residents but may also have broader impacts on recreation and tourism when units are located near coastlines.

4. Direct Solar Energy

Solar energy embodies the largest resource potential of any renewable or nonrenewable energy source. The amount of sunlight that can be collected and converted to energy at any time, however, is constrained by the amount of available land and the efficiency of energy conversion. Direct conversion of solar radiation into useful energy can be accomplished in many ways, e.g., solar architecture, solar thermal systems for hot water or electricity, and photovoltaic cells that convert solar energy directly into electricity.

a. Solar Thermal. Solar thermal systems collect heat from sunlight producing temperatures that can be used for industrial processes, electricity generation, or hot water heating. There are five predominant types of collectors: solar ponds, parabolic troughs, parabolic dishes, central receivers, and flat plate collectors. A central receiver system consists of an array of sun-tracking reflectors (heliostats) that focus light onto a receiver mounted on

---

[5]All monetary values are in United States dollars unless otherwise noted.

a tower. Solar energy absorbed at the receiver is transferred to a working fluid and converted into electrical energy via a steam turbine generator.

Application of these various technologies depends upon the end-use energy desired. Some sources believe that central receiver electric systems could become competitive for generating peak electric power by the mid-to-late 1990s. A study by Bechtel National and Pacific Gas and Electric predicts that central receivers of 100-200 MW could produce electricity in California for as little as 8-11/kWh by 1997 [Brower, 1990]. In the eastern Mediterranean, over 90% of the homes in Cyprus and 65% of the homes in Israel are equipped with solar hot water heaters. Despite the high initial costs of these systems, solar hot water heating in sunny climates is usually cost effective in comparison with electric water heating [Shea, 1988].

A distinct advantage of solar thermal systems (with the exception of central collectors, which are planned as large facilities of at least 30 MW capacity to take advantage of economies of scale) is that they are comprised of modular units that can be added or removed as demand changes, decreasing the risk in constructing facilities to meet predicted energy demand that may not materialize. Small modular units for the production of electricity may be economically competitive in rural areas which are costly to connect to the existing electricity grid and hot water heating units are even competitive in urban areas.

Environmentally, most solar thermal systems are relatively benign, producing waste only during routine maintenance periods. Solar collectors require large material inputs which is a one-time environmental and economic cost that is repeated at the end of the system's lifetime (currently estimated at 25-30 years). Land use for large station solar electric generation is comparable to the amount needed for electric generation from coal when land disturbances from coal mining are taken into account.[6]

b. Solar Photovoltaic. Photovoltaic (PV) cells convert sunlight into electricity by means of the photovoltaic effect. Photons of light strike the cell dislodging electrons from atoms. The charged electrons travel through the cell towards an oppositely charged contact drawn by a voltage created between two semiconductor materials. When the circuit is closed, an electric current is created.

The most dominant material used in photovoltaic construction is silicon. New manufacturing processes involving silicon as well as new exotic semiconducting materials are continuing to be developed. Conversion efficiencies of commercially available PV cells are currently about 15%, and laboratory tests involving single-crystal silicon, concentrating collectors and thin film systems have been demonstrated to have efficiencies in the high 20 percent and low 30 percent range [Brower, 1990].

The price of PV cells has fallen dramatically in just 15 years. In 1976 the cost per peak kilowatt of capacity was $44,000 (1986 dollars) and has fallen to the current estimated price of $4,000-$5,000 [Shea, 1988]. However, at this price, the cost of electricity generated from PV systems is 25-35 cents/kWh, usually beyond the price necessary to compete with current systems generating peak power. Nevertheless, PV systems have proven cost effective in some limited markets. For example, the largest market for PV systems is providing power for machinery and villages in areas far removed from utility grids.

---

[6]See Appendix Table B-7 in Foell et al. [1992].

As with solar thermal systems, most of the negative environmental effects of PV systems occur during the manufacturing process. PV cell fabrication requires exotic inputs and a number of toxic and explosive gases that pose a danger to plant workers and to the surrounding community if released. Land requirements for large scale PV electric generation are comparable to land requirements for coal mining for electric generation. In dispersed applications, individual cells can be placed on roof tops with little or no environmental effects.

c. Storage. An important issue with respect to solar and wind energy systems is energy storage. Because sunlight is variable, energy storage systems or backup systems will be necessary if power is to be provided on an uninterrupted basis. A number of technologies are currently available for providing energy storage for solar energy systems: hydroelectric, electric batteries, compressed air, thermal storage, and hydrogen. Hydroelectric storage is a simple form of storage that is already in wide commercial use.

Thermal storage usually involves heating or cooling a liquid or solid mass. Storage can either be short-term (storing excess energy by day for conversion to electricity at night or cloudy days), or long-term (using large, insulated underground storage to collect summer heat for use during winter months).

Although the need for energy storage in conjunction with renewable energy sources is an important issue, its significance should not be exaggerated. For many renewable utility applications, energy storage will not be necessary in the short-term. Some electric utilities have excess reserve capacity and some plants can be economically relegated to backup. In addition, variations in electricity demand are often matched closely with levels of solar insolation so that the energy will be available during times of high demand. Energy storage will be necessary, as solar and wind energy sources comprise a larger fraction of the total electric generating supply and in remote areas away from existing utility grids where renewable supply is the only means for heating or electricity generation.

5. Hydropower

Hydropower is a well proven source of power. Large scale plants are common throughout the world where river flow and geological conditions are favorable. This chapter focuses on small scale micro (up to 100 kW), mini (100 kW to 1000 kW), and small (1000 kW to 20,000 kW) plants [George and Van Schaik, 1988]. Plants are common at these scales. In Burundi, Costa Rica, Guatemala, Guinea, Madagascar, Nepal, Papua New Guinea, and Peru, small-hydro potential exceeds total installed generating capacity from all other energy sources. China is the world leader in small-hydro, with about 90,000 turbines supplying electricity to rural areas in 1988 [Shea, 1988]. The Philippines reported 3.9 MW of mini-hydro in place in 1980. In the United States by 1985, private enterprise had brought almost 1,000 MW of small hydropower on-line and electric utilities had installed twice that amount. Nearly 60 percent of the total 3,200 MW was installed during the 1980s [Shea, 1988].

The ***central economic question*** with micro-hydro and mini-hydro is whether the plants can be built and connected to grids, or directly to users, at costs competitive with other sources of power. Small scale hydro is particularly interesting in sites which are isolated from central grids, but where power is required, often generated by small diesel generation sets. Because of the finite number of potential sites in any region and the fact that the best sites are developed first, the cost of power from new sites is generally increasing. There is, however, tremendous variability from region to region as is the potential for and the extent of hydropower development.

The main environmental impact of major hydro facilities is the disruption of river ecologies and the inundation of land under the power reservoirs. Besides the ecosystems and often social disruptions caused by inundation, downstream areas are impacted by the change in sediment loads, disruption of fish migration patterns, changes in water temperature, etc. A dramatic example of these effects is represented by the Aswan Dam. The advantage of small scale hydro, including run of the river hydro, is that the areas of inundation are much smaller, and depending on the size of the facility, there may be no significant changes in sediment loads and other river characteristics.

6. Urban Waste

Although urban wastes are made up of an assortment of materials, some of which are not renewable, urban waste can be considered an ongoing and hence renewable source of energy. Renewable components of urban waste include organic material, which accounts for over half of urban wastes. The amount of urban wastes now being generated and landfilled can be considerably reduced by the adoption of recycling and composting, and a growing number of cities around the world are integrating recycling into their waste management plans. The benefits of recycling are the energy and material savings of avoiding the use of virgin materials and reduced pollution. For example, aluminum is an extremely energy-intensive material, however, recycling aluminum requires just 5 percent as much energy as producing it from bauxite [Pollock, 1987].

However, even after recycling, it is anticipated that there will continue to be a waste stream which can be combusted for the production of power or process heat. The facilities required for combusting urban wastes are similar to those for the combustion of biomass described in Section C.1 (Biomass). The main difference is the allowance for separation of combustibles which may take place prior to combustion, yielding refuse derived fuel (RDF) and other materials -- some of which may be recycled -- or the separation (of ferrous materials) after mass burn (i.e. after burning of the mass of materials).

Power generation from urban wastes does not generally compete with coal-based generation if transportation infrastructure is available to economically transport coal and if landfill costs are low. This is due to the high energy content and ease of handling of coal. However, in an increasing number of industrialized countries, landfill costs and environmental impacts, such as ground water pollution, are becoming so great as to make the use of urban wastes economical. Essentially, the higher cost of the fuel is more than offset by the avoided cost of landfilling. Waste to power plants are becoming increasingly popular although problems have been reported [Abert, 1985]. Worldwide, there are more than 1500 operating municipal solid-waste incinerator units built by selected major manufacturers [Penner et al., 1988]. In Switzerland 80% of municipal wastes are disposed of by incineration [Penner et al., 1988] and in West Germany 47 waste incineration plants serve 35% of its population [Barniske, 1989].

The production of power or process heat from municipal waste has a considerable environmental advantage of greatly diminishing solid wastes for landfill. Depending on their location, they may also reduce the distance that municipal wastes have to be hauled. Their environmental disadvantage relates to emissions of CO_2, sulfur oxides, particulates, heavy metals, and other pollutants. Particular attention has been focused on the emissions of dioxins and furans [Barniske, 1989; Penner et al., 1987]. While controversy continues, it appears that these emissions can be reduced to acceptable levels [Barniske, 1989] and that further work in terms of controlling input to the incinerators by prior recycling and source controls is promising. In addition, concern has been mounting over the disposal of the ash residues from incinerators. Because the ash often contains heavy metals from discarded batteries, lighting fixtures, and other sources, Sweden treats it as hazardous waste [Shea, 1987].

In planning disposal options for urban waste (recycling and incineration), program planners should include an assessment of the net energy gains from various materials. Wastes that prove more valuable when recycled should be separated from the waste stream rather than burned. Overbuilding incinerator capacity can result in a desire to meet the designed capacity by increasing the waste stream through the curtailment of recycling, a policy option that could waste more energy than it produces.

III. Framework for Energy Planning and Investment Analysis

The nature of and difficulties in selecting energy options in regions and countries were summarized in Part I. In Part II, the basic principles in describing any energy system were presented, followed by a summary discussion of a cross section of important renewable energy systems in terms of their environmental consequences, costs, energy balances, and uncertainties.

Energy policymakers and planners must be able to use this type of information for renewable resources and parallel information on conventional energy sources in setting policies influencing energy supply and demand and in making specific investments associated with these polices. There are two fundamental concepts that are useful in guiding choice. The ***first concept*** is integrated resource planning [see Hanson et al., 1991 forthcoming, for a description], also referred to as least-cost planning. This concept is particularly powerful within a multi-objective decisionmaking framework. The ***second concept*** is the combining of conserved and supplied energy into what is called an "integrated supply curve" [Bodlund et al., 1989].[7] The application of these two concepts provides a rigorous basis for aiding decisionmakers through the difficult, uncertain, and extremely important, ongoing process of setting energy policy and making energy investments, whose selection includes environmental considerations. This part describes both the concepts behind this prescriptive approach and the formulation of analytical and operational methods for applying it to investment decisions involving renewable energy resources.

A. Institutional Setting

As described in the introduction of this chapter, energy planning and investments in Africa, Asia, Europe, the Middle East, and Latin America are carried out primarily by governments working to various degrees with private firms. Governments and firms are

[7]The "integrated supply curve" is not really a curve but a connected set of discrete levels of different costs; if desired, the levels could be approximated by a smooth curve.

working within the broader context of international and domestic market forces. Energy supply of commercial energy sources is dominated by large organizations such as national electric power companies and national and international oil companies. Private firms may have major participation in activities such as producing oil, gas, or coal, refining, and marketing products to final consumers, as well as generating power. Even where private firms play one or more of these roles, the government (or a parastatal organization) usually has a strong position through determining production agreements, pricing, and profit sharing.

Energy demand planning is more diverse with more decision units, i.e. firms (state or private) and individual consumers. Government, however, has significant influence on energy demand through energy infrastructure provision and energy pricing. Governments may also influence energy demand via specific programs to encourage energy conservation. Such programs include audit programs, demonstration programs, investment incentives, grants, and loan funds.

The decision picture for the informal sector and for non-commercial fuels such as firewood is highly dispersed. Government has much less influence, although it can influence the use of non-commercial fuels by providing infrastructure and pricing policy for competing commercial fuels, including electricity.

In light of the large governmental role, the institutional setting that is used here as a point of reference is the government agency (or agencies) responsible for making decisions on commercial energy investments and determining energy prices.

B. Integrated Resource Planning

In the ***traditional approach*** to energy planning for electricity and other major commercial energy sources, a national utility or oil company is engaged in the following: (i) it forecasts demand; (ii) it screens supply options according to its economic and financial objectives and engineering constraints; (iii) it conducts detailed analyses of selected options; and (iv) it obtains financing and other approvals to invest in what appears to be the most promising option. In countries where there is an independent budgeting, regulatory, or planning agency with powers of approval for public sector investments, the fourth step includes requesting approval from that agency. This is often done within the context of a periodic (typically five year) planning process. In evaluating a request, the budgeting or planning agency typically considers three threshold questions:

(i) Is the proposed plant needed to provide sufficient capacity to maintain adequate supply reliability?
(ii) Are the technological aspects of the proposal sound?
(iii) Is the proposal financially feasible?

This traditional approach to planning is summarized in Figure 6 [Hanson et al., 1991 forthcoming].

The traditional energy planning process has several deficiencies. Planning is dominated by supply-side considerations while demand-side considerations, which frequently are more economically viable and less environmentally harmful, are ignored. Another deficiency is that traditional planning limits the criteria for project evaluation, generally focusing on financial and economic considerations.

Figure 6: Traditional Energy Planning

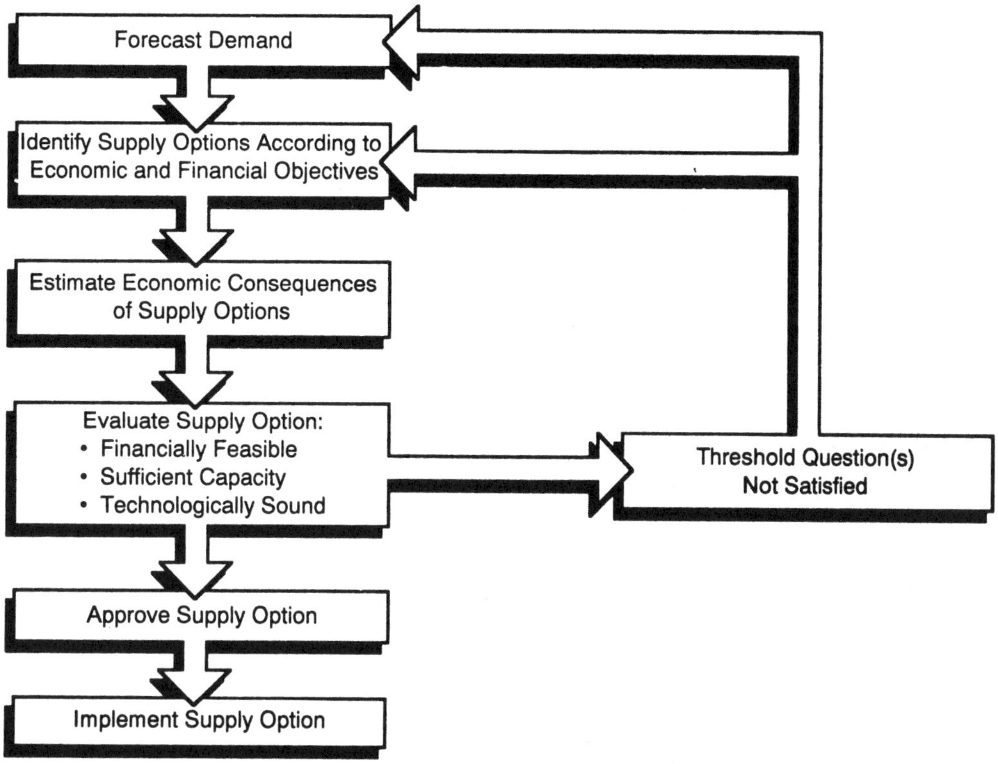

Source: Adapted from Hanson et al. [1991 forthcoming].

Integrated resource planning is a recent and important departure from traditional planning. A central aspect of integrated resource planning is the provision of energy services at minimum cost using demand and supply options. Minimizing the cost of energy services (such as heating, lighting, and mechanical drive in manufacturing processes) extends beyond achieving the lowest direct cost for energy supply; ***meeting energy requirements efficiently requires attention to economic, environmental, and social effects***. Thus, the intent of least-cost planning is to consider all relevant factors explicitly and balance competing interests to determine the method for meeting energy requirements.

A particularly useful technique for presenting and comparing direct costs of supply and demand side options is the use of "integrated supply curves" [Bodlund et al., 1989]. Integrated supply curves (in their simplest form) compare energy supply and demand options for meeting energy needs in terms of the direct per unit cost. An example (from the Swedish case study discussed in Part IV) of an integrated supply curve for electricity is shown in Figure 7 [Bodlund et al., 1989, p. 923]. Cumulative supply of energy is shown on the horizontal axis and the incremental cost of each supply addition is on the vertical axis. While the development of these supply curves is valuable in considering energy options, they are limited by considering only ***direct costs***. The challenge is then in augmenting such curves to consider other important costs and objectives, e.g.,social disruption, carbon emissions, sulfur dioxide emissions, solid and hazardous wastes [Vine and Harris, 1989]. The framework described in this part is designed to develop such supply curves and augment them with multi-objective decision support techniques.

1. The Setting: Global, National, Sectoral, and Facility Level

Energy planning and investment analysis take place continuously and simultaneously at the national, sectoral, and facility or household levels. While truly global decisions are seldom made, decisions at the national, sectoral, or facility level must be cognizant of global market and environmental conditions and trends. A familiar example of a global market is the international oil market.

The basic objective of selecting the least-cost option remains the same at each of the levels. As one ascends levels from the facility towards the global level, the choices become wider, the uncertainty and consequences larger, and the costs greater. The necessary analysis to support decisions also increases. For the purposes of this chapter, the discussion of the overall framework and specific techniques focuses on the sectoral planning level, for example electric power system investments, and the national level.

2. Identifying Potential Investment Sequences

Energy sector investments are continuous, and periodic decisions are required. At each decision point, choices have to be made as to the best investment, not in the context of just one point in time, but in the face of the sequence of investments required through time. Figure 8 provides a characterization of this planning process, which takes place every five years in a number of countries. For each iteration, demand is estimated and sets of investment options identified to meet this demand. The investments within each option set must be staged sequentially. In addition, consideration must be given to the longer-term implications of these investments and to the subsequent options that are opened up or closed off. For example, the Aswan Dam in Egypt delayed the development of gas-fired generation,

Figure 7: Example Integrated Supply Curve for Electricity

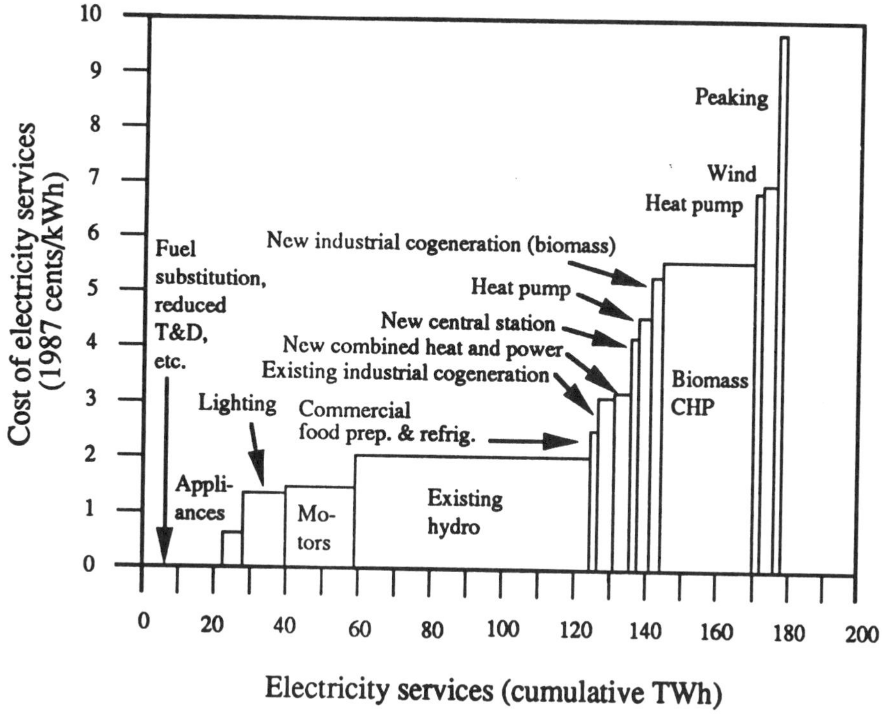

Source: Bodlund et al. [1989].

Legend: T & D = transmission and distribution losses; CHP = combined heat and power; cents/kWh = center per kilowatt-hours; TWh = terawatt-hours

Figure 8: Integrated Resource Planning

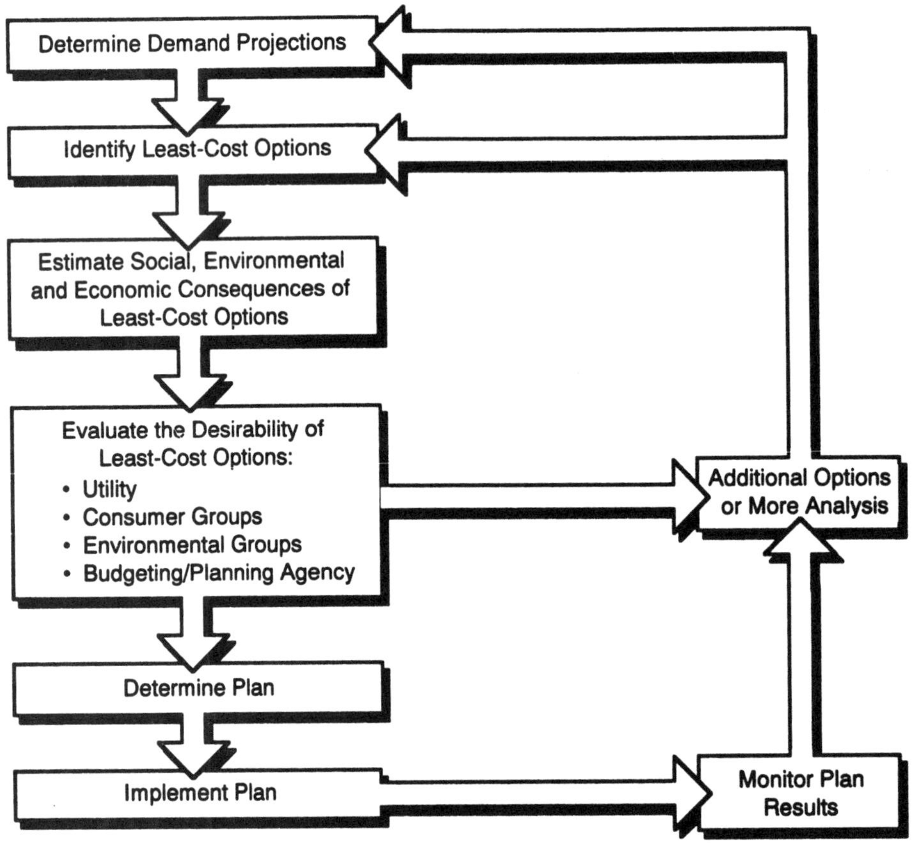

Source: Adapted from Hanson et al. [1991 forthcoming].

eliminated naturally flooded agriculture in favor of irrigated agriculture, and made Egypt's power planning subject to the varying flows of the Nile.

A central feature of the potential investment sequence options is uncertainty over a broad range of factors, including conventional costs, time required for implementation, environmental impacts, future prices of energy inputs, and social impacts. Decisionmakers must do the best that they can in choosing one investment sequence over other options. The periodic nature of the planning process, however, provides for continuous review of the status and progress of energy supply, whether derived from conventional or renewable investments, or from conservation investments.

3. Resource Supply Characterization

In order to compare renewable energy options to conventional energy and conservation options, systems for all relevant options are characterized in a consistent set of parameters or characteristics. The selection of characteristics is determined by the objectives of the nation and its decisionmakers.[8] As described in Part II, these and many other factors may be used to characterize renewable as well as conventional supply and conservation options. These factors encompass not only the direct effects at the point of energy use but the effects along the entire fuel cycle as well as the indirect effects.

The following provides an even more encompassing list of potential considerations in planning energy supply [Wisconsin Public Service Commission, 1986]:

- Health (such as respiratory disease);
- Safety (such as accident-deaths and injuries);
- Reliability (such as outages, certainty of conservation or energy production);
- Environmental -- primary and secondary impacts (such as physical and biological wetland impacts, loss of habitat, acid deposition impacts, water quality impacts, and endangered species impacts);
- Use of nonrenewable resources (such as coal, petroleum, and metals);
- Social (such as jobs, equity, loss of agricultural land, and production);
- Economic (such as taxes, economic development, and competition);
- Political (such as legislation and public relations);
- Flexibility (such as risks and adaptability to external changes);

---

[8] The characteristics provided in Appendix B and Appendix Table C-2 in Foell et al. [1992] include a number of factors that are likely to be of considerable interest to policymakers, such as rates, customer costs, sulfur dioxide emissions, solid waste, and employment.

- Technical innovation (such as new methods to serve load or achieve conservation).

Many of these factors are extremely difficult to estimate or project accurately. In part, this difficulty is due to the complexity of relating emissions emanating from and materials used in a given fuel cycle to impacts on the ecology, the economy, and society. ***Difficulty in estimating these impacts, however, does not justify their exclusion from the energy decisionmaking process.***

The point in identifying these factors is to make policymakers cognizant of those factors which are influenced in significant ways by choices in energy system investments. Different energy investments will have very different impacts. There is no "correct" answer as to which of these factors should and should not be used in choosing among investments. This is largely determined by what the citizens and policymakers in a given country value as being important. These factors will usually be the focus of the greatest effort in characterizing energy options.

4. Decision Criteria

Selecting decision criteria by which to evaluate energy investment options is an exercise of judgment and values. It is both necessary and desirable that these choices be made within the country or region which must make the investment. To the degree that these decisions affect other regions, however, policymakers should be cognizant of these external effects. The process is made difficult by the ***uncertainty*** in estimating effects as well as the uncertainty and differences of ***opinion*** as to what are important impacts.

As an example of decision criteria, Table 5 lists the criteria used in a previous study in which economic considerations were set aside to focus on human safety issues and other environmental effects in evaluating coal and nuclear power trade-offs.[9]

The intent of selecting decision criteria is to use them in identifying viable investment options and for comparing these options. The options which provide the necessary energy services and which perform the best in meeting the criteria will be the preferred choices. It is inevitable that some trade-offs will be necessary in choosing among options because decision criteria will generally be in conflict. For example, the option with the least direct cost may be the option associated with the greatest emissions of precursors responsible for acid rain. Specific methods for utilizing decision criteria are discussed below in Section III.C (Analytical and Operational Methods).

5. Sustainability Criterion

In recent years, sustainability has been the focus of considerable discussion related to strategies for development. It received prominent discussion in the United Nations World Commission on Environment and Development Report, *Our Common Future* [World Commission on Environment and Development, 1987]. A simple definition of sustainability

[9]Appendix Table B-1 in Foell et al. [1992] lists the decision criteria used in evaluating a mix of energy supply and conservation options for an electric utility in the United States. The table includes both conventional economic as well as environmental and social factors.

Table 5: Impact Factors Used in Study of Coal and Nuclear Power Options

Factors Considered	Units
1. Total quantified fatalities	Deaths
2. Permanent Land Use	Acres
3. Temporary Land Use	Acres
4. Water evaporated	10^{12} gallons
5. SO_2 emissions	10^6 tons
6. Particulate emissions	10^6 tons
7. Thermal energy needed	10^{12} kWh(th)
8. Radioactive waste	Metric tons
9. Nuclear safeguards	Tons Pu_f
10. Health effects of chronic air pollution exposure	Tons lead emitted
11. Electricity generated	10^{12} kWh(e)

Source: Buehring et al. [1976].

Legend: SO_2 = sulfur dioxide
Pu_f = fissile plutonium
kWh(th) = thermal kilowatt-hours
kWh(e) = electric kilowatt-hours

used in that report is "development that meets the needs of the present without compromising the ability of future generations to meet their own needs." Siddayao [in this volume] states that "economic growth is still the primary goal of development planning, but the criteria of sustainability will be viewed as ***necessary constraints***. This implies that economic development will be pursued in such a manner that an increase in output and consumption will not seriously impair the availability and quality, including the assimilative capacity, of natural resources over time."

From the perspective of selecting investment streams, short-term and long-term environmental implications must be considered in determining whether natural resources and ecosystems will be impaired or destroyed through time. Incorporating sustainability as a factor within the decision criteria suggests that one or more factors which measure sustainability be included in the list of factors [Section III.B.4 (Decision Criteria)] or that qualitative measures of sustainability be defined for use as a screening criteria. In other words, for an option to be considered, the sustainability of identified ecosystems and species must be reasonably assured. As with the other factors discussed previously, it is inevitable that there will be uncertainty associated with defining and measuring sustainability as well as differences of opinion as to whether an appropriate definition is used [Brown et al., 1988; Liverman et al., 1989]. What is crucial is that sustainability be explicitly considered and provided for as the energy planning process, as represented in Figure 8, proceeds through time.

6. Internalization of Impacts

The use of the broader decision criteria, such as those discussed in Sections B.4 (Decision Criteria) and B.5 (Sustainability Criterion), implies that conventional economic signals, such as prices of primary energy resources and final products, are not providing all of the information necessary decisions that result in economic efficiency. The use of broader criteria also recognizes the fact that many choices can not be made strictly on economic grounds, but rather are a matter of values.

Internalizing impacts, or in other words having the cost of side effects born by the producer or user, can serve to narrow the gap between the most desirable outcome and what may result if impacts are not considered. This may serve not only in making the choice of preferred investment streams somewhat easier for policymakers, but more readily acceptable to producers and users. For example, the price of electricity from coal production often excludes the negative environmental impacts of sulfur emission. Thus, coal-generated power appears to be less costly to society and the economy than it actually is. The external effects can at least be partially internalized by including the cost of environmental damage in the fuel cost and hence the price of power, or by requiring environmental controls to reduce external damage. Faced with more accurate economic signals power producers would then have incentives to control the sulfur emissions and consumers to reduce their consumption.

External costs cannot be internalized in all cases, but internalizing costs can be used to narrow the gap between existing investment sequences and more desirable investment sequences. This will also help eliminate conflicting economic signals to consumers and producers and make policy choices to protect the environment less politically difficult.

7. Choosing Appropriate Investment Sequences

The bottom line in an integrated resource planning framework is making the best possible energy policy and investment decisions. As outlined in Figure 8, the options identified and criteria selected for evaluating the options provide the basis for a decision on the best investment sequence or plan. Figure 8 also indicates that a number of interests will, or should, be involved in the planning process. It is useful to involve a number of interests in the planning process as they bring new ideas, perspectives, and values into the deliberations. Ultimately, however, the policymakers responsible for the energy systems will have to make the final choices. Once these choices are made, it is essential to monitor the results and begin preparation for the next set of choices.

There are numerous methods available for supporting policymakers in the difficult task of making and implementing the investment sequences. In the section that follows, specific selected methods will be considered which are particularly useful for including environmental considerations in evaluating energy investments.

C. Analytical and Operational Methods

1. Existing Methods

Numerous methods have been devised and applied to the evaluation of public and private investments. A few of the common methods include benefit-cost analysis, cost-effectiveness analysis, risk-benefit analysis, environmental impact assessment, and decision analysis. Siddayao [in this volume] notes that all decision rules within these methods: (i) define gains and losses according to some objectives and (ii) measure the gains and losses. Furthermore, definition and measurement requires judgmental weighing according to some scale of social and political criteria. In general, those options which are expected to result in the greatest net gains and which are politically and socially more acceptable are the preferred choice.

Environmental considerations are brought into energy policy development and investment planning to the degree that policymakers and analysts deliberately identify and measure environmental features. Environmental considerations are often ignored or understated due to inattention to the environment and due to lack of knowledge of ecosystems, which makes definition, measurement, and valuation extremely complex, uncertain, and open-ended tasks.

Within the context of evaluating means to incorporate environmental considerations into renewable energy policy and planning, there is little to be gained by attempting to demonstrate that one methodology is superior to all others in all situations. Indeed, ***appropriately applied***, many methods can be used to accomplish the same goal which is to provide information on the advantages and disadvantages, and hence the trade-offs of different investment streams. There are, however, two operational methods that we have found extremely useful in organizing complex environmental and economic information on both renewable and conventional energy sources.

The ***first operational method*** is to construct marginal cost functions for providing energy services whether supply-side or demand-side. These integrated supply curves can be based on direct costs only, or they may be adjusted to internalize some environmental externalities. From this basis, investment sequences for conventional and renewable energy sources and conservation can be compared to demand projections within the planning framework outlined in Figure 8.

The *second operational method* is to use a multi-objective decision analysis framework to explicitly evaluate environmental consequences, particularly for environmental concerns that are not amenable to incorporation into the integrated supply curves and are difficult to quantify. In Section C.3 (The Use of Multi-Attribute Decision Analysis in Selecting Energy Options), a particular version of decision analysis called multi-attribute decision analysis is identified. However, any number of multi-objective techniques can be reasonably adapted to the task of explicitly considering and weighing quantitative and qualitative environmental factors and helping policymakers sort through the tough and uncertain consequences of investment decisions.

2. Marginal Cost Approach to Selecting Energy Options

A conceptually powerful method for portraying options is a marginal cost approach using integrated supply curves. As shown in Figure 7, integrated supply curves may be used to summarize the relative direct cost and availability of supply-side (conventional and renewable) sources and demand-side measures. For a given region, a number of such integrated supply curves would be developed. A minimum of two curves would be required, one for energy needs that are best met with electricity and another for non-electrical energy needs. For regions with large and well defined sectoral energy requirements, e.g., industrial and commercial sectors, separate curves may be used for each of the sectors.

To apply these curves, base curves are developed for the current situation. Options for investments in the next planning period (Figure 8) are represented by separate curves which are then combined with the base curves to represent the energy system in the future. The integrated supply curves can be used to represent investment choices in the face of a number of changes in the energy situation, including:

- *New Technology*. New technologies, whether based on conventional or renewable sources, may be portrayed in terms of the cost of energy from the source and the amount of energy at any given cost. A specified technology may have a number of cost levels depending on such things as scale (for example a 5 MW wood-fired power plant versus a 50 MW wood-fired power plant).

- *Change in Prices*. The cost of energy services from existing technologies changes as a function of energy input prices or equipment costs. For example, the cost of oil-fired power would increase as a result of an increase in the world price of oil or the imposition of tariffs or taxes. The cost of providing conservation, say in the form of power savings from efficient motors, may also be changed as a result of changes in import fees on equipment. The result in both cases is that the cost of energy will change and the integrated supply curve will be altered to reflect the new conditions. If price changes are sufficiently large, a particular energy source or conservation measure will become too costly to utilize.

- ***Environmental Constraints.*** New provisions necessary to protect the environment may eliminate or limit certain options. For example, caps on the amount of carbon emissions may limit the amount of coal used in a region. Assuming no change in the level of controls, the cost of power from the coal may not change but the amount of power available from coal decreases.

The integrated supply curves may be used as a heuristic device for evaluating energy options or may be used in a formal energy planning model at varying degrees of sophistication. They may be used to reflect direct cost only, or they may be adjusted to reflect environmental and social costs. In other words, some of the external costs may be internalized. How these curves are developed formally is dependent on the analytical human resources and time available. Even when computer-based curves are not developed or implemented as part of a formal mathematical planning model, these supply curves are conceptually useful to policymakers faced with investment decisions.

a. Simplified Example of Integrated Supply Curves. The consequence of changes in technology and environmental constraints can be portrayed with integrated supply curves. This is demonstrated starting with the supply curve shown in Figure 9 and the following simplified situation:

- The only use for electricity is lighting.

- Demand for electrical services in 1990 is 3 terawatt-hours (TWh), all of which is met by coal-fired generation.

- The required level of electricity services for lighting at a future point in time, i.e. the year 2000, is 7 TWh.

- There will be five sources of electricity services: efficient lighting, coal-fired generation, oil-fired generation, central station solar, and photovoltaic generation.

- Coal-fired generation can not be expanded due to mine limitations within the region and a lack of facilities for importing coal into the region.

A base projection for providing electricity services in the year 2000 is shown in Figure 10. The least costly supply option is efficient lighting which provides 3 TWh equivalent. The coal-fired generation available in 1990 is maintained. Finally, 1 TWh of oil-fired generation is added to meet overall demand. Central station solar and photovoltaics are too costly to compete.

A future with a severe environmental constraint is envisioned in Figure 11. In this projection, an international treaty is implemented which requires dramatic decreases in carbon emissions from power generation due to climate impacts. The effect of this treaty for the region is that coal-fired generating capacity is retired. Oil-fired generation, which has lower CO_2 emissions is brought on-line as is 2 TWh of central station solar. A consequence of this change in supply is a higher average and marginal cost (private cost) of electricity services.

Figure 9: 1990 Integrated Supply Curve

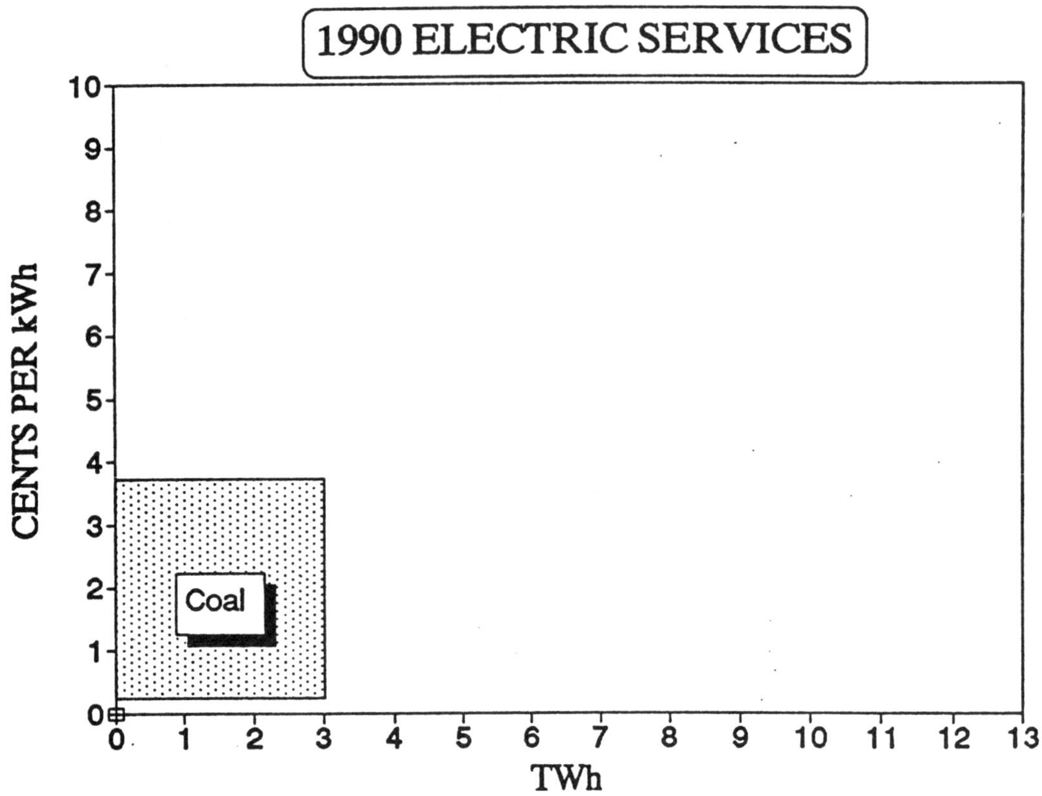

Source: Authors.

Note: The "integrated supply curve" is not really a curve but a connected set of discrete levels of different costs; if desired, the levels could be approximated by a smooth curve.

Legend: kWh = kilowatt-hours
TWh = terawatt-hours

Figure 10: Integrated Supply Curve for the Year 2000: Base Case

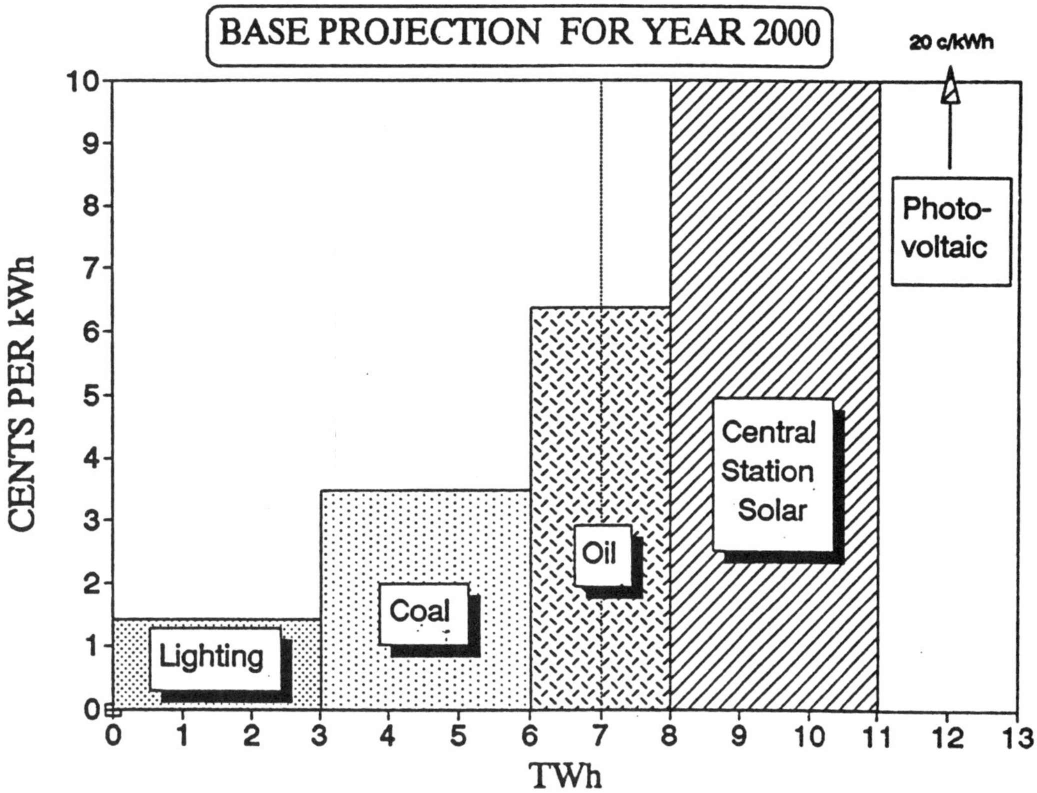

Source: Authors.

Note: The "integrated supply curve" is not really a curve but a connected set of discrete levels of different costs; if desired, the levels could be approximated by a smooth curve.

Legend: kWh = kilowatt-hours
TWh = terawatt-hours
c/kWh = cents per kilowatt-hours

Figure 11: Integrated Supply Curve for the Year 2000: Environmental Constraint Case

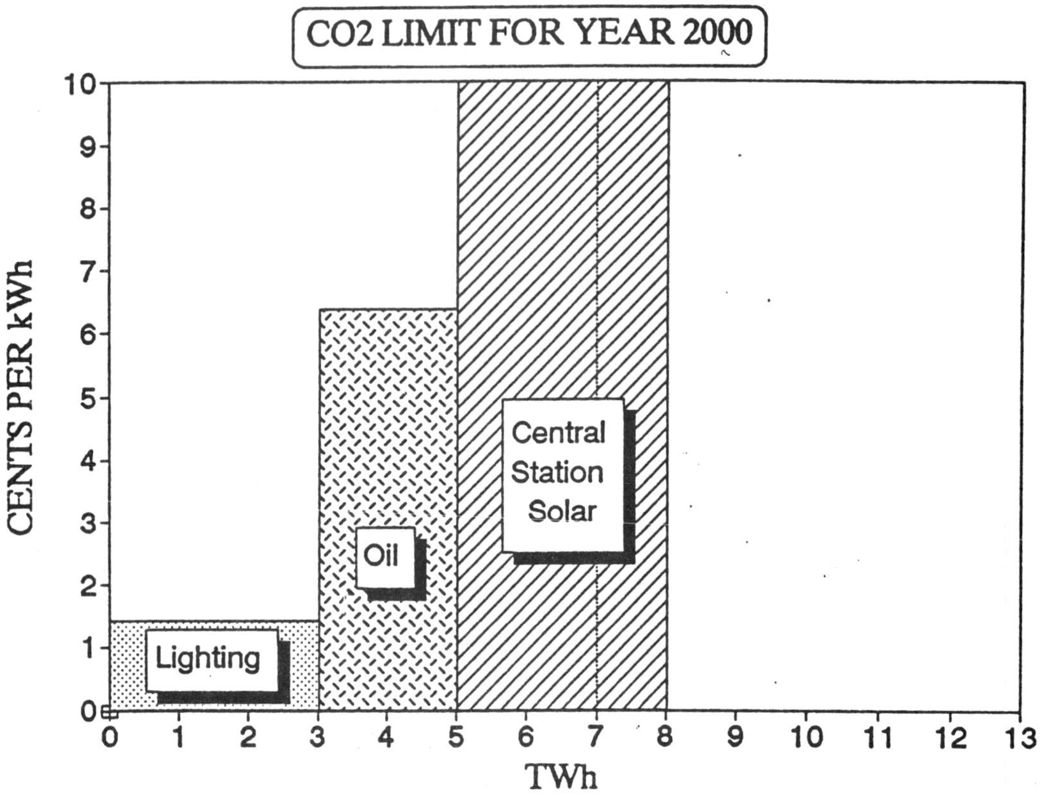

Source: Authors.

Note: The "integrated supply curve" is not really a curve but a connected set of discrete levels of different costs; if desired, the levels could be approximated by a smooth curve.

Legend: CO_2 = carbon dioxide
kWh = kilowatt-hours
TWh = terawatt-hours

Figure 12: Integrated Supply Curve for the Year 2000: Decline in Cost of Photovoltaics Case

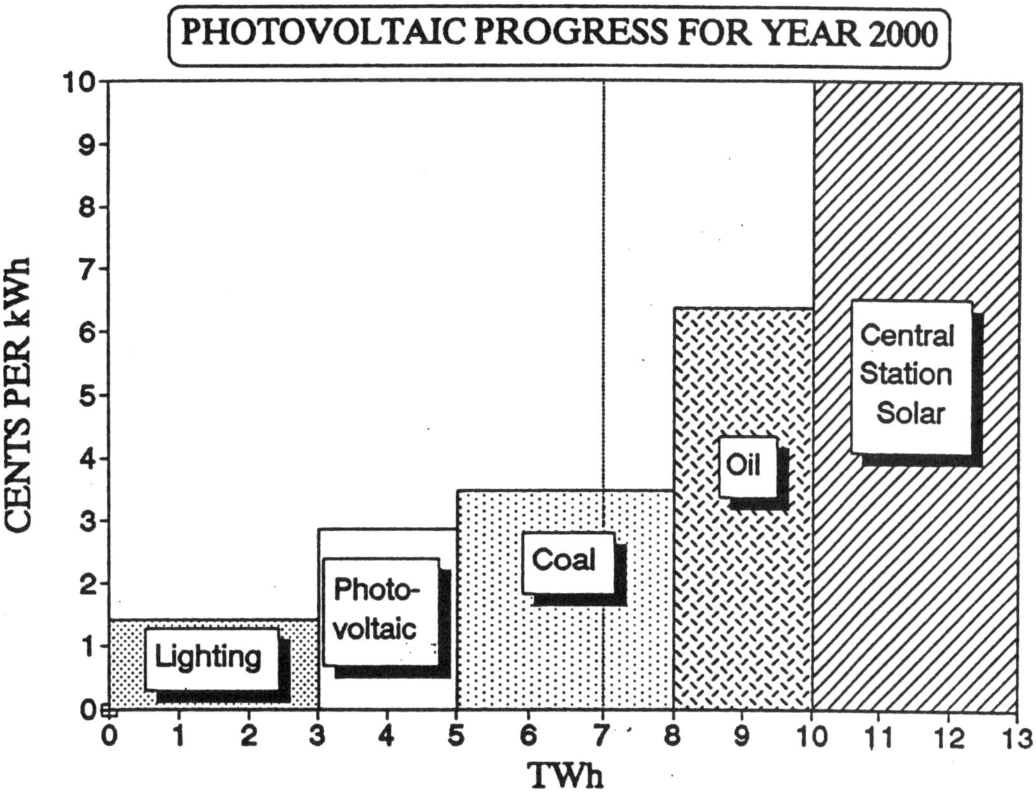

Source: Authors.

Note: The "integrated supply curve" is not really a curve but a connected set of discrete levels of different costs; if desired, the levels could be approximated by a smooth curve.

Legend: kWh = kilowatt-hours
TWh = terawatt=hours

A quite different scenario is shown in Figure 12 where continued progress in reducing the cost of photovoltaics results in a cost (private) slightly below that of coal. As a result, 2 TWh of photovoltaics are generated and coal-fired generation is reduced, relative to the base projection, from 3 to 2 TWh. The result in this case is a lower average and marginal cost of electrical services as well as a reduction in carbon emissions, although not as low as in Figure 11.

This highly simplified example demonstrates how integrated supply curves can be used to represent and evaluate energy service options and various changes in technology, prices, and environmental constraints. There are important environmental and social considerations which can not be reasonably addressed by the use of integrated supply curves because of the difficulty in assigning costs per kWh. Examples of variables that are difficult to quantify in economic terms include differences in carbon or sulfur emissions, in employment patterns, in the amount of equipment or primary energy that must be imported, in hazardous wastes that must be permanently stored, in the level of interaction with local economies and agriculture, and in the probability of accidents at different levels of magnitude. Some of these differences are particularly notable in comparing conventional and renewable sources of energy.

3. The Use of Multi-Attribute Decision Analysis in Selecting Energy Options

The choice of energy options inevitably involves trade-offs. Among fossil energy sources, there is the trade-off between the relative abundance and low cost of coal and the higher cost but lower emission properties of oil and particularly natural gas, both of which result in lower emissions of carbon, sulfur, and other pollutants. The trade-offs in comparing conventional and renewable resources become even more complex due to some features inherent to renewables. Renewable energy systems tend to have different types and locations of environmental impacts compared to conventional energy sources.

As noted in Section II.B (Summary Description of Selected Renewable Energy Systems), net emissions of carbon, sulfur, particulates, and other air and water emissions from renewables are either zero or extremely low. Much of the environmental impact of most renewables occurs at the point of manufacture, which can require extensive amounts of materials. After manufacture, most remaining impacts occur immediately adjacent to the point of energy conversion where, for example, visual and noise impacts may occur. The impacts of renewables are more localized and of a different nature than impacts from conventional energy sources. As will be described in the case studies in Part IV, renewables also tend to be more costly than conventional energy sources, based on conventional private cost (i.e. ignoring externalities and existing subsidies to conventional energy sources), and 1990 fossil energy prices.

In the case of biomass sources which are converted to gaseous form or combusted directly, air emissions are a consideration, although sulfur is much less a problem and carbon release equals carbon uptake if the feedstock is managed as a sustainable resource. Other air pollutants such as particulates can be effectively controlled. The major concerns with biomass sources are the land, soil erosion, and water impacts of crops raised as energy feedstocks. The conversion of local agriculture from traditional or export oriented commodity crops to biomass energy feedstock can also have important social impacts. Because of the relatively low density of biomass, long distance transportation is usually not economically feasible, one implication being that impacts of biomass harvesting are localized.

The fundamental underlying question in comparing renewable energy to conventional energy is how to balance the avoidance of more significant regional and global scale pollution with the higher direct private cost (at least at 1990 relative costs of oil, natural gas, and coal) of renewables. Furthermore, to the degree that risk of major increases in the price of oil exists, what value is derived from accepting somewhat higher direct private costs for renewables and thereby reducing the risk of large cost increases in oil? This is essentially an "insurance" argument.

Multi-attribute decision analysis (MADA) can facilitate decisionmaking within this complex situation by enabling systematic evaluation of alternative energy sources. Important advantages relative to more traditional policy evaluation methods (such as benefit-cost analysis) are that it explicitly recognizes and incorporates value judgments, and formally incorporates both quantitative and qualitative measures for evaluating outcomes of the energy options being considered. This evaluation proceeds by: (i) identification of objectives (economic, environmental, social etc.), (ii) estimation of outcomes for each option in terms of the identified objectives, (iii) explicit specification of the policymaker's preferences for each objective, and (iv) ranking options based on the options's attainment of the stated objectives. As with any decision support method, the overall process and ranking of options are aids to arriving at decisions in complex, dynamic, and uncertain situations with conflicting objectives. This method will typically be used in an iterative fashion as users struggle with difficult trade-offs between the various options.

Multi-attribute decision analysis utilizes a rigorous theoretical basis which may be explained in mathematical terms.[10] In less formal terms, the use of MADA involves the following elements:

- A *policymaker(s)* or some type of *committee* is identified as responsible for deciding on energy investments and policy. This policymaker within a developing country typically is at national power companies, oil companies, or national planning or economic development agencies. The analysts (staff and consultants) work with the policymaker in identifying the relevant options, driven by the need for energy services (see Figure 8).

- The next stage of using MADA is the determination of objectives in providing energy services, which typically include minimizing direct costs, but also are likely to include other qualitative and quantitative objectives such as political acceptability, employment, minimizing social disruption, and avoiding or minimizing various environmental impacts.

- Ways of measuring the attainment of these objectives are identified and analysis is then undertaken of the options to see how each option performs in meeting each objective. As an environmental example, if minimizing acid rain is an objective, one way of measuring how well an option meets this objective is to estimate the amount of sulfur dioxide and nitrogen dioxide emissions over the lifetime of each option.

- The policymaker also decides on the relative importance of the objectives and the importance of the level of accomplishment of each of the objectives. These are determined in a process called the elicitation of preferences. These preferences or

---

[10]A brief, mathematically oriented summary, some basic references, and an example application drawn from Hanson et al. [1991 forthcoming] are included in Appendix C found in Foell et al. [1992].

values are based on experience, scientific and technical judgment, and to some degree personal values. These values are present in any difficult decision, the point of MADA is to improve the decisionmaking by making these values explicit.

• Based on the weighting and utility functions determined above, the options are ranked. The policymaker then uses and often revises the weightings as the various investments and trade-offs involved are considered. The purpose is to support the policymaker in sorting through these complex issues. Should a major hydroelectric facility be built in the face of ecological and social disruption? Should coal-fired power plants be built instead which would not involve the social and ecological disruption but will result in higher power costs and more air pollution, acid rain, and carbon dioxide emissions? Ultimately, the policymaker in Figure 8 wants to find the mix of investments which work the best in providing the combination of energy at lower direct costs, with least social disruption, and least environmental impact.

The authors' experience is that MADA is a useful decision support tool. It may be used with other planning tools such as benefit-cost analysis to provide a different analytical perspective, or by itself.

4. Information/Data Needs

The thorough evaluation required for the large investments characteristic of energy systems requires extensive, systematic data, regardless of the evaluation procedures adopted. Because conventional supply sources are extensively relied upon, data for most aspects of these systems is generally available. Particular data needs exist, however, for systematic environmental data, as well as in the cases of conservation and renewable energy systems, for data on other aspects of the systems including technical, economic, environmental, and social data. For policy and investment purposes, options for meeting energy needs require a consistent basis of comparison. Reference energy networks, as described here, are an excellent means for providing consistent, system-wide data. Policymaking bodies need to assemble and continuously maintain this information to support their decisionmaking process.

5. Institutional and Implementation Issues

It is relevant at this juncture to consider the steps required in developing countries to advance the energy planning process to utilize integrated resource planning and the specific techniques described above in the evaluation of conventional energy supply, conservation, and renewable energy sources. Without such steps, energy planning will continue to follow the traditional process which often favors conventional sources at the expense of conservation and renewable sources and which limits the participation of other parties in the policymaking process. The adoption of integrated resource planning will encourage a more balanced, thorough, economically and environmentally efficient treatment of conventional, renewable, and conservation sources and will provide greater opportunity for a broader range of public input.

Specific opportunities to implement integrated resource planning are available within developing countries as well as within the international lending institutions. Lending institutions, as a condition of their loans, could require the adoption of an integrated resource planning framework. Developing countries with five year plans are well situated to adopt integrated resource planning because of the formal cycling that is built into their planning process. As depicted in Figure 8, a periodic reexamination of past accomplishments and future investments and policies is an integral part of the integrated resource planning process.

What would be a departure from traditional planning for most developing countries is the explicit focus given to ***environmental*** and ***social impacts*** of ***energy investments***, and the inclusion of broader ***public participation***, including newly emergent environmental groups. While this may appear to be a threat to effective planning, the experience in a number of countries is that the pressure brought by environmental groups has helped bring about wise, efficient long run decisions [see, for example, Foell and Hanson, 1980].

IV. Examples and Case Studies

The use of renewable energy is very substantial throughout the international community. Much of that energy is in the form of biomass used for cooking in low efficiency devices and large scale hydroelectric power plants. There are, however, a large number of additional renewable energy systems in place and an even larger array being considered. A central question for energy development policy and investment planning is which of these systems should be developed and when. A review of the experiences with large, recently implemented renewable energy programs is valuable for what is revealed about how these programs were identified, planned, financed, and implemented.

This part considers the experience of five major renewable energy programs in developing and industrialized countries.

A. Brazilian National Alcohol Programme (PROALCOOL)

The PROALCOOL program demonstrates that a very practical fuel (ethanol) can be produced from biomass in large quantities. Ethanol is an attractive fuel in part because it can be used in the transportation sector by mixing it with gasoline or using it directly in vehicles manufactured for the fuel. By 1985, the production of ethanol (anhydrous and hydrous) in Brazil had increased to over 9 billion liters from less than 1 billion liters in 1977, while transportation uses of ethanol had increased to almost equal that of gasoline consumption [Seroa da Motta, 1987]. By 1987, almost 90% of new cars sold in Brazil were designed for the exclusive use of alcohol fuel.

While the program is a technological success, various studies of the program reveal that at present oil prices, the program is not an economic success, i.e. not socioeconomically viable [Sperling, 1987; Seroa da Motta, 1987; and Duquette, 1989]. Indeed, Seroa da Motta [1987] and the sources that he cites indicate that oil prices on the order of $40 per barrel in 1987 were required to make the program economically viable. In other words, it would be less costly to the Brazilian economy to import oil than to produce ethanol from sugar cane.

It is notable that the literature reviewed did not directly deal with the environmental consequences of the alcohol program. There are both positive and negative environmental impacts associated with PROALCOOL. An important positive feature that has not been discussed is the reduction in urban air pollution that results from vehicles burning ethanol rather than gasoline. In addition, in an economic situation marked by depressed sugar prices, ethanol provides an alternative market for sugar cane helping to maintain employment and utilize the existing infrastructure. One study [Sperling, 1987] cites the creation of 1.7 million new jobs by the ethanol fuels industry. While that figure appears exaggerated, it can not be disputed that the industry has indeed created new jobs. Finally, if sugar cane is grown on a continuing sustainable basis, carbon release equals carbon uptake except for carbon releases from fossil fuels used in the construction and operation of the system. Negative features include the conversion of open lands into a monocrop production, conversion of agricultural land from other crops into sugar cane, and water pollution associated with the production of sugar cane. *To what degree these negative impacts are important needs to be assessed.* Furthermore, the negative and positive impacts have to be compared with the environmental impacts of using the alternative fuel, oil, or with using other means for providing energy services.

In light of these impacts, the fundamental question to be asked is whether "this uniquely Brazilian response" to the energy crisis represents a satisfactory investment. Sperling [1987], Duquette [1989], and Seroa da Motta [1987] find that the program was a response to a complex set of problems occurring in the late 1970s. During this period, the Brazilian economy faced depressed prices for its large sugar industry, an ambitious auto industry, and a large mounting foreign debt, driven in part by mounting oil prices and an energy sector that imported 80% of its oil. If oil prices had maintained their level of the early 1980s or continued to increase, Brazil's transition to renewable energy may have been well timed. As it is, it appears at least for the short run, that "Brazil erred on the side of starting too soon" [Sperling, 1979]. To maintain the momentum of the program, Brazil has found it necessary to provide subsidies to assure the auto industry and the public that the program is a permanent feature in the Brazilian economy.

In many respects, the primary issues concerning investment in renewable energy are the timing of the investment and the environmental advantages inherent in renewable energy sources. In cases where renewable energy, at a particular point in time, is more costly than fossil energy, a nation may wait too long to invest in renewables. By delaying a decision, the country may suffer losses in the future due to the possibly higher costs of fossil energy, assuming some combination of increasing fossil energy prices and declining renewable energy costs. If it moves too soon, it also suffers higher costs while fossil energy prices remain below that of the renewable sources. The dilemma is the critical role of fossil energy prices and the inability to predict future prices with reliability. The issue of environmental impact, including the issue of global climate change due to the combustion of fossil fuels, adds a new dimension to this dilemma. To the degree that renewable energy sources provide environmental benefits, the comparison to market prices is unfair in that market prices are relevant to private decisions but ignore the broader benefits to society.

An additional dilemma is that institutions, i.e. oil and gas companies and utility companies, are experienced with fossil and other conventional energy sources, but are less familiar with procedures to assess and implement renewable energy sources. Indeed, the end-user of energy will often be the provider of renewable energy.

B. Philippine Geothermal and Dendrothermal Programs

The Philippines launched a major energy program in the late 1970s to reduce its high dependence on costly imported oil, which at the time accounted for about 80% of its commercial energy use [Philippines Ministry of Energy (PMOE), 1981]. The program was a detailed plan which embodied a mix of renewable and conventional energy sources. The conventional options included increased exploration for and production of domestic oil and the opening of domestic coal mines. Two of the major renewable initiatives were geothermal-based power production and wood-fired power production, the latter called the dendrothermal program. The geothermal program has proven to be economically and technically successful while the dendrothermal has proven to be largely a failure.

The geothermal program began with three major installations with a combined capacity of 443 MWe by the end of 1980 [PMOE, 1981]. By 1987, 894 MWe of capacity was in place [Asian Development Bank, 1989]. The authors could not determine the exact cost of power from these sites, but they were believed to be competitive even before the power shortages of the last two years emerged in the Philippines.

The major environmental concern with the geothermal plants is the emissions associated with the spent steam and hot water emanating from the plant which are partially disposed of in locals rivers. Some of the steam and hot water are reinjected into dry wells drilled in the geothermal field. The significant environmental problems with the disposal of effluents in water bodies would have been greatly diminished or avoided with the reinjection of the waste streams. Air pollution and land use requirements have been minor concerns with these sites, particularly because of their isolated locations.

In contrast, the dendrothermal program was largely a failure, due to the inability to grow the feedstock trees for the plants, alternative markets for the fuelwood when trees were successfully grown, and some operational problems with the power plants themselves [Waddle, 1984; Waddle, 1990]. Plans for the dendrothermal program anticipated 72 plants with a capacity of 3-5 MWe each. By 1990, only 6 plants with a combined capacity of 16.6 MWe were in place, but not all of these were in operation and none of the facilities was operating at near capacity [Waddle, 1990]. Most of the operating experience occurred from 1984-87.

The reasons cited for the failure of this system include difficulties in growing the trees (Ipil-Ipil), both due to soil and other environmental conditions as well as for sociological reasons. In the areas where the tree plantations were relatively successful, the fuelwood market for tobacco-curing has been a major competitor for the Ipil-Ipil fuelwood. Finally, there have been operating problems with some of the British and French manufactured plants, which may possibly be attributed to lack of operator experience. Because the underlying concept of wood-fired power production or cogeneration has proven successful in a number of industrialized countries, e.g., Sweden and the United States, an important lesson from the Philippine experience is the importance of social and management issues. ***The lack of skilled people with appropriate economic incentives can undermine an otherwise sound concept.***

C. Thailand Hydroelectric System: The Nam Choan Dam

The controversy (1987-88) over the approval of plans for the construction of a large hydroelectric facility (580 MW) in the west-central region of Thailand represents an interesting case study which illustrates the need for adequate incorporation of environmental considerations into the planning process. Although the scope of this chapter deals with small rather than large hydroelectric facilities, the case, nevertheless, is a revealing one from the perspective employed here. Much of the information presented here is taken from the fascinating ex-post analysis by Phantumuanit and Nandhabiwat [1989].

As is well known, Thailand has been rapidly moving toward achievement of the status of a newly-industrialized country, with annual economic growth rates in the range of 8-10 percent in recent years. Concurrent with the rapid and sustained economic growth have been rapidly increasing energy demands, with electricity demand growing at double digit growth rates, i.e. on the order of 15 percent annually in 1987 and 1988. One of the key objectives of the Electricity Generating Authority of Thailand (EGAT) was to further, to the greatest degree possible, cheap and renewable hydroelectric power. The cornerstone of this policy would be the Nam Choan Dam, to be located on the Upper Big Kwai River. When completed in 1997, the dam would produce 1170 GWh of electricity annually, about two percent of anticipated national electricity demand in that year.

However, the siting of the project placed EGAT and the Thai government in a major dilemma: meeting electricity demands through construction of this dam threatened the preservation of the country's ***largest wildlife refuge and encroached on the nation's largest and finest remaining tropical forest***. In practical terms, the dam would also run counter to the National Forest Policy, which is attempting to preserve at least 15 percent of the country's land area as protected forest.

The conventional least-cost analysis carried out by EGAT and the government, as documented in Phantumuanit and Nandhabiwat [1989], argued strongly for the dam as the most economic alternative. With the then-anticipated 7 percent growth in electricity demand, it was estimated that the cost-saving of the proposed dam would be approximately 90 million dollars.

Public interest in the dam proposal was unprecedented. Intense, continuing media coverage combined with strong opposition by local and international environmental groups served to keep the government deliberations on approval in the center arena of public policy for the duration of the process. In response to this scrutiny, the government appointed a high level National Committee to evaluate the pros and cons of the project; a new and sharp departure from previous procedures for the decisionmaking arena.

The committee focused on five main areas of impact:

- Forest and wildlife;
- Seismic potential;
- Economics, energy, and finance;
- Archaeological values; and
- Water quality and public health.

The evaluation relied on two analytical approaches: (i) economic analysis of cost-saving, i.e. conventional economic analysis, based on calculated differences between capital investment, operation and maintenance, and fuel costs of competing fossil fuel power generating configurations and (ii) extended benefit-cost analysis which attempted to quantify major environmental impacts.

The first approach yielded the expected result that, "within a limited scope of energy, economic, and financial considerations, Nam Choan's 580 MW capacity would be genuinely beneficial to the country." However, in following the second procedure, it soon became apparent that there would be major difficulties in determining the true costs and benefits of this project. In hindsight the practitioners believe they had some degree of success in estimating some of the monetizable factors (e.g., value of timber cleared and value of fishery products) and quantifiable factors such as tourism, employment, and improved water supply.

However, in the end, the most decisive factors appeared to be the ***nonquantifiable*** ones. Two factors which were widely perceived as the most important were: (i) the degradation of the intrinsic value of Thailand's largest natural forest and (ii) the induced risk of earthquake. The final decision, made at the highest level by the Thai Cabinet, was to postpone the construction of the dam for an indefinite period.

The above process incorporated, albeit informally, many of the considerations laid out in the integrated resource planning methodology presented in this chapter. It attempted to take into account a wide range of environmental impacts and evaluated them vis-a-vis conventional economic costs. The process used a broadly constituted array of experts, and also relied heavily on a relatively open process with significant public input, which helped to increase the breadth and perspective of the evaluation. It did consider energy conservation as a possible way to lessen the impact of not choosing the option with least conventional costs, but unfortunately it did not go very far in examining the feasibility of implementation of conservation. In addressing environmental considerations it only alluded to the possibly serious environmental impacts of alternative options, e.g., to the magnitude of local air pollution impacts and acid rain effects caused by emissions from the lignite plants which would be likely alternatives to the dam. It is not suggested that these more penetrating analyses would necessarily have led to a different conclusion, but rather that they would likely lead to a process that over time, and with application to many difficult cases of this sort, would be more robust and productive in the long run.

D. California Wind Energy Program

In many respects the California experience with renewable energy is unique to California's political, economic and environmental conditions of the mid-1970s and early 1980s. Throughout this period, California provided a hospitable environment for renewable energy development. There was strong public interest in renewables, good private financing, and persistent political backing.

The early years of program development were fueled largely by fears of rising fossil fuel prices, diminishing quantities of fuel oil, and strong public motivation towards coastal environmental protection. Then governor of California, Jerry Brown, adopted these sentiments into his political agenda which became the initial motivating force behind the program.

Despite conventional wisdom which would forecast a steady, continuing rise in energy prices, California's electricity consumption was projected to rise on the order of 7% per year into the mid-1980s. Initial plans to meet this increasing demand called for the construction of a large number of nuclear power plants along the California coast. Strong public sentiment in favor of environmental protection and opposition from Governor Brown against proposed construction of these plants forced planners to consider alternatives to meeting the forecast demand.

In response to this dilemma, Governor Brown created the California Energy Commission and the Office of Appropriate Technology to assist with energy conservation efforts and small scale renewable energy development. The California legislature adopted PURPA[11] guidelines which required California utilities to purchase electricity from independent electricity producers at fair market prices. Initially PURPA created many long-term renewable contracts and natural gas cogeneration contracts with electric utilities. However, natural gas cogeneration was able to react more quickly than the renewable technologies and soon dwarfed the renewable energy's contribution.

To boost the participation of renewables, the legislature adopted a 55% tax credit for solar and wind energy in 1981. This high tax credit combined with the federal tax credits fostered a great interest in wind and solar projects. The rapid expansion in interest caused a number of problems, however, in quality control. The rapid growth in wind power moved too quickly for the energy commission to place regulations specifying quality standards for wind generators. It became profitable for companies to enter into the market with unreliable, inexpensive machines, using the tax credits to make a quick profit and then to swiftly leave as their machines deteriorated and failed. The large incentives, although fostering a great deal of interest, also created a measure of mistrust of wind power and a loss of credibility in the industry.

In some ways faith was restored in the mid-1980s by sharp reductions in the tax credits. With the loss of the large incentives, the fly-by-night investors disappeared as did interest in programs that could compete only in the heavily favored environment. What remained was an industry that was forced to compete at the margin; it included those who were oriented toward the long-term successes of their programs.

In 1989, California's 16,000 wind turbines met one percent of the state's electricity demand. The installed capacity produces a maximum of 15,000 MW at an installed cost of nearly 3 billion dollars. All of the turbines are on pasturelands, and good sites have the side benefit of bringing farmers $50-$100 per acre in rent. At current prices, even in the best locations, wind power is still not quite competitive with baseload fossil fuel and hydro plants. A study by Pacific Gas and Electric estimated the private cost of wind-generated electricity to be about 5.4 cents per kWh, slightly above the cost for fossil fuel generated electricity.

What is apparent in reviewing the Californian experience with wind energy is that it was implemented on a large scale without the benefit of the detailed analytical approach presented in this chapter. Although environmental considerations played a major role in selecting wind as the source of new energy, detailed planning and analysis were largely absent from the decision process. The wind program was also somewhat experimental, and some successes and failures can be expected in experiments. Whether in the long run the

---

[11]PURPA is the Public Utilities Regulatory Policies Act, Rep. 95-1750, United States House of Representatives, 95th Congress, 2nd Session, 1978.

California wind experiment proves to be a favorable investment depends in part on the importance of a number of factors: (i) the value assigned to the environmental damage avoided by employing wind energy rather than conventional energy, (ii) the future cost of fossil fuel, (iii) the future reliability of water flows for hydropower, and (iv) the technological knowledge gained with respect to wind energy systems which will increase their reliability in the future.

E. Swedish Power Planning

The final case study reported here is not based on a specific renewable energy supply system that has been implemented, but rather it focuses on an energy planning study for Sweden [Bodlund et al., 1989] which uses much of the framework for energy policy development and investment planning that has been described in this chapter. Where this chapter's policy and planning framework differs from that study, to a substantial degree, is in: (i) attention in greater detail to a range of environmental considerations associated with energy supply and (ii) application of multi-attribute decision analysis to help incorporate these environmental considerations into the decision process. The Swedish study accomplishes some of the same results by defining certain environmental constraints in their scenarios. Specifically, hydropower will not be significantly expanded due to environmental considerations, nuclear power will be phased out, and carbon dioxide emissions will be held constant. Within these formidable constraints, the study explores power options for Sweden which will maintain economic growth.

In brief, the Swedish study considers a set of electricity demand scenarios, based on residential, service, industry, space and water heating models, and electricity supply scenarios. The purpose of these scenarios is "to gain perspective on the current situation" by shedding "light on the various possibilities and their implications" [Bodlund et al., 1989, p. 884]. Demand and supply are integrated, considering the total cost of operating the system, by the use of integrated resource supply curves. Some important conclusions of the study include [Bodlund et al., 1989, p. 932]:

> The preceding scenarios illustrate some of the choices available to Sweden in determining her electricity future. It is possible from a technical standpoint to find paths that satisfy the demand for electricity services associated with continued economic growth, uphold environmental quality standards, and expedite the phase out of nuclear power as planned. The scenarios have very different CO_2 emissions, while other environmental aspects meet present environmental standards. These low-CO_2 scenarios would require the increased use of efficient end-use technology in all sectors as well as the installation of new low-CO_2 generating facilities. Use of coal and natural gas would lead to large increases in CO_2 emission compared with present levels. The economic differences are much smaller. In fact, the costs of the Efficiency and High Efficiency/Environmental Dispatch scenarios would be similar to or lower than those for the Reference/Economic Dispatch scenario, as calculated in this paper, based on today's knowledge about costs and prices.
>
> Experience suggests that such a development would not happen by itself. Individual decision-makers tend to optimize for themselves rather than for society at-large.... To capture some or all of these savings, policies would have to be shaped to make markets work better and stimulate actors in all sectors to make use of the technical opportunities we have described in the preceding pages. Information, education, and

training, rules, and regulations would have to reflect this by making the national good also be the actor's good.

Renewable energy sources that are included in the Efficiency/ Environmental Dispatch scenarios include conservation, additional industrial cogeneration based on biomass, combined heat and power production from steam-injected gas turbines fueled with gasified biomass (estimated at 4.5 to 5.6 cents/kWh), and wind power (7.0 cents/kWh).

While the specific findings are of interest, the important aspect of this study is that it is a full scale example which considered both investment streams and policy in a setting where conventional energy sources, renewables, and conservation were treated in a consistent fashion and environmental factors were considered as constraints on the investment options considered. The framework laid out in this chapter is intended as a broad guide which will result in studies similar to the Swedish study but will have a greater environmental focus and use additional techniques to incorporate and evaluate environmental information.

V. Summary

Historically, the energy planning process in developing countries has given little or no attention to environmental considerations. Energy policy has developed primarily in response to short-term economic and political pressures related to economic development, rather than on the basis of an understanding of the functions and roles of ecosystems, and the full costs and benefits of alternative policies which incorporate environmental and social considerations. Recently, however, an increasing awareness has become evident in some developing and industrialized countries of the overarching issue of sustainable development based on the efficient management of natural resources and the preservation of basic ecological systems. Energy policymakers are finding themselves, once again, in a position where they are beginning to question the future role of fossil fuel, based not only on the uncertainty in availability and price, but on the growing awareness of the potential social and environmental costs of global climate change and other long-term impacts brought about by increased fossil fuel consumption.

While economic growth is still the primary goal of development planning in developing countries, the sustainability criterion is beginning to be viewed as a necessary constraint. With this in mind, it will become increasingly essential for energy planners to weigh the environmental, social, and economic benefits and costs of renewables against the costs and impacts of more traditional energy sources. This chapter provides: (i) a framework for describing the quantifiable and unquantifiable environmental impacts of a broad range of renewable energy systems, (ii) a prescriptive planning and investment framework for simultaneously considering conventional and renewable energy options as well as conservation, and (iii) a set of case studies of experiences with renewable energy programs or planning studies which included renewables.

As part of the framework for describing environmental impacts, tables of impacts in quantitative and qualitative terms have been included for a set of renewable energy options. While these tables do not cover all potentially important environmental impacts, they do include many of the commonly encountered impacts. Estimating a comprehensive set of impacts for all renewable energy options is beyond the scope of this chapter. What the tables do provide, however, are specific examples of how impacts can be categorized and measured.

They also provide sufficient information to reveal the striking differences in environmental impacts between conventional and renewable energy sources.

The prescriptive planning and investment framework provides the means by which environmental information can be combined with more traditional economic information in evaluating energy supply and demand options. The core of the framework is integrated resource or least-cost planning. Integrated supply curves are developed for comparing options. Overlayed on the integrated supply curves is environmental information. The environmental information may be used as constraints on fuel use and technologies, or it may be considered as decision factors within a multi-attribute decision analysis framework. While a number of approaches can be used, the underlying goal is to provide a means for rigorously including environmental impacts in the trade-offs necessary in making energy policy and investment decisions.

By incorporating environmental considerations into the energy planning process in a rigorous and deliberate fashion, many energy investment decisions are likely to change significantly. The reason that energy investments are likely to change is in part shown by the exceedingly different patterns of environmental impacts between conventional and renewable energy systems. One major consequence of these changes will be the more frequent adoption of improved, sustainable development policies. Specific consequences of considering environmental factors could be the increased selection of renewable energy options, increased use of less environmentally-damaging conventional energy options, and increased reliance on conservation.

The case studies of renewable systems provide insight into how these programs were (or were not) brought into being, as well as their successes and failures. While the renewable systems provide some distinct environmental advantages, they, like any other system, must be implemented carefully or they will fail. It is instructive to note the degree to which environmental considerations were not a significant part of the rationale for the programs in Brazil and the Philippines at the time of those decisions. In the cases of Thailand and California, environmental factors played significant roles. The Swedish case study provides an excellent example of an integrated resource planning approach at the national level which considers a few environmental constraints. An important finding of that study is that options which meet strict carbon dioxide limits and incorporate significant amounts of renewable energy can be less costly than conventional energy options that do not take advantage of potential conservation measures.

References

Abert, James G. [1985]. "Municipal Waste Processing in Europe." World Bank Technical Paper No. 37. Washington, D.C.: World Bank.

Abrahamson, Dean Edwin [1989]. *The Challenge of Global Warming*. Washington, D.C.: Island Press.

Asian Development Bank [1989]. *Electric Utilities Data Book for the Asian and Pacific Region*. Manilla, Philippines: Asian Development Bank.

Barniske, Lothar [1989]. "Municipal Solid Waste Incineration in the Federal Republic of Germany." *Environmental Impact Assessment Review 35*, vol. 9, no. 3 (September): 279-290.

Bodlund, Birgit, Evan Mills, Tomas Karlsson, and Thomas B. Johansson [1989]. "The Challenge of Choices: Technology Options for the Swedish Electricity Sector." In Thomas B. Johansson, Birgit Bodlund, and Robert H. Williams (editors), *Electricity: Efficient End-Use and New Generation Technologies and Their Planning Implications*. Lund, Sweden: Lund University Press.

Brower, Michael [1990]. *Cool Energy: The Renewable Solution to Global Warming*. A report by the Union of Concerned Scientists. Cambridge, Massachusetts: Union of Concerned Scientists.

Buehring, W.A., W.K. Foell, and R.L. Keeney [1976]. "Energy/Environment Management: Application of Decision Analysis." International Institute for Applied Systems Analysis (IIASA) RR-76-14. Luxembourg, Austria: IIASA.

Cirillo, Richard [1989]. "Environmental Analysis." United Nations Development Program - World Bank Training Course on Energy Planning for European and Arab State Countries, December 8, 1989. Washington, D.C.: World Bank.

Clark, William C. [1986]. "Sustainable Development of the Biosphere: Themes for a Research Program." In W.C. Clark and R.E. Munn (editors), *Sustainable Development of the Biosphere*. Cambridge, United Kingdom: Cambridge University Press.

Duquette, Michel [1989]. "Le programme Proalcool et l'économie agricole au Brésil," *Energy Studies Review*, vol. 1, no. 2.

Electric Power Research Institute [1985]. "Electricity Outlook, The Foundation for EPRI R & D Planning." Palo Alto, California: Electric Power Research Institute.

Foell, W. K. [1979]. *Management of Energy/Environment Systems: Methods and Case Studies*. International Institute for Applied Systems Analysis, Wiley.

Foell, W. K. and M. E. Hanson [1980]. "Futurists and State Energy Policy: The Wisconsin Story." *Technology Forecasting and Social Change*, vol. 18: 341-358.

Foell, W. K. et al. [1981]. "The Wisconsin IIASA Set of Energy/Environment (WISE) Models for Regional Planning and Management: An Overview." Research Report RR 81-17. Luxembourg, Austria: International Institute for Applied Systems Analysis.

Foell, W.K. et al. [1992]. *Environmental Considerations in Renewable Energy Policy Development and Investment Planning.* EDI Working Papers, Energy Series. Washington, D.C.: World Bank.

Garabedian, Harold T. and Cedric R. Sanborn [1978]. "Environmental Aspects of Wood Fuel." *Conference on Environmental Aspects of Non-Conventional Energy Resources Proceedings*, September 26-29, 1978. Denver, Colorado: American Nuclear Society: 19-1 - 20-14.

George, Peter and David Van Schaik [1988]. "The Role of Small-Scale Hydro Development in Northern Ontario." *Energy*, vol. 13, no. 1: 25-31.

Goldemberg, Jose, Thomas B. Johansson, Amulya K.N. Reedy, and Robert H. Williams [1988]. *Energy for a Sustainable World.* New Delhi: Wiley Eastern Limited.

Hanson, Mark, Stephen Kidwell, Dennis Ray, and Rodney Stevenson [1991 forthcoming]. "Electric Utility Least-Cost Planning Within A Multiattribute Decision-Making Framework." *Journal of the American Planning Association*, vol. 57, no. 1: 34-43.

Heede, H. Richard, Richard E. Morgan, and Scott Ridley [1985]. *The Hidden Costs of Energy.* Washington, D.C.: Center for Renewable Resources.

Hohmeyer, Olav [1988]. *Social Costs of Energy Consumption.* Berlin: Springer Verlag.

Holdren, John P. [1987]. "Global Environmental Issues Related to Energy Supply: The Environmental Case for Increased Efficiency of Energy Use." *Energy*, vol. 12, no. 10/11: 975-992.

Holdren, J., G. Morris, and I. Mintzer [1980]. "Environmental Aspects of Renewable Energy Sources." *Annual Review of Energy.*

Holling, C.S. [1978]. *Adaptive Environmental Assessment and Management.* New York: John Wiley and Sons.

Inhaber, Herbert [1982]. *Energy Risk Assessment.* New York: Gordon and Breach.

International Energy Agency [1987]. *Renewable Sources of Energy.* Paris: Organization for Economic Cooperation and Development.

International Institute for Applied Systems Analysis [1981]. *Energy in a Finite World.* Cambridge, Massachusetts: Ballinger Publishing Company.

Jenkins, Alec [1990]. California Energy Commission. Personal communication, June.

Jhirad, David [1987]. "Renewable Energy in Developing Countries: Priorities and Prospects." *The Energy Journal*, vol. 8.

Keeney, Ralph L. [1980]. *Siting Energy Facilities.* New York: Academic Press.

Keeney, Ralph L. and Howard Raiffa [1976]. *Decisions with Multiple Objectives: Preferrences and Value Trade-offs.* New York: John Wiley and Sons.

Kilgroe, James [1989]. "Combustion Control of Trace Organic Air Pollutants from Municipal Waste Combustors." *Environmental Impact Assessment Review*, vol. 9: 199-222.

Liverman, Diana M., Mark E. Hanson, Becky J. Brown, and Robert W. Merideth, Jr. [1988]. "Global Sustainability: Toward Measurement." *Environmental Management*, vol. 12, no. 2: 133-143.

Manthey, Ch. [1980]. *Energy Technology Data Handbook, Volume 1, Conversion Technologies.* Julich, Germany: Kernforschungsanlage Julich, January.

Meridian Corporation [1989]. *Energy System Emissions and Material Requirements.* Alexandria, Virginia: Meridian Corporation, February.

Morris, G. [1980]. "Integrated-Assessment Issues Raised by the Environmental Effects of Biomass Energy Systems: A Case Study." Energy and Resources Group Report No. ERG-WP-80-6. Berkeley, California: University of California, March.

Moskowitz, P.D., E.A. Coveney, M.A. Crowther, L.D. Hamilton, S.C. Morris, K.M. Novak, P.E. Perry, S. Rabinowitz, M.D. Rowe, W.A. Sevian, J.E. Smith, I. Wilenitz [1983]. "Health and Environmental Effects Document for Photovoltaic Energy Systems." Upton, New York: Brookhaven National Laboratory, September.

Nahas, M.N., A.S. Mohamad, M. Akyurt, A.K. El-Kalay [1987]. "Wind Energy: An Engineering Survey." *Energy Sources*, vol. 9: 137-148.

National Academy Press [1980]. "Study of Nuclear and Alternative Energy Systems." In *Energy and the Fate of Ecosystems.* Supporting Paper No. 8. Washington, D.C.: National Academy Press.

Organization for Economic Cooperation and Development [1984]. *Biomass for Energy.* Paris: OECD.

Organization for Economic Cooperation and Development Compass Project [1988]. *Environmental Impacts of Renewable Energy.* Paris: OECD.

Pacific Gas and Electric [1988]. "Solar Central Receiver Technology Advancement for Electric-Utility Applications." Research and Development Department. San Ramon, California: Pacific Gas and Electric, August.

Penner, S.S., D.P.Y. Chang, R. Goulard, T. Lester [1988]. "Waste Incineration and Energy Recovery." *Energy*, vol. 13, no. 12: 845-851.

Penner, S.S., D.F. Wiesenhahn, and C.P. Li [1987]. "Incinerator Production, Fate and Health Effects of Polychlorinated Dioxins and Furans." *Energy*, vol. 12: 33-43.

Phantumuanit, Dhira and Widhanya Nandhabiwat [1989]. "The Nam Choan Controversy: An EIA in Practice." *Environmental Impact Assessment Review*, vol. 9: 135-147.

Philippines Ministry of Energy [1981]. "Five-Year Energy Program 1981-85." Manila, Philippines: Philippines Ministry of Energy.

Pollock, Cynthia [1987]. "Mining Urban Wastes: The Potential for Recycling." Worldwatch Paper No. 76, Washington, D.C.: Worldwatch Institute, April.

Rader, Nancy [1989]. *Power Surge: The Status and Near-Term Potential of Renewable Energy Technologies*. Washington, D.C.: Public Citizen, May.

Resource Policy Center [1980]. "Advanced System Demonstration for Utilization of Biomass as an Energy Source." In *Environmental Report*. Report No. 292. Hanover, New Hampshire: Thayer School of Engineering, September.

Richards, Bill [1988]. "Burning Issue Energy From Garbage Loses Some of Promise As Wave of the Future." *The Wall Street Journal* (June 16, 1988): 1, 13.

The Science and Public Policy Program, University of Oklahoma [1975]. *Energy Alternatives: A Comparative Analysis*. Washington, D.C.: United States Government Printing Office.

Seroa da Motta, Ronaldo [1987]. "The Social Viability of Ethanol Production in Brazil." *Energy Economics*, vol. 9 (July): 176-182.

Shea, Cynthia Pollock [1988]. "Renewable Energy: Today's Contribution, Tomorrow's Promise." Worldwatch Paper No. 81. Washington, D.C.: Worldwatch Institute.

Sorensen, B. [1976]. "Dependability of Wind Energy Generators with Short-Term Energy Storage." *Science*, November 26, 1976.

Sperling, Daniel [1987]. "Brazil, Ethanol and the Process of System Change." *Energy*, vol. 12, no. 1: 11-23.

Stein, Jay [1990]. "Hydrogen: Clean, Safe, and Inexhaustible." *The Amicus Journal* (Spring).

Suskind, Lawerence E. and Esther [1989]. "The Incineration Conflict: Addressing Public Concerns." *Environmental Impact Assessment Review*, vol. 9: 317-329.

Theodore, Louis and Anthony J. Buonicore [1980]. *Energy and the Environment: Interactions, Volume 1, Part A*. Boca Raton, Florida: CRC Press, Inc.

United States Department of Energy [1981]. *Technology Characterizations: Environmental Information Handbook*. Second Edition. Washington, D.C.: United States Department of Energy, June.

United States Department of Energy [1983]. *Energy Technology Characterizations Handbook*. Washington, D.C.: United States Department of Energy, March.

United States Department of Energy [1988]. *Energy Technologies and the Environment*. Washington, D.C.: United States Department of Commerce, October.

Waddle, D.B. [1984]. "Development and Utilization of Renewable Energy Technologies in the Philippines." Paper No. 84-5548. Presented at the 1984 Winter Meeting of the American Society of Agricultural Engineers, December, 1984, held in St. Joseph, Michigan.

Waddle, D. B. [1990]. Personal communication, June.

Wisconsin Department of Administration [1989]. *Wisconsin Energy Statistics-1988*. Madison, Wisconsin: Wisconsin Department of Administration.

Wisconsin Public Service Commission [1986]. "Findings of Fact, Conclusion of Law, and Order." Docket 05-EP-4. Madison, Wisconsin: Wisconsin Public Service Commission.

World Commission on Environment and Development [1987]. *Our Common Future*. Oxford: Oxford University Press.

World Resources Institute and the International Institute for Environment and Development [1988]. *World Resources 1988-89*. New York: Basic Books.

3

Oil, Gas, and the Environment

Dennis Anderson
The World Bank

I. Emerging Pattern of Energy Demand

To put environmental issues in perspective, it is first worth considering levels, trends, and geographical changes in world energy consumption. All available analyses show that developing countries have now emerged as the major growth centers, notwithstanding the economic shocks of the 1970s and 1980s. In 1970 they accounted for only 15% of world consumption, in 1989 for 25%, and within 20 years their consumption will probably exceed that of the Organization for Economic Cooperation and Development (OECD) economies combined, being over 100 million barrels of oil equivalent energy per day (mbdoe) assuming a gradual recovery of the African and Latin American economies. There are several factors contributing to the emergence of developing country markets: (i) high per capita income elasticities and population growth; (ii) growth of urban areas and industry; (iii) growth of vehicle fleets; and (iv) substitution out of fuelwood to commercial fuels, itself an important source of environmental improvement. Thus energy related environmental issues are likely to become more pressing in developing regions and to make the gains from environmental policy well worth seeking. This section introduces the paper by looking at the patterns of world energy consumption.

A. Current Patterns of Demand

In 1970, the developing countries' total consumption of commercial energy -- oil, gas, coal, nuclear, and hydro -- accounted for 16 mbdoe or 15% of the world total of 104 mbdoe. Despite the oil price shocks in the 1970s and the crises of debt in Africa and Latin America, consumption rose significantly in all developing regions in the next two decades. Consumption in these regions is triple the level of twenty years ago, currently around 45 mbdoe, accounting for 25% of world consumption and 44% of the growth during this period. (See Table 1.)

Table 1: Commercial Energy Consumption by Economic Grouping

	mbdoe		% distribution	
	1970	1990(e)	1970	1990(e)
OECD economies	66	85	73	50
Developing economies	16	45	15	26
U.S.S.R. & Eastern Europe	22	40	21	24
Total	104	170	100	100

Source: The British Petroleum Company p.l.c. [1989].

Legend: mbode = million barrels per day of oil equivalent
(e) = estimate
OECD = Organization for Economic Cooperation and Development
U.S.S.R. = Union of Soviet Socialist Republics

Oil, gas, and coal account for 50%, 15%, and 20% of total consumption respectively in developing countries, excluding China which alone has 10 mbdoe of coal consumption. Oil and gas shares of consumption in developing countries are on a rising trend and rather higher than in the OECD economies. (See Table 2.) Hydro obviously has an important role in overall energy supplies, though clearly fossil energy predominates.

Turning to future demand possibilities, the problem is best approached in two steps. The first is to estimate aggregate demands, the second to estimate the fuel and energy mix. The latter is much more sensitive to relative prices, as well as environmental concerns, than the former.

B. Long-Term Scenarios: Aggregate Energy Demands

The record of economic forecasting in the energy industry, as in many other areas, has not been a good one and has led to costly errors. In the 1950s, projections of exponential demand growth and limited fossil resources -- the latter greatly underestimated -- were used to justify major nuclear power research and investment programs. In the 1970s and 1980s, the capacity of the industry to discover new oil and gas resources, pessimism regarding costs, and again, demand optimism, led to predictions of oil prices rising indefinitely to $50-70 per barrel or more, perhaps a $100 per barrel in the early 2000s (in today's prices). Nevertheless, investment planning requires some view of the future, not least where environmental matters are concerned. The lead times for exploration and production investments may be up to 15 years in some regions when the time required for environmental studies, licensing, and permits are considered and 15 to 20 years for research and development (R & D). Most investment decisions being made today will not be operational until around 2000, with investment lifetimes extending to the period 2020-2030.

1. Assumptions

There is much that can be learned from the scenario approach to planning developed by the Royal Dutch Shell Group, in which the underlying assumptions are clearly stated and considered relevant for planning purposes [de Vries, 1988]. So what might be appropriate assumptions when examining issues in energy and environment? The following are suggested:

(i) Eventual peaking or saturation of OECD markets, helped by a "recovery" of real energy prices and - especially important - gains in energy efficiency [Davis, 1989];

(ii) Continued economic growth in Asia and an eventual recovery in Africa and Latin America.

(iii) Fairly rapid demand growth for commercial energy in the developing countries of around 4%. The growth rate in the period 1970-90 was 5.3%, despite the oil price shocks and the debt crises. For reasons discussed below it is likely to remain strong for some decades, barring economic calamities,

Table 2: Composition of Commercial Energy Demands by Economic Grouping 1990(e)

	mbdoe			% distribution		
	OECD	DCs	U.S.S.R. & E.E.	OECD	DCs	U.S.S.R. & E.E.
Oil	36.0	17.5	12.0	42	39	30
Gas	15.0	5.0	13.0	18	11	33
Coal	18.0	17.0[a]	12.0	21	38	30
Nuclear	7.5	0.5	1.5	9	1	4
Hydro & other	8.5	5.0	1.5	10	11	4
Total	85.0	45.0	40.0	100	100	100

Source: Trended up from the figures in The British Petroleum Company p.l.c. [1989].

Note: [a] Of which 10 mbdoe is China

Legend: mbdoe = million barrels per day of oil equivalent
DCs = developing countries
E.E. = Eastern Europe
U.S.S.R. = Union of Soviet Socialist Republics
OECD = Organization for Economic Cooperation and Development

even assuming major improvements in energy efficiency brought about by a recovery of prices and other factors.[1]

(iv) Moderate growth of the energy markets in Eastern Europe and the Union of Soviet Socialist Republics helped by economic recovery, but also dampened by significant improvements in energy efficiency.

These seem to be a consistent and operationally interesting set of assumptions. One could for instance be pessimistic about developing country growth prospects or for recovery in Eastern Europe. But this would not be a good basis for policy analysis. The main challenge ahead is to find a structure of policies that is consistent with and will help the aims of economic recovery and growth in the developing countries and elsewhere. These policies include meeting the demands for commercial energy in an economically efficient way and, of course, addressing the emerging environmental concerns.

2. Explanatory Factors

Six major factors which influence the aggregate demand for energy are identified below. Two of these -- managerial and technical efficiency, and prices -- often pull in opposite directions from the others.

(i) ***Managerial and technical efficiency***. These factors include, for example, improvements in the thermal efficiency of power stations, reductions in vehicle fuel consumption (miles per gallon), and improvements in the efficiency with which energy resources are managed and used in industry and homes. The scope for energy demand reduction through such efficiency improvements both in the developing and the industrial countries is appreciable [World Bank, 1989 and Davis, 1989];

(ii) ***Per capita income growth***;

Combined with:

(iii) ***The positions of the various regions on the 'S' curves for energy using machines, equipment, and vehicle fleets***. Developing countries are still on the early to middle ranges of the 'S' curves for energy using appliances, equipment, and vehicles. Also, the share of industry in output tends to rise rapidly in the middle and higher income developing countries;

(iv) ***Population growth***;

(v) ***Prices***;

---

[1]Numerous people have drawn attention to the potential for energy efficiency improvements in developing countries. See, e.g., World Bank [1989]. (ESMAP is the Energy Sector Management Assistance Programme.)

(vi) ***Substitution for fuelwood.*** Fuelwood still accounts for about half of energy demand in developing countries, over 90% in parts of Africa. Substitution alone is likely to raise overall demand in developing countries by perhaps half or more in the long-term.

Table 3 presents a broad summary of how these factors might influence energy demand in different regions. In a fairly "energy efficient" scenario which assumes a gradual increase in real energy prices, either through taxation or a rising call on the Organization of Petroleum Exporting Countries' (OPEC's) resources or both, a long-term growth rate of less than 1% for OECD countries, 4% for the less developed countries (LDCs), and 1% to 2% for Eastern Europe and the Union of Soviet Socialist Republics, seems a reasonable starting point for analysis.

3. Geographical Demand Patterns

The main upward pressures on world commercial energy demand are therefore likely to arise from the growth of per capita incomes and populations in the developing countries. Table 4 presents a scenario of overall demand based on the assumptions stated above. It is worth emphasizing that this is a scenario of fairly modest demand growth for developing countries. As noted, trend growth rates in the 1970s and 1980s were over 5%. More countries are likely to enter the high growth ranges of the 'S' curves in the coming decades than are likely to leave it, especially with the growth of industry, vehicle fleets, and household assets. Assuming economic recovery in Africa, it is not difficult to defend a scenario of 5-6% growth in developing regions, with their demands rising to 130-150 mbdoe by 2010 and to over 300 mbdoe in four decades. Under the scenarios summarized in Table 4, developing country per capita demands would still be low relative to the OECD countries today, even allowing for four decades of sustained growth. (See Tables 4 and 5.)

4. An Aside on Scenario Choice

The above scenarios are in the middle of a broad range of possibilities reviewed by Keepin et al. [1986] [see, Bolin et al., 1986], who rightly counsel against working with only one scenario. There are three reasons for beginning with the one above, in the mid-range, before turning to other possibilities. ***First,*** using higher demand figures would merely reinforce the policy conclusions reached without materially altering them. ***Second,*** turning to lower demand scenarios than the one developed here it must be noted that those analysts who have considered such scenarios are focusing on the greenhouse effect and often make the rather strong assumption that the greenhouse effect can be solved by energy efficiency.[2] The greenhouse effect is of course only one of several environmental problems to be addressed. As noted above, demand growth in developing countries is likely to be fairly rapid even under optimistic assumptions on energy efficiency. Assuming the greenhouse effect is as serious as many climatologists believe, energy efficiency may help to address it, but energy efficiency alone will not solve it. ***Third,*** for this and other reasons, one needs to consider how the aggregate demand for energy can be met by various fuel types, including the use of renewables in the long-term as substitutes for fossil fuels. This issue is considered now.

---

[2] E.g., the scenarios of A.B. Lovins whose work is cited by Keepin et al. [1986]. See also "The Role of Release of CO_2 as a Function of Future Energy Developments," Chapter 2 in Bolin et al. [1986].

Table 3: Factors Influencing the Demand for Commercial Energy

		Economic Group/Region			
		OECD	Developing Countries	Eastern Europe & Russia	Comment
i.	Energy Efficiency	strong	strong	very strong	-1%
ii.	Per Capita Income Growth	2%	2-6%	2%	) Combined effects: weak in OECD; very strong in LDCs
iii.	Position on 'S' curve	mature phase	high growth phase	upper ranges	)
iv.	Population growth	0.2%	2%	1%	
v.	Price	strong	strong	strong	Currently, prices are weak. May recover in long-term
vi.	Substitution for fuelwood	0	1%	0	
	Overall assessment	<1%	>4%	1-2%	

Source: Author.

Note: The percentage figures represent the author's assessments of the influence of the various factors on long-term growth rates.

Legend: OECD = Organization for Economic Cooperation and Development

Table 4: Energy Demand Scenarios by Economic Group (mbdoe)

	Actual			Scenarios	
	1970	1980	1990(e)	circa 2010	circa 2030
OECD	66	75	85	100	90
Developing countries	16	28	45	100	200
Eastern Europe & U.S.S.R.	22	30	40	50	60
Total	104	140	170	250	350

Source: Actual data from Shell Petroleum Company Ltd. [1989a] and The British Petroleum Company p.l.c. [1989]. (The 1990 estimates are trended up from 1985-89 data.)

Legend: (e) = estimate
mbdoe = million barrels per day of oil equivalent
OECD = Organization for Economic Cooperation and Development
U.S.S.R. = Union of Soviet Socialist Republics

Table 5: Per Capita Consumption of Commercial Energy[a]

	barrels of oil equivalent per capita per year			ratio relative to the United States (%)		
	1990	2010	2030	1990	2010	2030
United States	58	53	45	100	100	100
Western Europe	26	27	26	45	50	60
Developing Countries	4	7	10	7	13	23
Eastern Europe & Russia	36	40	45	62	75	100

Source: Author.

Note: [a] Based on Table 4 and supporting calculations. [For Africa and South Asia, per capita demands are only 3% of those of the United States today, for China 8%, the Far East (excluding China) 7%, and Latin America 11%.]

C. Long-Term Scenarios: Oil, Gas, and Substitutes

When determining how the aggregate demands for commercial energy might be met, there are broadly four factors to consider: initial conditions, relative prices, technical change, and the environment.

1. Initial Conditions

Prices, environmental concerns, technical progress, and other factors may suggest larger shares of demand being met by some fuels, such as gas or renewables, and less by others. However, investments have long lead times (up to 15 years) and lifetimes (20 to 30 years) and this sets a limit on the rate at which changes can be made. For high growth sectors, there is also a limit at which new technologies can be introduced without raising inefficiencies and prices. Thus sectoral shares may change slowly even under quite strong incentives.

2. Relative Prices

The growth of demand for oil in relation to world reserves must ultimately increase the call on OPEC resources appreciably. In 1987, OPEC accounted for 75% of the world's proven oil reserves of 900 billion barrels. Prices and OPEC's share of world markets declined appreciably in the 1980s as a consequence of the growth of non-OPEC production brought about by OPEC policies. But a growth of world markets at the rates discussed above -- or possibly higher, since in actuality the world may be less "energy efficient" than assumed above -- would inevitably increase the call on OPEC and raise the demand for non-oil alternatives such as gas, coal, nuclear, and renewables.

3. Technical Change

Costs of offshore exploration and development declined dramatically by around 50% in the 1970s and 1980s and were a major factor in reducing oil prices. Exploration and production (E & P) costs of $30/barrel declined to $15/barrel in many regions. In the longer-term, tar sands and shale oils may be commercially attractive at less than $30/barrel; synthetic liquid fuels (synfuels) from natural gas or coal are other options. These developments are due to major advances in refining and conversion technologies.

Another area where technical progress has been important is renewables, particularly in liquid fuels from biomass and in electricity production from photovoltaics. Both are likely to reshape the energy market over the long-term for both commercial and environmental reasons. The costs of liquid fuels from ***biomass*** have fallen significantly over time [van der Toorn, 1988][3] from over $100/barrel in the 1970s to $60-70 per barrel or less today [World Bank, 1988]. Investments in this area were widely shelved by the oil companies following the collapse of oil prices in the 1980s, but would soon be revived if oil prices recovered or if carbon taxes were introduced. Progress in photovoltaics (PVs) has been even more dramatic,

---

[3]Also see Shell International Petroleum Company Ltd. [1987b].

with costs falling from $200,000 per kilowatt of peak capacity (kWp) in the early 1970s, to $25,000/kWp in 1980, and $5,000/kWp today. Current expectations are for costs to drop to $1,500/kWp to $2,000/kWp in the next ten years, with average costs for grid-fed systems declining to United States cents 6-10 per kilowatts per hour (kWh), depending on discount rates.

4. Environment

Regulations or taxes on acid deposition would affect the relative prices of fuels and are expected to favor gas. Carbon taxes would likewise favor gas and renewables.

5. Energy Demands by Energy Type

With these factors in view, Table 6 puts together a long-term scenario of commercial energy demands by energy source and by region. From a policy viewpoint, most attention will be focused on developments in the next two decades, and thus in the fuels that dominate the markets today. However, the scenarios are extended out further for two reasons. ***First***, the greenhouse effect (GHE) is too important a concern to be neglected in the analysis of environmental policies towards fossil fuels. ***Second***, even making strong assumptions as to the plausible growth rates of renewables, in response to GHE, it is clear that the dependence on fossil fuels, particularly on oil and gas, will increase rather than decrease for three, perhaps four decades, even assuming a major acceleration of investments in renewables. The reasons are (i) the historical factors given earlier, namely the long lifetimes and lead times of existing investments, (ii) the point that institutional and management structures (indeed consumers) are adapted to existing technologies and have major asset holdings in them, and (iii) the difficulties of developing and investing in renewable technologies. Thus the scenario shows oil and gas still to be the preponderant fuels for the next 20-30 years[4].

II. Environmental Problems Related to Oil and Gas

A. A Classification of Problems

The range of problems related to oil and gas is very wide and, for this reason, it may be useful to begin with a classification of sources and effects in order to organize analysis and identify priorities. Gaseous emissions from refineries are important to address at the design stage, in the reaching of agreements on operating procedures and the choice of standards, and

---

[4]Even more draconian assumptions on the growth rates of the renewables industry are unlikely to change this outcome. The basic problem is that the industry still has to establish a sizeable technological, managerial, and commercial base which realistically would take 20 years. Many might regard 7 mbdoe of output from the industry in 20 years time, from its base today, would be difficult to achieve. But once a sizeable base is established, historical experience shows that an industry's growth rate can be very rapid (as the history of the industry itself shows), in the order of 10 to 15% for several decades until market saturation approaches. Hence, the high output figures in this scenario are projected in the outer years but not in the near future.

Table 6: A Scenario of Energy Demand by Fuel Type with Rapid Growth of Renewable Energy Sources (mbdoe)

	1980	1990(e)	circa 2010	circa 2030	circa 2050
OECD					
Oil	36	37	40	25	10
Gas	15	16	25	30	20
Coal	15	18	16	10	5
Nuclear	3	7	8	7	7
Hydro	5	8	8	8	8
Renewables[a]	~0	~0	3	20	50
Total	74	85	100	100	100
Developing Countries					
Oil	12	18	40	45	25
Gas	3	5	25	65	35
Coal	12	16	20	20	10
Nuclear	<0.1	0.5	1	~0	~0
Hydro	2	5	10	20	30
Renewables[a]	<1	<1	4	50[b]	200[c]
Total	29	45	100	200	300

Source: 1980 data from The British Petroleum Company p.l.c. [1989]. The 1990(e) figures are trended up from past data. The *BP Statistical Review* does not list renewables, which are however fairly minor.

Notes: [a] Non hydro. Also excludes firewood.
[b] 13% annual growth rate in the 20 year period.
[c] 7% annual growth rate in the 20 year period.

Legend: mbdoe = million barrels per day of oil equivalent
(e) = estimate

have significant influence on costs and location. The various options are well understood from a technical viewpoint and design manuals and guidelines are widely available [see, for example, Royal Dutch Shell Group [1983].[5] But by far the greater sources of gaseous emissions are those arising from combustion in end-use activities, and it is here where abatement policies related to such emissions need to be focused. On the other hand, the problems of effluents, wastes, leakages, spills, and accidents arise mainly on the industry side, much less than in end-use. This suggests a classification of environmental problems according to the principal source (see Table 7).

It will be seen later that this classification also works well when one turns to the choice of policy instruments. The policy of taxing polluters is much more feasible and economically attractive in relation to end-use activities, while the instruments of regulation and legal liability are more appropriate, and often the only workable options, on the industry side.

B. End-Use Gaseous Emissions

Five types of emissions give most cause for environmental concern: the acidifying gases sulfur dioxide (SO_2) and nitrogen oxide (NO_x); the toxic and also "dirty" gas carbon monoxide (CO); unburned hydrocarbons or particulates; and the greenhouse gases carbon dioxide (CO_2), a product of combustion; and methane (CH_4) which, outside agriculture and natural sources, arises mainly from leakage. These emissions have several effects on the environment and health.

1. Health Effects

High concentrations of sulfur dioxide in urban areas have been associated with bronchial health problems, and have been studied at length by the World Health Organization. Extensive controls in the industrial countries have resulted in significant reductions. Carbon monoxide, the use of lead in fuels, and ozone arising from photochemical reactions of nitrogen oxides and hydrocarbon leakages (photo-oxidant formation) are also well-known health hazards. They also lead to dense smogs ("photochemical smogs") under certain weather conditions.

2. Forests and Soil/Water Acidification[6]

Pollutants originating primarily from sulfur dioxide and nitrogen oxides can be carried for long distances in the atmosphere and converted into acids (acid deposition). In parts of Europe and North America there has been extensive damage to forests, much of it attributed to acid deposition. Soil acidification occurs if the soil's ability to neutralize acidic inputs becomes exhausted. In addition to the potential damage to trees and crops, the effects often extend to the acidification of streams and lakes which become unable to support life.

---

[5]For a recent discussion of problems, see Corbett [1990], pp. 33-38.

[6]See Shell Petroleum Company Ltd. [1987a], for a particularly clear commentary, from which the following is extracted.

Table 7: Principal Sources of Environment Problem by Activity (denoted by •)

	Industry Side			End-use			
Problem Area	E & P	T & S	R & M	Industry	Transport	Electricity	Domestic
Gaseous Emissions:							
SO_2, NO_x, CO, CO_2, Particulates				•	•	•	•
Wastes:							
Systemic: Effluents & Leakages	•	•	•				
Accidents & Spills	•	•	•				

Source: Author.

Legend: E & P = Exploration & Production
T & S = Transport & Shipping
R & M = Refining & Marketing
SO_2 = sulfur dioxide
NO_x = nitrogen oxide
CO = carbon oxide
CO_2 = carbon dioxide

Soils and waters differ in their capacity to neutralize acids. If the receiving environment is rich in calcium carbonates, then acids can be effectively neutralized. On the other hand sand, non-carbonate rock, and soft water have little neutralizing capability.

3. Buildings and Materials

The main problem effecting buildings and materials is acid attack leading to corrosion and discoloration from the deposition of particles on the surface.

4. Gaseous Pollution in Developing Countries

The gaseous emissions discussed so far and their possible effects on health and the environment have been extensively monitored and researched in the industrial countries and have been the subject of considerable legislation over the past forty years. There has been much less monitoring and research done on the situations in developing countries. The development of pollution monitoring networks, and scientific and social analysis of the effects of gaseous emissions on local environments is unmistakenly a matter of some urgency, not least of all because of the rapid growth of emissions, as can be inferred from the energy growth scenarios presented in Part I. Figure 1 describes the effects of gaseous pollution in Cubatao, Brazil. The following summary by the author testifies both to the huge social costs of pollution when it reaches extreme levels and, equally, the social and economic gains of abating it:

> The case of Cubatao demonstrates, perhaps more dramatically than any other in the world, the most extreme results of unregulated occupation of land by mixed uses in a sensitive ecological setting: a large nation's most important and most polluting factories concentrated in a small area subject to atmospheric inversions and interlaced with thousands of homes; tens of thousands of people bathed in toxic effluent and sleeping directly over pipelines carrying flammable and explosive substances; acid rain defoliating adjacent mountainsides and causing landslides that threaten not only the factories and residences but the highways, railroad, pipelines, and harbour connecting the community to the outside world; and public officials at all levels seemingly in a state of paralysis, obsessed with the goal of economic development and striving to ignore the environmental catastrophe they have allowed ...
>
> Since 1985 there has been real progress toward ameliorating some of the worst aspects of the environmental fiasco in Cubatao. A tremendous amount of pollution control equipment is being installed in industrial plants, which also have been switched to less-polluting fuels, thousands of residents are being assisted in relocating to more suitable living areas, CETESB has become more aggressive in using fines and temporary plant closures to deal with recalcitrant polluters, and the Ministerio Publico has initiated public civil actions seeking restoration of damaged wetlands, waterways, and hillsides. Moreover, through extensive national newspaper and television coverage of the agony and progress of Cubatao, all of Brazil has received an environmental education.

5. The Greenhouse Effect

In contrast to the effects on health and the environment of the gaseous emissions discussed so far, the greenhouse effect of CO_2 and other gases is notable for three reasons: it is long-term, highly uncertain, and potentially far more calamitous. The amount of CO_2

Figure 1: Atmospheric Pollution in Cubatao, Brazil

The following is a summary by Findley of a pollution crisis in Cubatao that reached extreme conditions in the 1980s.

Additional air quality monitoring by scientists at the University of Sao Paulo had disclosed, in the dust and smoke perpetually shrouding the city, "an infinity of ... chemicals, invariably toxic," as well as sulphates, phosphates, and nitric and phosphoric acids, in concentrations "at least a dozen times higher than the maximum acceptable levels." Although CETESB's preferred course of action was "evacuation [of residents] from the city, pure and simple," there seemed to be little chance of that happening. Meanwhile, acid rain continued to denude the slopes of the Serra do Mar, and the threat of massive landslides was described as a "geological time bomb."

On September 3, 1984, in the midst of an atmospheric inversion, officials of CETESB and SEMA visited Cubatao. A few hours later the governor of Sao Paulo, for the first time ever, decreed a "state of emergency" in Cubatao, citing particulate concentrations in excess of the ambient standard of 876 micrograms per cubic meter. CETESB promptly required nine industries in Vila Parisi to shut down and ordered residents to evacuate the district. Police were sent from the city of Sao Paulo to assist in the evacuation and to prevent looting of empty homes. Although the mayor of Cubatao protested that he had not been consulted before these measures were taken, he agreed to make the soccer stadium available for displaced residents and to provide food and blankets. Eventually, atmospheric conditions improved, the state of emergency was downgraded to a state of alert (defined as concentrations of particulates in excess of 625 micrograms per cubic meter), the eighth such alert of 1984, and people were allowed to return to their homes. A few months later, in the early morning of Saturday, January 26, 1985, there was a massive, prolonged release of ammonia gas from a ruptured pipe at a fertilizer plant in Vila Parisi. Six thousand residents were evacuated; more than sixty persons were hospitalized. On Sunday, after the gas had dissipated, people were allowed to return to their homes. On Monday, CETESB assessed a penalty of twenty-four million cruzeiros against the owner of the plant. Later that day, after the Governor of Sao Paulo said the penalty was too small, the mayor of Cubatao signed a decree ...

Since 1985, in response to national media attention, public pressure, and the realization that public health and safety no longer should be sacrificed completely, state and municipal officials finally have moved to deal with Cubatao's problems.

(the main greenhouse gas) has risen by 15% this century and is projected to rise by around 50%, under the sort of scenarios discussed above, in the next 50 years or so. Since the effect has received much technical and public discussion, it is sufficient here to summarize the main carbon sinks and fluxes involved; the following figures relate to the present (the figures are generally regarded as approximate):

Atmosphere (sink)	740 billion tonnes
Fluxes (billion tonnes/year):	
Photosynthesis	- 60
Respiration	+60
Oceans - absorption	- 103
- release	+100
Fossil Fuels	+ 5.5, rising to >10 in 30-40 years
Net Annual Additions	~ 3 (rising at around 2% per year)

It is estimated that the sinks in vegetation and soils are 800 and 3,000 billion tonnes respectively, in the oceans 39,000 billion tonnes and ocean sediments over 60,000,000 billion tonnes. Fossil fuel reserves, proven and unproven, amount to about 4,700 billion tonnes. [See Shell Petroleum Company Ltd., 1987d]. Carbon dioxide allows ultraviolet and visible radiation to reach the earth's surface, but traps part of the infra-red energy that is radiated back. The potential effects on climate and their possible social consequences have been much discussed and are being extensively researched.

Given the uncertainties and lags involved, it seems likely that policy decisions will have to be taken (i) when the effects on climate are unknown and (ii) if the problem is solved, the damage avoided may also remain unknown. It is perhaps the most difficult of the policy dilemmas facing the fossil fuel industry and governments today.

C. Offshore Operations and Shipping

When blow-outs or accidents occur onshore, it is generally possible to contain the spilled oil within a relatively small area and recover it. With blow-outs or accidents offshore, however, the oil quickly spreads over large areas and, depending on weather conditions and distances, may contaminate beaches, shell-fish beds, and fish-spawning grounds, and injure and poison wildlife. It continues to be a significant source of economic damage to other activities, principally fishing and tourism, as well as to wildlife.

1. Sources of Oil Pollution in the Seas

The United States National Academy of Science (NAS) occasionally publishes information on oil pollution in the seas. In 1985, approximately 750 million tonnes of oil, or one quarter of world production, was produced offshore, while trade movements of oil between the major exporting and importing regions, most of it shipped, amounted to 1,200 million tonnes. Of this total, 0.05 million tonnes or 0.007% of offshore production entered the sea, and a rather larger figure, 0.64 million tonnes or 0.03%, entered from tanker operations. Accident figures vary appreciably from year to year; the NAS studies have found that, on average 12 percent of oil pollution in the seas (about 0.4 million tonnes per year) is due to accidents and spills. Figure 2 summarizes the main sources of pollution, under the following headings:

- coastal refineries and terminals (6% of total pollution)
- tanker accidents (12%, on average)
- offshore exploration and production (E & P) (2%)
- tanker operations (ballasting, etc, 20%)
- non-tanker shipping (10%)
- sewage, industrial effluents, urban river run-off and rain (40%);
- natural sources (seeps, sediments, erosion, 10%.)

The contribution of industry related sources (the first four of the above list), is about 40% of the total of 3.2 million tonnes per year, has declined by over half in the past decade [Siddayao, 1980, pp. 393-405],[7] and is quite small in relation to the overall offshore production levels and shipping. Nevertheless, it is still a major environmental concern, not least of all because of the growth of the industry and the geographical spread of markets to developing countries. Consider, therefore, to two aspects of the offshore pollution problem, namely systemic wastes, which as seen above arise mainly from tanker operations, and accidents and spills.[8]

2. Systemic Wastes from Tanker Operations

As noted, these have been the largest sources of pollution historically, though because the pollution is more dispersed and controlled the ecological damage has been less. Tanker operations have, in the past, caused significant pollution by discharging the sea ballast and tank washwater that contains oil. This practice continued for some time even after the 1954 International Convention for the Prevention of Pollution of the Sea by Oil came into force. This convention allowed such discharges to be made at a distance of 50 nautical miles from land. However, with the rapid growth of international shipping, it soon became apparent that the measures adopted by the convention "were insufficient to prevent serious pollution of the seas and shores, but [it should be noted] it took several years for effective legislation to be adopted." [Royal Dutch Shell Group, 1983].

In addition, significant technical advances in cleaning, ballasting and waste recovery procedures were required. In the 1960s, in the absence of shore facilities capable of receiving and treating contaminated water from tankers, the industry developed a procedure for treating oily water aboard ship. The procedure, known as the "Load on Top System" (Figure 3), reduced oily discharges to low levels and led to a major recovery of oily wastes. Another method is to use segregated ballast tanks in which the water is never contaminated with oil. It is an international legislative requirement, arising out of the Marine Pollution Convention

---

[7]Siddayao cites the following NAS data for 1975: coastal refineries and terminals, 450 thousand tonnes/year (7% total); tanker accidents, 200 thousand tonnes/year (3%); off-shore E&P, 80 thousand tonnes/year (1%); tanker operations, 1,700 thousand tonnes/year (28%); sewage, effluents, etc. (non-industry), 2,500 thousand tonnes/year (41%); natural sources, 1,200 thousand tonnes/year (20%); totalling 6,130 thousand tonnes/year.

[8]Shell Petroleum Company Ltd. [1987c], provides an admirable overview of these matters. See also Royal Dutch Shell Group [1983], pp. 649-653, and Wardley-Smith (editor) [1983].

Figure 2: Origins of Oil in the Sea

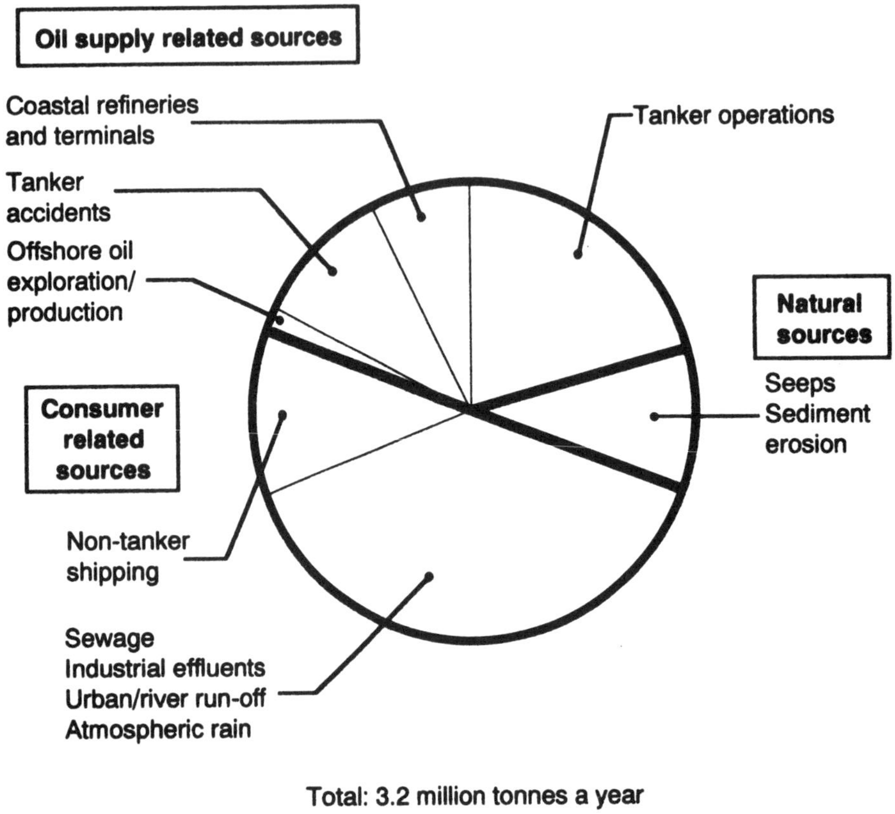

Source: United States National Academy of Science [1985]. (Copied from Shell Petroleum Company Ltd. [1987c].)

Figure 3: "Load on Top" System of Tank Cleaning

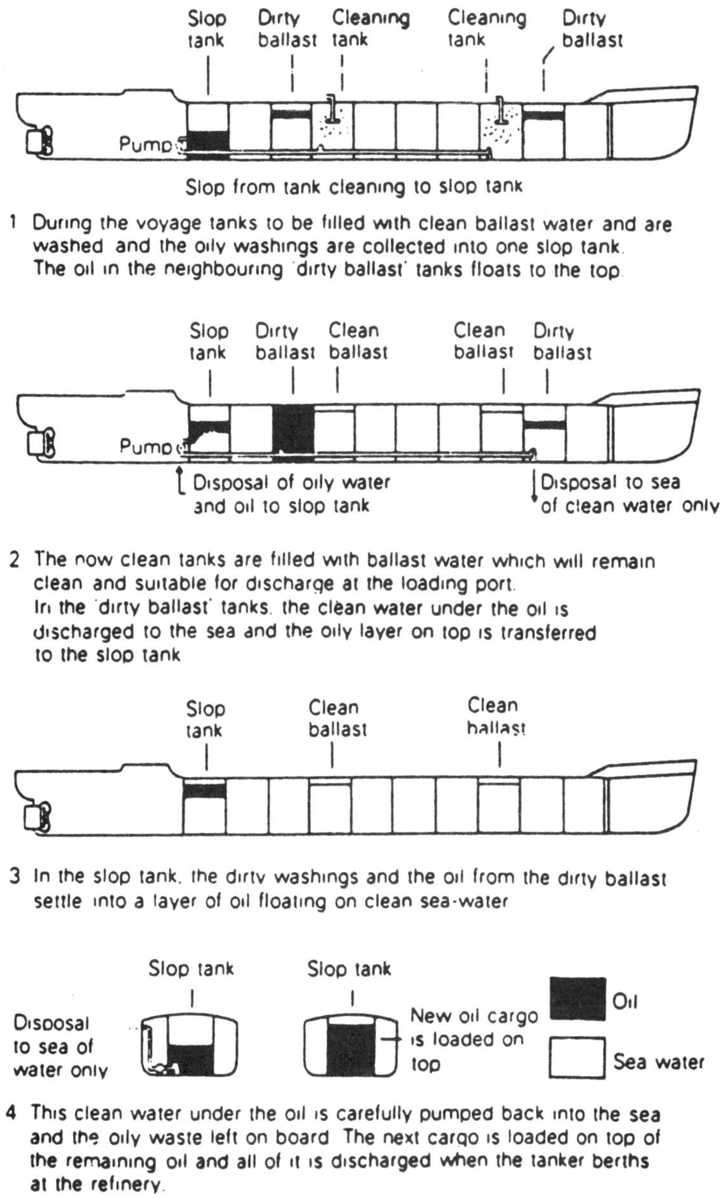

Source: Wardley-Smith (editor) [1983].

(MARPOL) of 1973 and Protocol (MARPOL) of 1978 that all new tankers are equipped with such tanks. An industry report comments that:[9]

> Since the 1970s, industry practice and MARPOL have become even more stringent. MARPOL now prohibits the discharge of oil or oily mixtures from tankers anywhere at sea, except in minute quantities in low and harmless concentrations and then only 50 miles or more from land.
>
> New crude oil tankers must be equipped with segregated, clean ballast tanks. Existing tankers must eventually either be similarly equipped, or must use a crude oil washing technique that minimizes oil residues. Discharged ballast must be monitored for oil content and the pumps shut down automatically if set levels are exceeded. Effluents from engine room bilges have to be processed through separators and the oil content must not exceed specified levels.
>
> These measures, if obeyed, are sufficient to keep sea pollution to harmless levels. Coastal states are increasing surveillance of ships at sea ... MARPOL requires all ships to keep an oil record book ... If violations are detected, prosecution follows.

What is learned from this, as far as pollution policy is concerned? There are four points worth noting, and which will be drawn upon later when the formal discussion of policies is addressed. ***First***, under an appropriate regulatory framework, whether national or international, pollution levels can be reduced significantly despite the growth of the industry. ***Second***, changes in operating practices and technologies are required, not restrictions in overall demand. Demand reductions by themselves would accomplish very little, even assuming they are feasible; technical progress and improvements in operating practices, on the other hand, lead to major reductions in pollution. ***Third***, pollution control adds to costs and, for this reason alone, the policies must apply equally to all. Cheating cannot be allowed, otherwise, there is a modern version of Gresham's Law where the "bad drive out the good" and policies fail. This of course is a general point applicable to all aspects of environmental policy. ***Fourth***, extra expenditures are also required on the government side to monitor compliance with policy and to ensure uniformity and fairness in its application.

3. Accidents and Spills

"Poor housekeeping," the industry notes, "in the operation of oil fields, or in transporting oil, may lead to accidental spillages." [Royal Dutch Shell Group, 1983, p. 643]. But it is important to recognize that no matter how well designed and operated equipment may be, or how well trained the staff, it is impossible to prevent accidents entirely. What can be done is to reduce the probability of occurrence of accidents and the ensuing damage to levels where the benefits of damage avoided bear a reasonable relation to costs. There are three aspects to the problem: (i) prevention, (ii) damage control when accidents and spills occur, and (iii) conservation.

(a) Prevention. Although operational or systemic pollution contribute to perhaps two-thirds of the oil discharges at sea, such discharges involve low concentrations over large areas and are much less damaging than those arising from accidental damage. For many years it has been found that accidents are more frequently the result of human error; indeed, it is the primary cause in 80% of the reported cases. "Adequate training of masters, officers and

---

[9]See Shell Petroleum Company Ltd. [1987c], p. 3.

crews is the key to preventing them. Recommended sailing routes, traffic separation schemes and the use of sophisticated navigational equipment can help prevent collisions and strandings. Special traffic regulations frequently apply for oil and gas tankers in harbour approaches." [Royal Dutch Shell Group, 1983, p. 652]. Advanced training has now become a requirement of the International Maritime Organization Convention and also extends to "hands on" training in well-drilling operations. The reduction in the number of tanker accidents over the past two decades (see Table 8) is generally attributed to attention paid to training. Spillages from vessels of 25,000 tonnes or more amounted to about 160 thousand tonnes in the period 1985-1989, as compared with 660 thousand tonnes in the preceding five years and 1,550 thousand tonnes between 1975-1979. Developing countries have been affected almost as often as the industrial countries.

Yet, despite the efforts to improve operating practices and standards, there was again a rise in big oil spillages in 1989. The United Nations International Maritime Organization has recently drafted a plan to combat oil pollution at sea. Four key measures are:

(i) setting up national centers to cope with oil pollution in every state;
(ii) mandatory contingency plans for tanker crews;
(iii) standardizing spillage combat equipment to make coordinated efforts easier; and,
(iv) pooling of R & D information on tackling spills.

The plan was drafted by the organization's 134 member countries in May 1990, who are to be asked to ratify the convention in November 1990.

(b) Damage Limitation and Clean-up. The "polluter pays" principle has been interpreted by industry and governments to mean that the ship-owner or well operator has a legal responsibility for accidents resulting in spills. It has two aspects: (i) responsibility for damage limitation and clean-up costs, and (ii) compensation to the polluted parties, discussed separately below.

A recent review of contingency planning for oil spills comments that:

> Experience has shown that action to contain and control an oil spill must be taken well within the first 24 hours in order to be effective. There will probably be insufficient time to mobilize federal and state governmental resources before the effects of a spill become widespread ... Facility specific plans should be prepared for coastal and off-shore exploration wells and production facilities, terminals, and other oil-transfer facilities, and any other sites with a potential for spills of hazardous substances.[10]

Aside from the obvious need for contingency planning, training of personnel, and ensuring damage control facilities and materials are within ready distances of those potential spill areas where the ecological damage of the spills would be significant; it must not be overlooked that liability schemes need to be worked out and clearly laid down by each country. This is an essential aspect in the proper working of the "polluter pays" principle in

---

[10] See Anderson and Starer [1990], pp. 41-46.

Table 8: Accidental Spills from Tankers of Over 25,000 tonnes and Over $5 Million Indemnity

	Quantity Spilled		Countries Affected	
Year	Number	(000 Tonnes)	Industrial	Developing
1967[a]	1	121	1	0
1968	2	65	1	1
1969	2	55	1	1
1970	2	70	1	1
1971	4	110	3	1
1972	5	217	1	4
1973	2	42	1	1
1974	3	104	2	1
1975	8	255	6	2
1976	6	170	3	3
1977	6	222	3	3
1978[b]	6	344	5	1
1979	11	558	6	5
1980	4	256	2	3
1981	4	41	3	1
1982	0	0	0	0
1983	3	265	1	2
1984	2	98	0	2
1985	2	131	0	2
1986	0	0	0	0
1987	0	0	0	0
1988	0	0	0	0
1989[c]	1	35	1	0

Source: Organization for Economic Cooperation and Development [1990].

Notes: [a] Torrey Canyon
[b] Amoco Cadiz, 228 thousand tonnes spilled
[c] Vaidez

relation to accidents and spills. Although liability schemes may differ between countries, it may be of interest to note recent shifts in the United States' policy following the Valdez spill:[11]

> Under the Clean Water Act, the spiller is ... strictly liable, up to the specified limits for the actual costs incurred by the government in containing and removing the oil. If the discharge is from a facility, the current limit is $50 million; if the discharge is from a large vessel, the limit is currently $150/gross ton of ship or $210,000, whichever is greater. As a result of the Exxon Valdez spill, legislation is pending which would significantly raise these limits ... to the greater sum of $1,200/gross ton or $10 million ... For off-shore facilities, the limit would be set at $75 million plus unlimited removal costs ... When the discharge is the result of willful negligence or misconduct, the discharger is liable for the full clean-up costs without limit ... .

Furthermore, the companies, of course, must bear their own costs directly or via their protection and indemnity or insurance clubs.

(c) Compensation. Another element in the "polluter pays" principle is compensation to polluted parties, invariably supported by legal suits where voluntary compensation is deemed insufficient. The processes and options now take on a well defined, if not complex structure which is summarized in Figure 4. The reader is referred to the source materials cited above and the organizations listed in the figure for further details.[12]

It is of special interest to note that compensation payments, whether voluntary or otherwise, have risen appreciably in recent years. There are two reasons for this, one economic, the other political. The economic reason is that the costs of damage to polluted parties is rising in real terms over time as the value of natural resources, such as fisheries, coastal lands, and beaches, and the value placed on wildlife increases with (among other things) economic growth. The political reason is that public awareness and concern are rising continually with the growth and international spread of media attention.

(d) Assessment. In relation to accidents and spills, there are four points that might usefully carry forward to the analysis of policies in Part III. The ***first*** is that the "polluter pays" principle remains a fundamental principle of policy, although to implement it requires an elaborate international and national network of institutions and laws. ***Second***, clarity in the application of the principle and in the laws that support it is also required for the industry to respond appropriately. ***Third***, once again, the equal application of the principle to all parties is required for the policy to work. ***Fourth***, it is worth recalling that most accidents are still attributed to human error notwithstanding intensive training programs, contingency plans, and heavy investments in modern control and information technology.

---

11 See Anderson and Starer [1990], p. 41.

12 Again an especially useful and concise summary is to be found in Shell Petroleum Company Ltd. [1987c], pp. 6-9.

Figure 4: Compensation Schemes

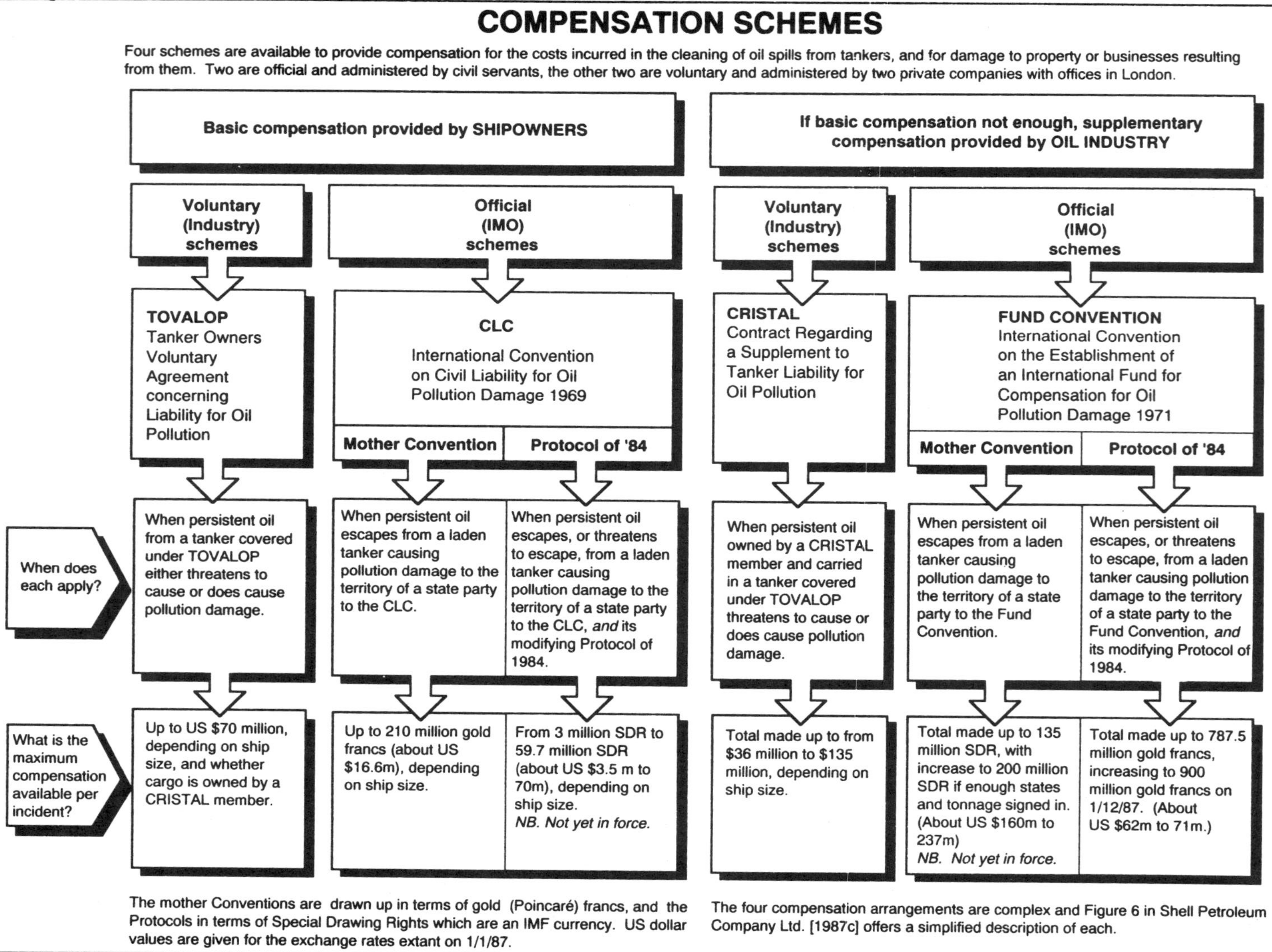

Source: Shell Petroleum Company Ltd. [1987c].

D. Refineries[13]

Refineries have two types of problems to address, one relating to their own emissions and wastes, the other to meeting increasing demands for "cleaner" fuels, such as low sulfur, unleaded fuels. The following summary will discuss them under five sub-headings: gaseous emissions, aqueous effluents, hazardous wastes (such as spent catalysts), decommissioning, and the demands for cleaner fuels.

1. Gaseous Emissions

The main gaseous emissions from a refinery are combustion gases, principally SO_2 and NO_x, from fuel burning; tail gases from sulfur recovery units; leakages from valves, pump seals, flanges, drainage systems, etc; and, combustion gases from flares.

The tighter standards that many countries are applying to the gaseous emissions of industry and transport apply equally to the refinery industry. The once seemingly cost-effective solution of building high stacks is being replaced by sulfur dioxide (SO_2) and nitrogen oxide (NO_x) reduction systems. The quantity of SO_2 in the stack gases depends on the sulfur content of the refinery fuel and the efficiency of the sulfur recovery units and treatment systems. Recovery efficiencies (reductions in SO_2 emitted) of 91-99% have been achieved through modern recovery units and treatment systems.

NO_x is a more difficult emission to control and for many years the main approach was to seek modifications in combustion techniques. Two technologies recently introduced to reduce NO_x emissions are selective non-catalytic reduction and selective catalytic reduction.[14] The former requires the injection of a reducing agent, such as ammonia or urea, the latter works with ammonia injection only. Both convert NO_x to nitrogen and water vapor. It has been found that the non-catalytic process can remove 50-70% of the NO_x from the flue gas, while the catalytic process can remove up to 90%.

Leaks from valves and other sources are small, but often contain odorous compounds like hydrogen sulfide. The main approach to controlling them is, as one would expect, pollution conscious design and good maintenance. "Emissions from the storage of volatile products and crudes can be controlled by the use of floating roof tanks." [Royal Dutch Shell Group, 1983, p. 336].

2. Aqueous Effluents[15]

In any refinery there are a large number of wastewater streams requiring treatment. The most contaminated streams are condensates from the various processing units and the

---

[13]See Corbett [1990] and Royal Dutch Shell Group [1983] for good discussions. Also see Shell Petroleum Company Ltd. [1989b].

[14]The following draws on Corbett's [1990] recent review, p. 35.

[15]Royal Dutch Shell Group [1983], p. 337-340, for a good discussion. The following paragraphs draw extensively on the handbook.

water drained from the storage tanks; they contain volatile, malodorous compounds, hydrocarbons, dissolved organics and suspended solids. Other streams can become contaminated by oil in the event of maloperation and equipment failure.

Royal Dutch Shell Group [1983] notes that in the industrial countries refineries have developed a number of measures to reduce their impact on neighboring surface waters. Before turning to this, however, it is worth recalling how serious the problem can be if the temptation to cut refinery costs by ignoring pollution is not resisted. For example, oil contamination in the Red Sea has recently been estimated to be 14.6 kilograms (kg) of oil per square kilometer (km^2) per year, as compared with 9.2 kg of oil per km^2 per year for the world's oceans; of this 6.6 kg or 45% stems from refinery effluent sources as compared with 0.6 kg or 6% for the world's oceans [Hassan, 1989, pp. 235-243].[16] As will be seen, it is in fact possible to reduce the pollution of aqueous effluent to low levels.

There are three approaches:

(i) In-plant control measures aimed at minimizing pollution at the source, for instance by recirculating water for cooling instead of once-through cooling water and by applying a high level of water re-use.

(ii) Drainage systems designed to prevent complications in treatment units, principally through the use of segregated sewer systems for the different categories of waste water.

(iii) End-of-pipe treatment units which is typically a five-stage process involving oil separation; removal of emulsified oils and colloidal solids; removal of dissolved organic material by biological oxidation; further treatment involving aeration and filtration prior to discharge; and sludge dewatering and disposal. [See Royal Dutch Shell Group, 1983, for further details].

The costs of such processes are not negligible. An important issue in refinery economics is the differing environmental standards across countries. Countries with low emission and effluent treatment standards act to lower prices; this can be expected to reduce the refiners' margins in countries with higher standards, at the expense of the local environment. The issue is taken up further in Part III.

3. Hazardous Wastes[17]

There are several categories of hazardous wastes in refineries [Corbett, 1990]:[18] various "floats" or foams containing toxic substances; slop-oil emulsion solids; separation sludges; heat exchanger cleaning sludges; tank bottoms containing lead compounds; and spent catalysts. Corbett reports on the various technical options being followed for the treatment and disposal of the wastes. Some can be dealt with through in-plant solutions (treatment of slop-oils and sludges), incineration, biochemical treatment of organic material in wastewater

---

[16] The above figures were taken from the computerized abstracting services.

[17] See Corbett [1990] upon which the following paragraphs are based.

[18] The categories are defined by the United States Environmental Protection Agency.

streams, and recycling of catalysts. It is beyond the scope of the present paper to adequately summarize the technical options being pursued, and the interested reader is referred to Corbett's paper and his source material. Suffice it to note here that an expansion of refining in response to a long-term rise in demand for the industry's products *and* a reduction of hazardous wastes are both technically and economically compatible goals if (and only if) there is a reasonable harmony of standards among countries.

4. Decommissioning Refineries[19]

Dickey and Jones comment that "...it has become readily apparent that even a modern carefully designed facility can cause numerous, costly environmental problems [for decommissioning]. The operating practices at the plant are undoubtedly a major cause of the problems, and it is important that the eventual shutdown of the facility should be part of its long-term operational strategy. So much of the environmental work [in decommissioning as in other areas] depends on full and accurate records being available." [Dickey and Jones, 1987]. Some environmental issues they cite relate to soil quality, groundwater resources, lead, disposal of spent catalysts and chemicals, and disposal of other toxic materials and substances. Restoration of sites to safe and functional conditions, which is increasingly a regulatory requirement, is now a significant aspect of costs and operating procedures.

5. Demands for Cleaner Fuels[20]

The demands for clean fuels and associated environmental regulations and taxes are perhaps posing the major challenges for the refinery industry. The issues are complex and wide ranging, affecting both gasoline and diesel fuels, and cannot be covered adequately in the course of a short paper. The following issues are listed as partial background to the discussions of policy principles in Part III.

(a) Unleaded Gasoline. This is coming to dominate the gasoline markets in the OECD countries following legislation in the 1980s and more recently. Unleaded gasoline had been introduced to allow use of catalytic converters both to control exhaust emissions and to reduce lead emissions. The three way catalytic converters, which substantially reduce the emission of unburnt hydrocarbons, carbon monoxide, and nitrogen oxides, are deactivated by the lead in conventional leaded gasoline. (The use of lead compounds was the cheapest, least energy demanding way of raising octane quality.) The phasing out of lead required changes in refinery facilities to produce high-octane components based initially on aromatics. [Shell Petroleum Company Ltd., 1989b, p. 8 and Seymour, 1990].

(b) Evaporative emissions. This step also increases gasoline volatility and thus the evaporative emissions of hydrocarbons, which are also coming under increasingly stringent regulation in the industrial countries. The industry notes that: "this is putting further pressure on refiners. Possible options to reduce [such] emissions include reducing gasoline volatility, fitting carbon canisters, or installing vapor recovery equipment. Of these options,

---

[19] See Dickey and Jones [1987].

[20] The author is grateful to Adam Seymour of the Oxford University Institute of Energy Studies for making available to him some of his material on this issue, especially his draft paper, Seymour [1990]. See also Shell Petroleum Company Ltd. [1989b].

reducing vapor pressure specifications exerts an even greater pressure to meet gasoline octane requirements, since the volatile components have good octane qualities ... Considerable attention is, therefore, being given to the production of methyl tertiary-butyl ether (MTBE). MTBE is a gasoline component that plays a major role both to boost octane levels and to control volatility ... MTBE production [expanded by] 70% in the United States and 100% in Western Europe in the period 1986 to 1988."

(c) Low Sulfur Fuels. Compliance with more stringent goals for reducing acid deposition has required the reduction of sulfur levels in transport fuels and fuel oils. This, too, raises investment requirements. Table 9 shows for instance the incremental costs of removing sulfur from gasoil for high sulfur crude.

It is noted that hydrogen addition conversion processes can also make important contributions to sulfur reduction "as they not only convert heavier products into lighter, higher quality products, but also necessarily [by the nature of the process] lead to the reduction of sulfur contents to low levels." [Shell Petroleum Company Ltd., 1989b].

E. Summing Up

The above discussion does not exhaust the range of environmental concerns faced by the oil and gas industry, whether in the industrial or the developing countries. One should, for instance, include oil and gas pipelines and safety issues in liquefied natural gas (LNG) production transport in any comprehensive survey.[21] But the range of issues covered -- gaseous emissions from end-use, systemic and accidental wastes and spills from offshore drilling and from shipping operations, and the wide ranging environmental problems to be addressed in refining -- serve to make a number of points that need to be kept foremost in mind in any discussions of policy. To recapitulate they are:

(i) That technical options are generally available or can be developed which address most environmental problems, although they continue to tax the innovative capacity of the industry greatly;

(ii) The costs of the options are often appreciable, and need to be weighed against the environmental benefits;

(iii) In some cases they take significant periods of time to develop, so that proper phasing will be important in policy;

(iv) Uneven standards across countries in an internationally competitive industry can erode the margins of those producers having to work to the highest standards.

(v) There is much evidence in the historical record, and in the analyses of technological options and management processes, that an expansion of output of the industry can be accomplished with environmental improvements.[22]

---

[21]Further guidance on this can be found in several sources, including Royal Dutch Shell Group, [1983].

[22]The GHE would, of course, require more profound adjustments, though the point remains valid, as discussed in Part III.

Table 9: Cost of Removing Sulfur from Gasoil

Gasoil specification % sulfur, by weight:	0.43%	0.4 to 0.2%	0.2 to 0.15%	Under 0.15%
Incremental cost of reducing sulfur to below 0.43% ($,1983)	0	1900	7000	9000

Source: Shell Petroleum Company Ltd. [1987a].

This chapter now turns to the policy approaches for achieving environmental improvements as output expands.

III. Policy Options and Approaches

From an economic viewpoint, the primary aim of environmental policy should be to achieve an environmental, as well as an economic improvement, and there are indeed many ways by which this can be achieved. In this sense, economic and environmental policies are working towards common ends, and trade-offs only begin to arise at the margins of policymaking; e.g., when deciding how stringent environmental standards should be. In this part of the paper, the following will be discussed:

- external costs and the "polluter pays" principle;
- instruments of policy for implementing the principle;
- how instruments work in practice, with special reference to the use of environmental taxes;
- instruments suited to the oil and gas industries;
- some issues for local analysis, such as the setting of standards, effects on trade, and effects on income distribution.

There are a large number of texts on the first three items listed, and so the summaries are brief.[23]

A. External Costs and the "Polluter Pays" Principle

External costs are the negative effects on well-being (often in the form of measured income) born wholly or partly by agents other than the producers or consumers responsible for them. The costs of pollution or environmental damage are classified as external costs when the costs to polluted parties (e.g., the effects of gaseous emissions, effluents, or environmental accidents on health, property, and economic well-being) are not accounted for in the decisions of industries or of the consumers responsible for pollution. The idea of the "polluter pays" principle is thus to reflect or "internalize" the costs (strictly, the marginal costs) of pollution damage in the decisionmaking of those responsible for it. An environmental gain results because there is an incentive to reduce pollution. An economic gain results when the costs of reducing pollution are less than the costs of the pollution damage avoided (i.e. the benefits of environmental improvement).

---

[23]With special reference to developing countries, some readers may be interested in the author's review for The World Bank. See Anderson [1990].

This is a well-known principle and has already received widespread, if sometimes faulty, application in the oil, gas, and other industries. There are broadly two ways in which it can be implemented:

(i) through environmental taxation or

(ii) through regulation, which broadly requires polluters to introduce pollution control and other measures to comply with defined standards.

These options are considered further.

B. Instruments of Policy

Table 10 provides a brief listing of instruments of policy under the headings of (a) economic instruments and (b) instruments such as regulation and negotiations that are legally enforceable by law in the event of non-compliance. Different countries may often use different instruments to address a similar problem. Some have opted to regulate for the use of unleaded fuels and catalytic converters, others to provide tax incentives. Approaches also differ as to the use of taxes, subsidies, or regulations to deal with acidifying gases, or to the finance of research and development in environmentally related areas, and so forth. It is also not unusual to apply more than one instrument to deal with a problem; e.g., to regulate discharges of residuals and yet to use environmental taxes to meet the public financial requirements of environmental policy [see Opschoor and Vos, 1989].[24] The relative merits of the various approaches will be discussed shortly (Section 3.4). But the main point to be noted for the moment is the variety of options that the public authorities have when implementing environmental policies.

The question is often raised whether interventions such as those listed in Table 10 are in any way at odds with the working of market systems. In fact, they are intended to internalize environmental concerns into market systems by correcting defects in structure. All open market economies operate within a regulatory framework established by law and government, and the values of their citizens. This framework includes the setting of standards, safeguards, and regulations relating to health and safety in the production of goods and services, enforced by law and legal liability; the abilities of governments to tax, subsidize, and provide grant aid; and the influence of numerous public and private organizations and institutions on values and moral restraint in economic and public affairs. Few economic activities are left untouched by these instruments of social policy -- in foods, manufacturing, transport, and public and private services -- and it is likely that they will be applied increasingly in areas of environmental policy.

---

[24]If an environmental policy is successful, however, environmental tax revenues would often be small in the long-term.

Table 10: Environmental Policy Instruments

Instrument	Applications (Examples)
	Economic Instruments
Taxes	• Acidifying gas emissions • Greenhouse gases (carbon taxes) • Congestion charges
Subsidy/Tax Relief	• Energy research • Unleaded fuels; catalytic converters • Energy conserving investments
Public Investment/Grant Aid	• Research and development Regional development programs
	Law
Regulation and legal liability	• Chlorofluorocarbons • Toxic wastes • Environmental accidents • Unleaded fuels; catalytic converters
Negotiated arrangements (enforceable by law in event of non-compliance)	• Localized issues: emissions; wastes; aesthetics; compliance with local land use and building codes

Source: Author.

C. The Practical Effects of Environmental Policy

In terms of their long-term effects on economic growth and the environment, the regulatory and the tax approaches to environmental policy can be so designed as to be equivalent. The choice between the two rests on such practical matters as administrative feasibility and costs, and the costs to polluters of complying with policy. It has long been known that, in theory, the tax approach to environmental policy, by giving industry and consumers more flexibility in responding to policy than regulations, reduces the costs of implementing policy; but this result neglects the costs and difficulties of administration, which vary from one situation to another. In practice both approaches tend to be used.

The following discussion of the practical effects of environmental policy will initially concentrate on the tax approach; comparisons between the two are reserved for Section 3.4.

1. Quantitative Effects (Other things equal) of Tax as a Policy Approach

An initial aim of environmental taxes is to raise the prices of polluting products or practices such that the external costs to other parties are reflected in the price. The immediate effect is a quantitative reduction in the polluting activity via the effects of price on demand and supply. However, such effects are a small part of the story, the least important and the least interesting. If a tax were to add 25% to marginal production costs, pollution damage may fall by 10% to 15% in cases where demand and supply are fairly elastic -- a rather small effect for such a large price increase, and one which would soon be eliminated in the case of energy by added demands arising from income growth. It would rarely be sufficient to allay environmental concerns.

2. Technological Response and Substitution to Taxation and Regulation

A much more important effect (which applies equally to taxes and regulation) is to encourage substitution towards less polluting fuels, such as gas and low sulfur coals and oil in the case of sulfur taxes, or to induce changes in production technologies to reduce pollution. Two recent publications of the OECD [OECD, 1988 and OECD, 1990a] have provided an admirable overview of the rich range of options here, which are classified into four groups:

(i) add-on technologies, such as scrubbers and catalytic converters;

(ii) "clean technologies," involving redesigns and reconfiguration of the combustion process: lean burn engines, fluidized bed combustion in boilers (reduces SO_2 and NO_x), and lower temperature combustion (reduces NO_x);

(iii) fuel substitution; and,

(iv) greater energy efficiency in consumption.

3. Past and Current Examples from Oil, Gas, and Electricity

Some of the options and their characteristics are summarized in Table 11, for the case of electric power. The main point is that technological innovations may bring about dramatic reductions in emissions once the rents are created for their introduction by environmental policies. Looking at the cost data presented it is clear that, in the case of electric power, major reductions of the order of 90% to 95% may be achieved over the long-term, as the new approaches are brought on stream, even with quite moderate environmental tax incentives.

The industry examples provided in Part II, i.e. treatment of systemic wastes and emissions from refineries; introduction of unleaded, low sulfur fuels; "top-down" loading systems to reduce oil wastes from tankers; and, indeed, in the steady if faulty and incomplete progress on the reduction of oil spills, may all be cited as evidence of technological or innovative responses to environmental policy. An important historical example from the industrial countries has been the introduction of clean fuels and the reduction of smogs following the Clean Air Acts. [See, for example, Brimblecome, 1987]. While this led to a loss of major markets for coal and lignite, it was a huge stimulus for the development of the gas and electric power industries. More recently, Clean Air Acts are focusing on the reduction of "photo-chemical smogs" (more formally, photo-oxidant reduction) brought about by the interaction of sunlight with nitrogen oxides and hydrocarbons. (This is also one of the reasons for new policies regulating the use of aromatics, discussed in Part III.) Further examples are the industry pollution controls and pollution abatement investments in Cubatao, Brazil, discussed in Part I.

In sum, technological innovations and substitutions in response to environmental policies become widespread once satisfactory policies are in place, and are by far the most important means of abating pollution. Further, they make output growth and pollution abatement compatible objectives.

4. Examples from Road Transport

Road transport is another area where technical innovations have brought about significant reductions in pollution in response to environmental regulation or taxation. In the OECD countries, policy has focused on limiting specific pollutants such as carbon monoxide, sulfur dioxide, nitrogen oxide, hydrocarbon vapor and particulates. The policy approach has varied between countries. Some countries' approaches, e.g., those of the United States, focuses exclusively on the regulatory approach, while others use a mix of regulation and taxation. It is worth contrasting emission levels in the United States with more of the European Economic Community (EEC), since the United States (where standards are still being tightened) has generally introduced its policies earlier. (See Table 12.)

The technologies for reducing such pollution have been well reviewed in a number of documents, such as OECD [1990a]. For example, for gasoline engines there are two routes. The first is the use of three-way catalytic converters using unleaded fuels and is winning favor in OECD. This is an expensive add-on, which raises consumption, but meets new legislative requirements. The second route is "lean-burn" engines which also use unleaded fuels with an oxidation catalyst to reduce the hydrocarbon and CO emissions. For diesels, "trap" and "trap oxidizer" systems have been developed to reduce emissions of particulates.

Table 11: Potential for Emissions Reduction: Examples from Electric Power Generation

A: Fuel Substitution

Fuel	Sulfur Content, %	SO_2 Emissions mg/MJ	NO_x Emissions mg/MJ
Coal	1	720	245
Coal-low sulfur	3	2200	
Fuel oil - heavy	3	1400	155
Fuel oil - low sulfur	1	480	
Gas oil	0.3	140	
Natural gas	0.002	0.73	115

B: Technology Options (selected examples)

Technology	% Reduction SO_2	% Reduction NO_x	Status	Costs, as % generation costs
Pre-combustion				
Coal cleaning	10-30		Commercial	
Advanced coal cleaning	90		R & D	
Combustion control				
Low NOx		30-50	Commercial)	
Advanced low NOx		Up to 70	R & D)	
Catalytic		80	)	1%
Sorbent injection	60-75		Demonstration)	
Fluidized bed	70-95		Operational; R & D	
Post Combustion				
Fluegas desulfuration (FGD)	80 Up to 90		Several options: commercial & R & D	10-15% for coal & oil
Selective catalytic reduction (SRC)	80-90			10% for coal, 2-5% for oil and gas

Source: Organization for Economic Cooperation and Development/International Energy Agency [1988].

Legend: mg/MJ = milligrams/Megajoule; R & D = research and development; SO_2 = sulfur dioxide; NO_x = nitrogen oxide

Table 12: Emission levels in the United States and the European Economic Community

Emission type	United States	EEC
CO (grams/km)	6.9	18-38
Hydrocarbon (grams/km)	0.28	4-6
NO_x (grams/km)	1.2	2.3-3.4
Leaded fuel (lead, g/l)[a]	0.026	0.15
Unleaded fuels[a]	0.013	00.013

Source: Organization for Economic Cooperation and Development [1990], Annex B.

Note: [a] Legislated levels, see Shell Petroleum Company, Ltd. [1987a].

Legend: EEC = European Economic Community
grams/km = grams per kilometer
g/l = grams/liter
CO = carbon oxide
NO_x = nitrogen oxide

5. Summing Up of the Policy Response Process

Suppose the extra marginal costs of using low pollution options are denoted by MUC and the marginal costs of the polluting options were MC. Then if prices (including the environmental taxes) are greater than MC plus MUC, low polluting options would gradually be introduced; taxes would decline to low levels because low polluting options are virtually tax exempted, prices would decline to MC plus MUC, and the environmental concerns would be fully internalized in the pricing system. The extra value added by the low polluting options will be roughly MUC times total demand, an important source of employment and earnings opportunities and of returns to capital invested.

The process is summarized in Figure 5, where three effects are shown:

(i) Quantitative reductions, accompanied by rapid growth of tax revenues and a moderate reduction of environmental damage.

(ii) Innovation and substitution, as the new technologies, substitutes, or practices are introduced; in this phase, tax revenues (and prices) begin to decline.

(iii) Environmental concerns are fully internalized, the switch to low polluting options is virtually completed, tax revenues are negligible, and prices reflect the marginal costs of the environmentally unoffensive produce or practice.

As noted, the same effects can in principle be achieved through the regulatory approach to policy (it is sometimes known as "command-and-control"). This approach forces through the required technical and managerial innovations by placing conditions on emissions levels and on the treatment of wastes and effluents.

6. The Greenhouse Effect

In principle, the same model would apply to policies to address the greenhouse effect, assuming its implications for the climate are as serious as many scientists believe it will be. The most widely discussed of the policy proposals made so far have been concerned with demand side adjustments to encourage energy conservation and reduce losses and unnecessary waste -- so called energy efficiency improvements. Such proposals will be very important, as noted in Part I, but in and of themselves will not solve the problem. It will be necessary to examine long-term supply side options as well. Several policy proposals on the supply side have been made,[25] of which two might be mentioned:

(i) Solar energy based on photovoltaics and thermal schemes, and

(ii) Biomass as a source of liquid fuels (synfuels) such as ethanol and methanol.

---

[25] For a remarkable compendium, see Organization for Economic Cooperation and Development [1989].

Figure 5: Responses to Environmental Policies

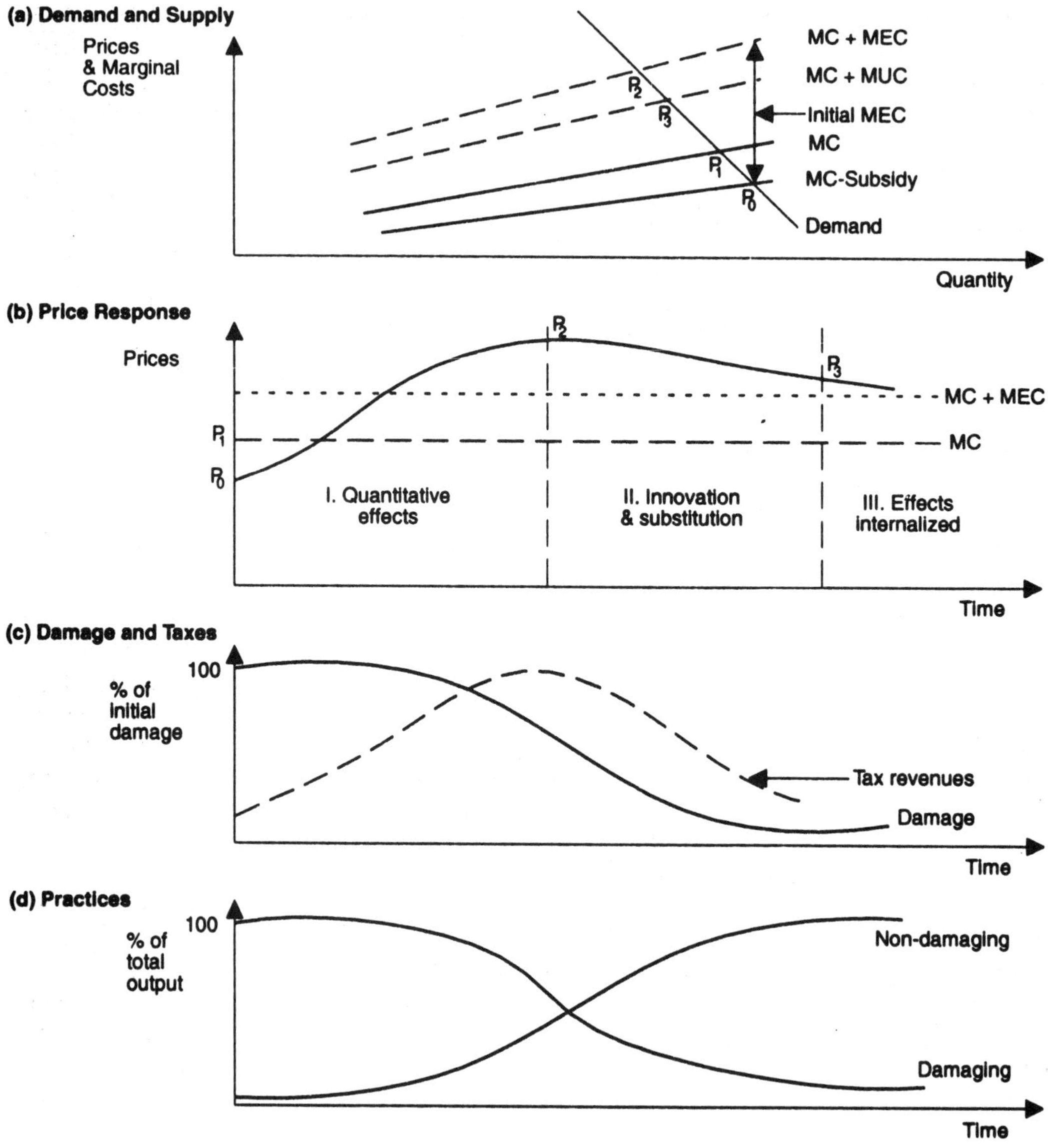

Source: Author.

Note: Case considered is one where taxes are introduced gradually from an initially subsidized program.

Legend: MC = marginal costs; MEC = marginal external cost; MUC = marginal user cost

Commercial interest in both was extensive in the period of high oil prices (1973-1985) but subsided following the oil price collapse in 1986. It would revive again under the influence of carbon taxation (which is widely being discussed in OECD countries), a recovery of oil prices, or (more surely) of both.

In fact, photovoltaics (PVs) and also solar-thermal energy gained ground throughout the 1980s as possible sources of commercial energy due to major improvements in efficiency and reliability and reductions in costs. Conversion efficiencies for field systems now range from around 7% for low cost, thin-film amorphous silicon devices to 20% for crystalline silicon devices using concentrators to focus the sunlight onto high grade cells. Costs have fallen from $200,000/kWp capacity in the early 1970s, to around $25,000/kWp in 1980 and under $6,000/kWp for grid-tied systems in 1990. In the 1990s they are expected to fall appreciably again under the influence of three factors:

(i) Scale economies in production. World output rose from under 5 megawatts peak (MWp) per year in the early 1980s to 42MWp in 1989; numerous larger scale operations are now being developed and production levels of several hundred MWp are expected by the late 1990s.

(ii) Technical progress in production methods, both for thin-film and for high grade crystalline silicon cells.

(iii) Further improvements in conversion efficiency, into the 10 to 15% range for thin-film devices and over 25% for high grade cells using concentrators.

Cost expectations of $2,100/kWp are widely regarded as plausible for the late 1990s and $1,500/kWp in the following decade if production levels rise into the gigawatt range, representing over a hundred-fold decline in costs since PVs were first seriously considered (and rejected) as a possible source of commercial energy at the time of the first oil price shock. Table 13 summarizes some recent cost estimates for PV energy and also includes estimates for biomass based liquid fuels such as ethanol and methanol.

It is apparent that a major new source of commercial energy is becoming available. Whereas the 1980s saw much experimentation with the technology in developing and industrial countries - mainly for remote, small-scale, stand-alone electricity systems, and for some pilot electricity general projects linked to the grid -the 1990s are likely to see the technology used increasingly for power generation in areas of high solar insolation [high kilowatt hours per square meter (kWh/m^2)]. Solar-thermal generation has also made major strides.

It is beyond the scope of the present paper to discuss greenhouse effect policies and options in detail; and it is quite possible that other technologies than the ones just noted may be more attractive, or that a mix of the technological options will be followed. The point to be made here is more elementary. It is that, with respect to the greenhouse effect, as with other environmental problems, technological options are available and would become commercially attractive under an appropriate incentives structure brought about by environmental taxation regulation.

Table 13: Recent Cost Estimates for Some Renewable Energy Sources

	Cost Expectations	
	Late 1990s	2005-2010
PV Electricity (Grid-Tied Systems)		
Low Insolation Areas[a]	23c/kWh	15c/kWh
Medium Insolation Areas[b]	15c/kWh	10c/kWh
High Insolation Areas[c]	12c/kWh	7c/kWh
Thermal Electricity		
Nuclear		6.5c/kWh
Coal-fired (large-scale)	5.5c/kWh[d]	
Gas-Combined Cycle	6-8c/kWh[d]	
Small-scale Coal	8c/kWh[d]	
Diesels (5-15MW)	12-15c/kWh[d]	
PV Hydrogen (at source in high insolation areas)		
$/boe	250	140
$/United States gallon oil equivalent	6.0	3.3
Biomass Liquid Fuels		
$/boe	40-50	--
$/United States gallon oil equivalent	1.1-1.2	--

Source: Derived from United States Department of Energy data supplied by the United Kingdom Department of Energy. See United States Department of Energy [1987].

Notes: [a] E.g., Central and North Europe, Canada
[b] Southern Europe, Asia, South America, Southern Africa
[c] Southern United States, Middle East, Sahel, Tropics, Australia
[d] Would rise with any rise in fuel prices. For example, a $10/boe adds 1.3 cents/kWh to costs (2c/kWh for diesels).

Legend: PV = photovoltaic; c/kWh = cents per kilowatt hour; MW = megawatts
boe = barrels of oil equivalent; oe = oil equivalent; -- = information not available

D. Instruments Suited to the Oil and Gas Industries[26]

Which policy instruments are best suited to the oil and gas industries and their consumers? It was noted above that much the same end-results in terms of environmental benefits and industry response can in principle be achieved by the regulatory and the tax approaches to environmental policy. The main differences between the two approaches lie in the short-term and medium-term, and the question to be addressed is, which is the best way of bringing the transition about?

As with most questions of this kind, the answer rarely rests on economic efficiency alone, but on administrative and institutional practicalities as well. It also varies with the problem. Regulations backed by legal liability and law are better suited, for instance, for hazardous wastes and environmental accidents; while the tax approach is better for congestion, and a combination of the two is better in other situations. Further, neither approach can work properly without certain elements of the other. Regulation requires significant funds for administration, research, and monitoring compliance with policy, and thus requires tax revenues from one source or another. The tax approach, on the other hand, has many of those features normally associated with regulation, such as setting environmental standards, monitoring emissions (or the practices responsible for them), and regulating the use of common resources; like regulation, it also relies heavily on the instruments of law and legal liability, if only to take defaulters to court.

In practice, therefore, the proper choice of instruments tends to vary with the situation and the problem at hand. Taxes are better suited as an incentive to use clean fuels and install emission control devices, while the instruments of law and legal liability are better for dealing with environmental accidents and spills. Table 14 presents a rough classification of instruments in relation to the oil and gas industries and indicates where the balance of advantage would generally lie.

Some further comments on the classification might be useful. Although the regulatory approach uses the instruments of negotiation, law, and legal liability, this does not preclude the use of indirect taxes to provide for the costs of administering environmental policy, monitoring emissions and wastes, and monitoring compliance. It is essential to a successful policy for compliance to be widespread and applied equally to all. A policy should not, therefore, be undermined by weak and lax administration brought about by revenue scarcity. Thus taxes for revenue raising purposes (as opposed to their use as an environmental incentive) would often complement the regulatory approach well.

In contrast, when taxes are preferred as the main instrument of policy, they have two advantages. ***First***, they lower the costs to polluters of complying with policy.[27] Polluters facing high costs of pollution abatement would prefer to pay a charge or tax while those facing low costs would prefer to avoid it by installing the necessary equipment or changing practices. Hence, the least-cost forms of abatement are introduced first and there is a better ranking of priorities. ***Second***, since they take the form of indirect taxes, they can often be grafted onto existing administrative structures for the taxing of commercial energy. This

[26] A further discussion of instruments is provided in Anderson [1990].

[27] This is a classical argument for the tax approach, and is due to Baumol and Oates [1971].

Table 14: Environmental Policy Instruments and the Oil and Gas Industry: Where the Balance of Advantage Lies (denoted by •)

	Balance of Advantage	
	Regulation	Taxes
End-Use		
SO_2, NO_x emissions		•
Unleaded fuels		•
CO_2		•
Energy efficiency		•
Urban congestion		•
Industry		
E & P	•	
Shipping	•	
Pipelines	•	
Refineries - emissions	•	
effluents	•	
wastes	•	
Marketing	•	

Source: Author.

Legend: SO_2 = sulfur dioxide
NO_x = nitrogen oxide
CO_2 = carbon dioxide
E & P = Exploration & Production

makes them administratively convenient and practical to apply. Indirect taxes have long been favored forms of taxation in developing countries because of their administrative convenience. Further, by being levied at wholesale or bulk supply points, problems of non-compliance with policy as well as administrative costs are minimized.

Table 14 also includes one item which is not, strictly speaking, an oil and gas issue, but which is an environmental problem in and of itself, and would have a significant bearing on the industry's development. It is the use of taxation or licensing schemes to alleviate urban congestion. Very few countries have pursued the approach, with the Singapore Area Licensing Scheme introduced in 1976 being the most successful example.[28] Not only would the wider adoption of such schemes reduce congestion and raise revenues for urban development, but they are widely accepted as being a good means for reducing gaseous emissions and for reducing fuel consumption.

E. Applying the Policies: Further Issues for Local Analysis

The main issues to weigh concern setting standards, internal consistency of policies, compliance, and distributional effects. The outcome of the analyses of these issues (most notably on standard setting and in distributional effects) tends to vary with the local situation, but some general points can be made on each.

1. Environmental Standards

The marginal costs of pollution abatement tend to rise sharply as abatement standards rise while the marginal benefits fall -- a typical case of diminishing returns. (Some examples of rising marginal costs were provided in Part II in relation to refining, though the effect is quite often encountered.) The situation is summarized in Figure 6.

The marginal benefit curve is a curve of what are called social benefits, e.g., the benefits to health of a cleaner environment. Although the benefits of pollution abatement, such as improved health or reduced pollution of fisheries and spawning grounds, are difficult to quantify, analysis shows that the process of classifying them and attempting to assess their economic or social significance can have an important bearing on policy.[29] For example, it may often be found that major improvements in the environment can be achieved at moderate cost. It is only when standards are tightened greatly (often for small gains) that costs rise steeply.

If there is reasonable compliance with policy (an important qualification), the effects of regulations or taxes on pollution should be to raise the prices of outputs to cover the marginal costs to industry of installing the low polluting options or producing the low-polluting fuels. The optimum reduction of pollutants occurs when the marginal net benefits and the marginal profitability of further reductions are both zero, and thus when there is a convergence of social interests in the policy.

---

[28] See summary in Anderson [1990].

[29] For a review of approaches, see Pearce and Markandya [1989].

Figure 6: Comparing the Marginal Costs and Benefits of Pollution Abatement

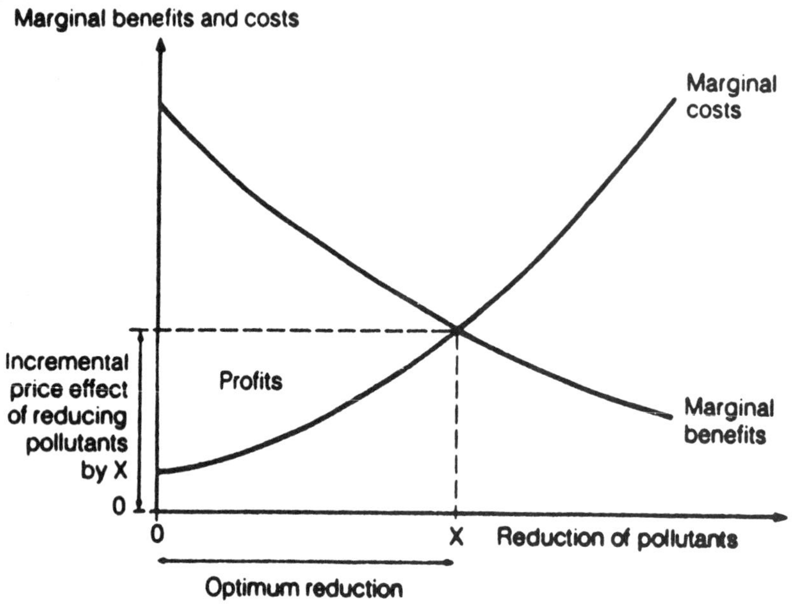

Source: Author.

Another question which the cost benefit analysis can help to revalue concerns the affordability of environmental policies. Standards, even in theory, should ideally differ between countries because circumstances, and thus costs and benefits, differ. For example, the policies will generally impact more on trade and investment in some countries than others and this needs to be allowed for in the analysis. The attraction of the cost-benefit approach, even if approximately applied, is that it yields less ambiguous answers on questions as to the effects of policies on such matters as trade, incomes, and affordability than other approaches.

2. Compliance

There are two conditions for a policy to be a success. They have already been alluded to on a number of occasions in the preceding analysis, but are worth singling out separately to emphasize their importance.

The *first* is that any regulatory framework or environmental tax system must apply equally to all. A policy's effectiveness depends on this. It cannot work if cheating is widespread. This condition may be easier to achieve at the national than international level, though discrimination between domestic and foreign investors is unfortunately often reported.

The *second* condition is that policies need to be internally consistent such that the tax and regulatory structures are not mutually contradictory. The consistency of policies over time along with technological options is also required, i.e. phasing may be important.

3. Income Distribution

Lastly any policy analysis must look into its impact on various income groups. Some general points were set out on this in a separate World Bank paper [Anderson, 1990] and will not be repeated here. Suffice it to note that environmental policies impact on income distribution in two ways via their effects (i) on labor demand and productivity and (ii) on health and living conditions. In a large number of cases the effect may often be favorable. For example, emissions levels and effluents are often highest in low income areas; to take another example, pollution of fishing grounds may affect a labor-intensive industry and be a health hazard as well. Even where distributional effects are adverse, it is generally possible to design compensatory policies that neutralize them; revenues from environmental taxes may often be well used for this purpose.

IV. Conclusions and Assessment

The emerging demands for commercial, primarily fossil, energy in the developing countries are very strong and will probably be far greater than those of the OECD countries within 15 to 20 years, four times those of Eastern Europe and the Union of Soviet Socialist Republics combined. LDC energy demand growth rates were 6% per year in the 1970s, curiously about the same in Asia, Africa, and Latin America, despite the oil price shocks; they were 6% again in Asia in the 1980s, though had declined to 2% in Africa and Latin America owing to the crises of internal balance and debt. Per capita consumption is less than one-tenth of that of the OECD countries today and would still be less than one-quarter in four decades time assuming 4% growth (2 percentage points below the expected rate, assuming an eventual economic recovery in Latin America and Africa). The countries are still low on their 'S' curves for practically all forms of energy using durables, equipment and vehicle fleets. The growth of populations and per capita incomes, along with the substitution from fuelwood to commercial energy, are all likely to exert strong effects, even making generous allowances for the very important potential of efficiency improvements in the production, conversion, management, and uses of energy.

Hence, a major geographic shift in the demands for commercial energy is taking place and, with it, backward linkages into the engineering industries providing the supporting infrastructure such as exploration and production, refining, conversion (i.e. synfuels, electricity generation), distribution, and marketing facilities. The demands of Eastern Europe and the Union of Soviet Socialist Republics are also potentially important; however, like those of OECD, demand growth could eventually be tempered by efficiency improvements and price increases.

Such an expansion of demands in developing countries will, of course, require increased attention to environmental policy including the monitoring of emissions, effluents, spills, accidents and wastes; the designing of policies; and, the monitoring of compliance with policies. The above report reviewed the various environmental problems related to the oil and gas industry and the policy options. Since summaries or assessments were provided in the course of the review, they need not be repeated here. The key areas reviewed were:

(i) *Gaseous emissions.* The control or abatement of acid deposition, particulates, toxic emissions, photochemical smogs, and greenhouse gas accumulations.

(ii) *Offshore exploration and production (E & P) and shipping.* The reduction of systemic wastes (especially ballasting operations), spillages, and accidents. And,

(iii) *Refining.* The reduction of systemic gaseous emissions, aqueous effluents, and wastes (e.g., spent catalysts).

On the policy front, it was shown that there is a wide range of instruments open to governments, which were summarized in Table 14. They were grouped under two headings: (i) the economic instruments of environmental taxes, subsidies, and public investment, both to discourage pollution and encourage investments and innovation in pollution abatement; and (ii) the various instruments of regulation, legal liability, and negotiation (with negotiated arrangements being enforceable by law in the event of non-compliance). It was found that the instruments of environmental taxation were especially suited to gaseous emissions in the end-uses of oil and gas; and that the instruments of law, regulation, and legal liability were especially suited to E & P, shipping, transport and refining, or more generally to the industry side of oil and gas activities.

The range of technological possibilities and product and process substitutions for dealing with environmental problems is also very wide. Notwithstanding the criticisms often levelled at the industry, its capacity to respond to environmental problems in an innovative way has been remarkable. Significant problems remain both on the industry side and in the end-users of oil and gas, and it can be anticipated that environmental policies will become increasingly stringent in all regions, not least in the developing countries. The historical record shows, however, that output increases have often been achieved with a reduction of environmental damage where policies have encouraged it. The emerging problem of the greenhouse effect should not prove to be the exception: a range of technological options, mainly in renewables, are being delineated that may still prove the rule just stated and carbon taxes, like taxes (or their regulatory alternatives) on other emissions, may lead to a major restructuring of the industry in the long-term in environmentally less troubling ways.

Thus at the economic and technological levels, the conclusions are not discouraging. Moreover, much can be gained, in economic and in environmental terms, without necessarily resorting to best practice techniques. Concerns as to the effects of environmental policies on such diverse matters as income distribution, trade, and investment can also be addressed in a number of ways without compromising the policies. Indeed, environmental goals in the production of energy and in its end uses often mesh well with those of economic efficiency and poverty alleviation, though of course there are exceptions. The main issues ahead relate to the willingness of the public authorities to pursue the options open to them, not to the response of the industry or its consumers to policies, and to ensure that the policies are equally applied to and complied with by all. Compliance and fairness in application are, of course, fundamental for a policy's success.

References

Anderson, Charles B. and Brian B. Starer [1990]. "Contingency Planning Is Crucial to Oil Spill Response." *Oil and Gas Journal* (March 5, 1990): 41-46.

Anderson, D. [1990]. *Environmental Policy and the Public Revenue in Developing Countries.* Environment Working Paper No. 36. Washington, D.C.: World Bank, July.

Baumol, W.J. and W.E. Oates [1971]. "The Use of Standards and Prices for Protection of the Environment." *Swedish Journal of Economics*, vol. LXXIII (March).

Bolin, Bert, Bo R. Doos, Jill Jager, and Richard A. Warrick [1986]. "Emissions of CO_2 into the Atmosphere." Chapter 2 in *Scope 29: The Greenhouse Effect, Climatic Change and Ecosystems.* Chichester and New York: John Wiley and Sons.

Brimblecome, Peter [1987]. *The Big Smoke.* London and New York: Reutledge.

The British Petroleum Company p.l.c. [1989]. *BP Statistical Review of World Energy.* London: Britannic House.

Corbett, Richard A. [1990]. "Refineries, petrochem plants focus on new waste challenges." A subsection of a special survey entitled "Environment and Safety Report." *Oil and Gas Journal* (March 5, 1990): 33-38.

Davis, Ged [1989]. *Global Warming: The Role of Energy Efficient Technologies.* Shell Selected Papers. London: Shell Centre.

de Vries, Joop [1988]. *Images of the Nineties.* Shell Selected Papers. London: Shell Centre.

Dickey, Peter and Murray Jones [1987]. *Environmental Aspects of Decommissioning a Major Oil Refinery.* Shell Selected Papers. London: Shell Centre.

Hassan, Awad [1989]. "Oil Contamination in the Red Sea Environment." *Water, Air and Soil Pollution,* vol. 45, nos. 3-4 (June): 235-243.

Keepin, W., I. Mintzer, and L. Kristoferson [1986]

Opschoor, J.P. and H. Vos [1989]. *The Application of Economic Instruments for Environmental Protection in OECD Member Countries.* Paris: Organization for Economic Cooperation and Development.

Organization for Economic Cooperation and Development (OECD) [1988]. *Emission Control Technologies in Electric Power.* Paris: OECD.

Organization for Economic Cooperation and Development (OECD) [1989]. *Energy Technologies for Reducing the Greenhouse Emissions of Greenhouse Gases.* OECD Seminar Proceedings, OECD Seminar, April 12-14, 1989, held in Paris. Paris: OECD (in two volumes).

Organization for Economic Cooperation and Development (OECD) [1990a]. *Energy and the Environment: Policy Overview.* Paris: OECD.

Organization for Economic Cooperation and Development (OECD) [1990b]. *Handbook of Environmental Statistics.* Paris: OECD.

Organization for Economic Cooperation and Development (OECD) [1990c]. *Substitute Fuels for Road Transport.* Annex B. Paris: OECD.

Organization for Economic Cooperation and Development/International Energy Agency (OECD/IEA) [1988]. *Emission Control in Electricity Generation and Industry.* Paris: OECD/IEA.

Pearce, David W. and Anil Markandya [1989]. *Environmental Policy Benefits: Monetary Valuation.* Paris: OECD.

Royal Dutch Shell Group [1983]. *Petroleum Handbook.* Amsterdam: Elselvier.

Shell Petroleum Company Ltd. [1987a]. "Air Pollution: An Oil Industry Perspective." Shell Briefing Service Publication No. 1. London: Shell Centre.

Shell Petroleum Company Ltd. [1987b]. *Renewable Energy - A Global View.* Shell Selected Papers. London: Shell Centre.

Shell Petroleum Company Ltd. [1987c]. "Safeguarding the Seas." Shell Briefing Service Publication No. 3. London: Shell Centre.

Shell Petroleum Company Ltd. [1987d]. "Synthetic Fuels and Renewable Energy." Shell Briefing Service Publication No. 2. London: Shell Centre.

Shell Petroleum Company Ltd. [1989a]. "Energy in Profile." Shell Briefing Service Publication No. 3. London: Shell Centre.

Shell Petroleum Company Ltd. [1989b]. "Issues in Refining." Shell Briefing Service Publication No. 6. London: Shell Centre.

Seymour, Adam [1990]. "Environmental Regulation, Refining and Marketing." Oxford University Institute of Energy Studies. Draft paper, April.

Siddayao, Corazón M. [1980]. "Submarine Hydrocarbons in Southeast Asia." *Geo Journal,* vol. 4, no. 5: 393-405.

United States Department of Energy [1987]. *Five-Year Research Plan 1987-91.* Washington, D.C.: United States Department of Energy, May.

United States National Academy of Science [1985]. (Copied from Shell Petroleum Company Ltd. [1987c]).

van der Toorn, Betus [1988]. *Strategy for Biomass Conversion*. Shell Selected Papers. London: Shell Centre.

Wardley-Smith, J. (editor) [1983]. *The Control of Oil Pollution*. London: Graham & Trotman.

World Bank [1988]. "Impact of Lower Oil Prices on Renewable Energy Technologies." Energy Series Paper No. 5. Washington, D.C.: World Bank, May.

World Bank [1989]. "Energy Efficiency Strategy for Developing Countries: The Role of ESMAP." Energy Department Background Paper. Washington, D.C.: World Bank, November.

4

Sustainability and the Energy/Environment Connection: Overcoming Institutional Barriers to "Doing the Right Thing"

Morris Miller
University of Ottawa

I. Introduction

> In the three years since *Our Common Future* appeared we have gone through an explosion of conferences and meetings on sustainable development around the world. We have gone through a change of rhetoric, but so far we have seen very little action. All of the indicators are moving in the wrong direction...Action is not only urgent, it's long overdue. Hopefully, this will turn around within the next decade.
>
> - Jim MacNeill, former Secretary-General of the United Nations' World Commission on Environment and Development (the Bruntland Commission)[1]

A. The Approach: Focusing on the Global Energy/Growth/Environmental Nexus

When an estimated 200 million people in 140 countries turned out to participate in the 1990 celebration of the twentieth annual Earth Day, the event reflected a high point of environmental consciousness. This degree of popular support for environmental issues brings to mind the popularity of the conservation movement in the early part of the century. At the time, some environment-enhancing measures were enacted in response to public pressure, principally the establishment of nature preserves and national parks. But the strength of the movement ebbed and for the next half century there was only localized concern and agitation. The revival of a broad-based movement as a political force began in the 1960s, peaking in the

[1]MacNeill's comment is contained in an interview he gave to the editor of *New Environment* [1990].

mid-1970s when the environmental concerns were so frequent and so strident that a columnist was moved to characterize the mood as "environmental hysteria." During the 1970s the environmental issue begot a proliferation of organizations that collectively took on the attributes of a movement, though each had its own agenda with a focus on one or two facets of the environmental spectrum. "Green" political parties won elections and entered the legislatures of many industrialized countries, and traditional parties adopted planks to show their support.

Each of the recent peaks in popular concern gave rise to and, in turn, was reinforced by well-publicized international conferences and commissions, e.g., the United Nations Conference on the Environment in Stockholm in 1971 and the World Commission on Environment and Development (the Brundtland Commission) in the late 1980s. The upcoming United Nations (UN) sponsored environment conference, scheduled for 1992 in Rio de Janeiro, may sustain the momentum that seems to be flagging. While this commission and conference approach undoubtedly has a consciousness-raising impact, the recent surge of popular support for the idea could well be interpreted simply as the public's concern for the future in reaction to fears about impending environmental catastrophes akin to the Exxon Valdez oil spill, the Chernobyl nuclear meltdown, and the Bhopal gas tragedy that are still very much in the collective consciousness.

To this fear of hazards, there has been added, as an ominous background, a great deal of publicity of scientific findings that tell of atmospheric trends that could have grave implications, namely, the increasing global levels of emission of chlorofluorocarbons (CFCs), carbon dioxide (CO_2), and other gases which may lead to ozone layer depletion and climate change. The scope of environmental concern has thus gone global.

In spite of appearances that the quality of the global environment has clearly become a major issue which politicians are being forced to address, the progress on this front of the battle to save the environment has been slow and unsteady. While there has been a proliferation of plans enacted by governments to respond to environmental concerns, they all seem to suffer from the same weakness that characterized the Canadian government's Green Plan proposed in 1990. As an editorial in *The Ottawa Citizen* of December 12, 1990 observed, the Green Plan is too typical in its lack of "details, draft legislation, secure financing, and political muscle."

The nub of the difficulty is simply that there is a close and complex relationship between environment, energy, and development. Their symbiotic connection makes it impossible to deal with environment policy, energy policy, and development policy separately, either at the national or the international level. This complexity is most clearly evident when tackling the problem of the "greenhouse effect" which is believed to threaten significant climate change or global warming.[2]

A great deal of attention has also been focused on large-scale deforestation that contributes to the greenhouse effect by reducing the environmentally-beneficial absorption

---

[2]"Radiative trapping," otherwise known as the "greenhouse effect" is the atmospheric retention of CO_2 emissions. This is discussed in greater detail elsewhere in this volume.

of CO_2 from the atmosphere.[3] Deforestation is, however, less environmentally damaging than carbon emissions and, from a global perspective, would appear to be less directly related to the development process. However, in many Third World countries there is a direct connection between deforestation and development, since forests provide both fuelwood and lumber as well as a frontier available for agricultural exploitation and settlement.[4]

Global energy model-builders all agree that, without some dramatic change in trends, the conventional sources of energy -- oil, gas, coal, hydro, and nuclear -- will continue to play a large role even 50 years into the future with resultant high rates of carbon emission, but these changes require accompanying changes in the institutional framework.[5] The challenge facing policymakers in their efforts to reduce dependence on fossil fuels -- or, at least, reducing the rate of increase of its use in all its forms -- is thus formidable. So far, however, there has been an impressive display of rhetoric which has not been matched by action.

With few exceptions, in both the industrialized and the developing countries, the legislative record, the policy positions taken, and the resources committed with respect to almost all key environmental issues have fallen far short of what might have been expected in light of the public's avowed concern about the seriousness of the environmental problem as a life-threatening issue of global proportions. This somber assessment raises the question: Why is it so difficult to do "the right thing" when there appears to be so much public support and so much appears to be at stake? At both national and international policymaking levels, it is important to understand the reasons behind the barriers to action. Once identified and understood in context these barriers will be better overcome. It is useful to consider them under three headings:

(i) ***inertia*** with its related sources and attributes: ignorance, skepticism, fatalism, alienation, etc.;

(ii) the ***aversion to risk-taking*** exacerbated by the exceptional degree of uncertainty about environmental processes and their implications -- and about the associated costs and benefits;

(iii) the ***resistance to change*** by those having a ***vested interest*** in the *status quo* and are unwilling to countenance anything more than slight, but not sufficient, modifications thereof -- and are fearful of the costs in financial and other terms.

---

[3]The consensus scientific estimate, as cited in United States Department of Energy [1990], is that in 1987 fossil fuel combustion released 5.5 billion metric tons of carbon into the atmosphere while the destruction of tropic forests allowed the release in that year of as much as 1.65 billion metric tons that would otherwise have been absorbed by the vegetation.

[4]The deforestation aspect of the environmental problem is distinctive in so far as it is not directly related to the use of energy, and in so far as it poses the question of who pays and who benefits in a more dramatic way. The question presents itself in the following way: Should countries that still have large-scale forests be obliged to constrain their growth (so far as forest clearing can be said to contribute to such growth) for the sake of maintaining the planet's environmental quality and, therefore, for the sake of humankind?

[5]For the most up-to-date review of such forecasts, see Worldwatch Institute [1990], especially the section in Chapter 2 by Christopher Flavin entitled "Alternative to fossil fuels," pp. 22-27.

All of these are related and sometimes mutually reinforcing, but it is useful to distinguish them if one is to understand how they operate to impede the necessary changes. Thus, this chapter will focus on these institutional barriers, but from the special vantage of the energy and environment relationship and of the relationship of each of these to sustainable development. After considering the barriers of inertia, risk aversion, and vested interests one can better address the questions: what needs to be done and what could be done about overcoming these barriers at different levels of governance?

B. The Necessary Energy Conditions for Reconciling Growth and Environmental Objectives

Conventional wisdom held that a trade-off had to be made between the pursuit of economic growth and attainment of environmental quality. As long as the maintenance of an acceptable environmental quality was assumed to be a goal attainable only at the expense of higher incomes and improved levels of welfare, the environment was bound to lose out to growth. The conception of this issue as a "zero-sum" proposition began to fade when, in the early 1970s, the idea took hold that the development process was not only compatible with environmental quality but could be augmented by environmental protection measures. Over the last two decades this view of a mutually reinforcing relationship between environment and growth has itself become the conventional wisdom.

Key to the resolution of this seeming conflict between growth and environment are far-reaching institutional changes that both reflect and reinforce that concern for environmental quality while, at the same time, promote "*new* patterns of growth." In the words of the chairman of the 1971 United Nations Conference on Environment, Maurice Strong, two basic steps are called for:

> (i) a ***major transition*** to a less physical kind of growth, relatively less demanding of energy and raw materials; and,
>
> (ii) on the global level, a ***revamping*** of the present international system of arrangements and institutions to better serve the interests and aspirations of the developing world. (Emphasis added.)

The issues have been reiterated over the years. See, for example, MacNeill [1989].

This re-orientation and re-structuring has profound cultural, social, and political implications, in addition to economic ones. Indeed it would have to be profound to change the global historic trend of increasing energy use per capita leading to a four-fold increase in total energy use over the last four decades and an almost fourteen-fold over the last century, as is evident from Table 1.

Historical trends are not easily reversible under the best of circumstances, but they are especially difficult to even slow down when so many in the global community live in poverty and aspire to higher living standards that imply higher energy use and carbon emissions. This dilemma has given rise to academic consideration of draconian measures that, in effect, would slow or stop global growth as a matter of deliberate policy. Needless to say, such a policy would meet with fierce resistance in both the industrialized countries and the developing countries.

In the industrialized countries, growth is a key cultural and political attribute of all the prevailing economic systems. A foretaste of the reaction to the prospect of a slow growth or a no-growth future is provided by the heated controversies of the early 1970s which are reflected in an exceptional outpouring of books on the theme of the probabilities and the dire consequences of a zero rate of growth. In the case of the developing countries, the hunger for the tantalizing fruits of growth is even more palpable. This group of countries have over three-quarters of the world's population and are in a phase of development that is very energy intensive, as Table 2 illustrates.

On the basis of past trends modified by energy conserving policies that are judged to have modest impact, world primary energy demand has been forecast to increase by two-thirds to three-quarters by the year 2010 from 1980 levels. Table 3 indicates forecasts made in the mid-1980s by various entities.

A glance at the forecasts for the world's electric supply can indicate the magnitude of the increase and some factors underlying it, principally, their programs of energy development as a necessary condition for industrializing and for providing the amenities of convenient electrical energy for heating and cooking. The Third World's demand is projected by the World Bank to grow to about a third of global demand by the year 2000 which implies that they will account for about 60 percent of the increased global demand. With the electric power demand expected to grow as much as 7 percent per year and with each kilowatt of capacity costing at least $2000, the developing countries will need about $100 billion per year.[6] The constraint on the demand side will, therefore, be the availability of capital to build new power plants or expand existing ones. But even the most constrained program has profound implications with regard to the global increase in the use of fossil fuels. See Miller [1992].[7]

Thus, the challenge of the "new growth" approach on a global scale is daunting. It would, as one commentator observed, call for a change of historic scope, comparable, "to only two other changes: the agricultural revolution of the late Neolithic and the Industrial Revolution of the past two centuries, both of which were gradual, spontaneous, and largely unconscious." He added, "if we actually do it [in the timeframe that is required], the undertaking will be absolutely unique in humanity's history" [Ruckelshaus, 1989].

---

[6]This is based on an assumption that these countries will grow at the rate of 4.5 percent, the World Bank's medium forecast. That would call for an increase in generating capacity of 1,500 gigawatts, an investment of $125 billion each year which is more than double the present rate of investment by these countries in expanding their electric power supply. See United States Agency for International Development [1988]; Churchill [1988], pp. 11 & 12; and *The Economist* [1988], p. 82. The electricity bills for these countries (when subsidies to electricity consumers are added) is exceptionally high in relative as well as absolute terms, absorbing an estimated fifth of their government's budgets and accounting for as much as 40 percent of their foreign indebtedness.

[7]These details are discussed in some chapters in this volume.

Table 1: Population, Per Capita and World Energy Use Increase, 1890-1990

	1890	1950	1990
World Population (billions)	1.49	2.51	5.32
Industrial Energy Use (kilowatts per capita)	.32	1.03	2.30
World Energy Use (terawatts)	1.00	3.26	13.73
Cumulative Industrial Energy Use since 1850 (terawatt-years)	10.00	97.00	393.00

Source: Holdren [1990], p. 160.

Note: A terawatt is equal to a billion tons of coal or 5 billion barrels of oil per year.

Table 2: Economic Growth and Commercial Energy Consumption, 1970-86

	Average Growth Rates in %		
Region	GDP	Energy Consumption	Elasticity of Demand
Industrialized	2.9	0.9	0.31
Developing	4.5	6.2	1.38
World	3.4	2.4	0.71

Sources: United Nations [1990a] and United Nations [1990c].

Legend: GDP = gross domestic product

Table 3: World Primary Energy Demand (in millions of tons of oil equivalent)

Source of forecast	1980	1990	2000	2010	% increase (1980-2010)
European Community	7,270	10,800	--	--	--
International Institute for Applied Systems Analysis	6,800	8,000	9,900	11,300	66%
World Energy Conference	7,700	9,400	11,100	13,300	73%

Source: United Nations [1990b], pp. 122 & 123.

Legend: -- = information not available

II. The Institutional Barriers to Making the Changes Necessary for the "New Growth" Future

A. The Inertia Factor as a Barrier to Change

1. Inertia: Innate Human Characteristic or System-Conditioned?

Despite the enthusiastic popular support for environmental causes, as exemplified in the impressive turnout for Earth Day 1990, few have a true idea of the meaning of the term, "good environmental management."

There is a cyclical pattern in movements of this nature. The phenomenon of ebb-and-flow is normal, the pattern is more likely attributable to the force of the inertia factor which makes public involvement for change extremely difficult to sustain a movement and to achieve the stated goal.

Inertia embraces two concepts, the concept of "perception" and that of the "response to perception":

> (i) The perceptual aspect refers to the tendency to see things only in ways that are familiar and acceptable. This is a societal characteristic that is a concomitant of ignorance, indifference, lack of imagination, and parochialism.
>
> (ii) The response aspect refers to the tendency in almost all societies, whether democratic or authoritarian, to accept the continuation of past and prevailing conditions with their supportive institutions, even when this acceptance is seen as likely to lead to unacceptable outcomes. Conditions have to become exceptionally uncomfortable in terms not only of physical discomfort or hardship but also in terms of the level or intensity of anxiety before the aversion to the risks of change tip in favor of some form of action to achieve change.

Social behavior, it seems, is influenced only slowly over time by its history. People tend to respond to situations in a manner which is based on past or learned experience but no society has, as yet, demonstrated an ability to respond to predicted events -- unless they threaten to be catastrophic and unless there is a societal memory of such occurrences within the lifetime of the past generation or two. While the rationalization for this passivity or high level of tolerance often manifests itself as skepticism or cynicism, it is cultural conditioning, in large part, that induces widely shared views that accepts the main features of the prevailing order or is alienated to a point of fatalistic acquiescence.

Leaders of every society, if they are to remain leaders, have to inculcate attitudes that reinforce the established order. One of the most powerful of these forces is the inertia factor which can manifest itself as fear of change, passivity, skepticism, cynicism, alienation, and fatalism. A central element of this defensive strategy of system-conditioning is the propagation of supportive mythology that can rationalize the *status quo* as a system.

Perhaps the most dramatic example of this process of selling a system that is already in place is provided by Malthusianism. At the dawn of the Industrial Age in England, the economist, Reverend Thomas Malthus, put forward a simple doomsday model relating how the growth rates of population and of food were periodically brought into balance by pestilence, famine, and wars, all of which were then frequent occurrences. The model served to lay the blame for the misery of the working poor on their tendency to procreate at a faster rate than the food supply could be increased. The model was a heaven-sent theory to divert attention from the prevailing institutional arrangements as a causal factor. William Pitt, the British Prime Minister at the time, found it in the interest of the establishment to promote it as a theory, even before the empirical basis for its substantiation could be established. Within a short time it was disproven, and to this day continues to be invalidated by facts: on a global basis over the last forty years population has doubled and food production has tripled.

Over many centuries there have been similar instances of collective anxiety initially articulated by intellectuals. In the early 1970s there was a resurgence of Malthusianism focused on oil. When oil prices soared in 1973, the dynamic models of the Club of Rome propounded the "limits to growth" (LTG) thesis with the key factor identified as resources depletion, particularly energy resources, and most specifically, oil. The impact of the Club of Rome and the best-selling book *The Limits To Growth* was pervasive [Meadows et al., 1972]. The book made publishing history on a global scale by coming as it did in 1973 just as the "oil shock" was being felt around the globe. Its message caught the people of the industrialized world in a receptive mood as they lined up for gasoline and saw prices for resources rise, generating what one commentator described as a "frenzy of morbidity." Speaker after speaker, article after article, book after book publicized the deplorable prospects of the world and many advocated a "no growth" solution because of the imminent exhaustion of supply of one or more key resources in the face of exponentially increasing demand.

Subsequently, the panic subsided as oil prices dropped dramatically and have since remained at comparatively low levels. Since the anxiety about energy supply has subsided, the neo-Malthusians have come to be recognized as false prophets. This may explain the cool reception of many key decisionmakers to the warnings about the environmental threat; likewise the public's response to "doomsday scenario" remedies may be enthusiastic until the bills are presented. The support appears to be shallow. While it is true that there is a finite capacity of the air and water of this planet to absorb the gaseous and solid wastes that are dumped and pumped into them, there is now an understandable degree of skepticism about theories that again point to the physical limits to growth.

The fatal flaw of the LTG model is a misspecification of the limiting factors to the physical aspects of nature's bounty and to the degree and manner in which they would be exploited. Like other doomsday models, the LTG model neglects or under-rates the role of a response-adaptive process. Most environmentalists have recognized this weakness in these models and have, accordingly, provided a central role for adjustment through the operations of market forces. In their models, the market system is presented as an adequate institutional arrangement to avoid environmental catastrophe and achieve the very daunting environment and development objectives. For those with this outlook, the environmental challenge is not a sufficiently compelling reasons to get off the inertial pathway of reliance on the prevailing market-based system, albeit slightly modified. In large measure this approach is based on the inertia principle of opting for the minimum amount of change that might be necessary to realize any given objective -- or its converse, opting for a downgrading of the objective to conform to a minimal degree of change.

2. The Market Approach: The Inertial Path and Its Limitations

The confidence in market forces may be the product of ideology or the result of experiences during the more recent "oil crisis." There can be little doubt that that experience has influenced many in their assessment of the current environmental crisis in terms both of its gravity and urgency, as well as proposed solutions. Like swings on a pendulum, the exaggerated fears in the early 1970s of a severe shortage of oil and natural resources have been replaced by an exaggerated confidence in the effectiveness of the market process in which the price mechanism was perceived to have significantly reduced the dependency on oil, and thereby, its price.

Consumers did indeed respond to the higher energy prices by buying smaller cars, improving the insulation of their homes and factories, and adopting other energy-saving measures with the result that the energy/output relationship changed perceptively, though hardly enough to make a significant impact on the overall demand for fossil fuels. Studies show that the United States used 20 percent less energy after 1973, two-thirds of the conservation response being attributed to higher prices and the remaining third to a variety of measures such as automobile fuel economy standards.[8] This favorable change in the energy/output relationship was, of course, bolstered by financial measures in the form of direct government subsidies and tax allowances designed to bring on new sources of energy and develop more efficient ways of using the conventional sources. The institutional changes were minor, leading some to the conclusion that the necessary and sufficient changes to resolve global crises need only be very limited and consistent with the prevailing economic and social systems.

Even in terms of the limited objective of reducing dependence on fossil fuels this confidence in a strictly market approach can be seen to be premature. The days of dependence on oil are not over, and the market's regulatory influence has weakened, far short of achieving the desired shift in the global energy mix in a reasonable time span. Reliance on the price elasticity of demand for oil and other conventional forms of energy to dampen their consumption has been effective in a limited way, but when viewed in relation to the minimum target that environmental considerations would call for, the verdict is a failing grade. The demand for fossil fuels has thus continued to grow in absolute terms despite efforts by Third World countries to reduce or shift their reliance away from fossil fuels. There are serious reasons for this - among them the fact that less developed countries (LDCs) are in the very early stages of development and are still in the process of increasing the capital stock that uses oil (e.g., transport and machinery). Even in the industrialized countries, the fossil fuel-GNP ratio has ceased to improve since the mid-1980s. Thus, despite

---

[8]Chandler [1985] observes that "the overall conservation response could have been greater but the U.S. was slow to decontrol oil prices, still controls the price of half of all natural gas used, and prices electric power at average costs which is typically below the cost of new power." He cites the experience of Canada and other countries, noting that Canada's energy demand in 1982 was a third lower than would have been expected if pre-1974 trends had prevailed and that two-thirds of this reduction can be attributed to higher energy prices. After reviewing the pricing practices in a host of other countries, Chandler observes that "energy scarcity alone [as reflected in higher prices] may not be enough to encourage a level of conservation measures consistent with a low energy future."

the favorable trend of a fall in the ratio of carbon emissions per unit of GNP, the net effect has been a doubling of the volume of carbon emission over the last quarter century, most of this attributable to the industrialized countries [Worldwatch Institute, 1990].[9]

Underlying this doubling of carbon emissions are trends showing a substantial increase in global population and GNP combined with a substantial rise in carbon emissions per capita. The per capita rise has brought the level of the United States to over 5 tons per capita (tpc) annually and confers on the United States the unenviable distinction of world leadership in carbon emissions, far outstripping the other industrialized nations with their average of 3 tpc, and astronomically above the levels for developing countries that, with almost no exception, are well under 1 tpc.[10] Evidently, prevailing policies are not working to achieve the desired environmental effect, particularly in the United States where the reliance on the market has been strongest. Though some countries, such as Japan, were able after 1973 to reduce their dependence on oil in relation to economic growth and to attain a per capita consumption of energy that is less than half that of the United States, there is a question as to how much of such savings can be attributed to responses to price changes as distinguished from cultural and political factors.

The continued rise in global emission should not be surprising. Past history reveals that major shifts in the global energy mix have taken a long time to achieve, as changes in the energy mix are both a causal factor and a reflector of structural change in the economies that use the energy. The shift from peak use of coal to peak use of oil took over three generations and was concurrent with a major transformation of the global economy. Action of the requisite scope and speed would call for the identification of the minimally necessary institutional changes needed to get onto the adjustment path to achieve the desired growth and environmental goals without waiting for a calamity to force action.

A realistic understanding of the broader institutional, cultural, and political framework within which policies are made would reveal the necessity of going well beyond the proposed policies and programs that give a central role to market forces as a means of achieving the "new growth" that is required. The prevailing economic system engenders a cultural condition that has been well characterized as a "consciousness of unsustainability." This cultural attribute is reinforced by the prevailing market system with its advertising messages that, of late, has begun to co-opt the "green" movement to promote sales with questionable environmental benefits.[11]

In any case, with respect to the energy market, it is too often a misnomer to append the label "free market" to the prevailing process. In the *first* place, particularly with respect to utilities that generate electricity and do not operate at arms length from their political masters, there are institutional rigidities that severely constrain the price setting process from

---

[9]More details are available in [Miller, 1992].

[10]The range of the per capita figures is instructive: less than 1 ton per capita (tpc) of carbon emissions for all the developing countries (except Korea with just over 1 ton) and about 3 tpc for the Group of Seven (G-7) industrialized countries, with the United States in the lead at over 5 tpc. The source for these figures is Worldwatch Institute [1990], Chapter 2.

[11]The classic case in point is illustrated by McDonald's abandonment of its plastic containers for paper bags, a move that may have questionable long-term impacts, but has short-term public relations and commercial gains for the seller.

operating freely, and from operating with environmental costs taken into account. It would be naive to dismiss the host of market failure symptoms as exceptional; they are the norm when account is taken of the political rationale for the rigidities that pervade most economies:

- Electricity and natural gas pricing for households and for gasoline for cars and public transport are usually set at a level that is below cost on the grounds that these commodities are basic goods and thus raising their prices would be regarded as regressive, that is, as imposing an additional strain on the poorer segments of society.

- The source of power generation is generally determined on the basis of its employment-creating attribute in the locality or region, rather than on the basis of comparable costs for alternative fuels or ***costs that take account of the environmental diseconomies.***

- Prices are rarely allowed to rise commensurate with rising costs, a phenomenon that could be attributed to weak "market discipline" that allows poor management, nepotism, and corruption to prevail.[12]

The pervasiveness of such conditions should give pause to policies that place all the weight on the price mechanism and market forces. This is not to dispute the key role of the market mechanism. It works if there is a requisite institutional framework. It is a question of whether both the necessary and sufficient conditions (or only one of either) are present.

There is a *second* significant factor that would limit reliance on the role of the market as a sufficient instrument in environment policy, namely, the common property nature of environmental services. This attribute plays havoc with the incentives system that is normally relied upon to lead to socially, economically, and environmentally desirable outcomes. When the activities using common property create what are called "environmental external diseconomies," the outcome can result in collective disaster -- and often does, a phenomenon that inspired a seminal essay entitled "The Tragedy of the Commons" [Hardin, 1968, pp. 1243-48].

This outcome does not necessarily arise from a lack of intellectual appreciation by the users of "the commons" about the possibility or even the probability of an adverse environmental impact as a result of their manner and degree of usage. The reason is found in the difficulty of integrating environmental considerations with economic and financial factors into the decisionmaking process of both the public and private sectors when this entails taking into account both (i) non-market cost phenomena such as ecological deterioration or damage, depletion of irreplaceable resources and other deleterious effects, and (ii) benefits related to recreation, aesthetic, health and other conditions that do not enter into the market process or are not meaningfully measured, even if they could be sold in some semblance of a market.

A ***third*** reason for limiting reliance on the market is evident when environmental quality is recognized as a public good and when account is taken of the biases of both public and private decisionmakers in favor of actions that have short-term payoffs (a high discount

---

[12]See Chandler [1985], pp. 43-49, for a discussion of policies related to maintaining the profitability or to limiting the subsidies of parastatal utilities and the role of markets in determining energy prices.

factor) and the accumulation imperative that is a basic characteristic of the private market system.[13] Both of these biases are likely to be prejudicial to environmental quality which the market can neither measure nor factor into the calculus of these decision-makers. They operate with narrow criteria that (i) take little or no allowance for non-financial factors, and (ii) cannot respond to the consequences of environmental damage that is cumulative and dangerous only over the long-term, at which time they may be irreversible.

These limitations of the market process have stimulated economists to apply economic approaches to environmental regulation. For example, a plan is now being applied, in a limited way, to auction off transferable pollution permits. This plan is considered valuable because it is seen as providing an incentive for existing or potential polluters to reduce their pollution levels. Because they can sell the unused part of their pollution allowance, these polluters have a chance to profit from reducing their pollution levels. One proponent sees "the power of the market [thus] being harnessed to economic incentive policies for the achievement of environmental goals, [in effect, turning] the market into a powerful environmental ally." See, for example, Tietenberg [1990].[14]

This type of market-based scheme provides a license to pollute within a regulatory framework and, in so doing, legitimizes activities that are environmentally damaging. This approach is, of course, a bow to reality: all economic systems have their environmental downside that cannot be reduced beyond a certain point except at the unacceptable costs of a slowing down of growth or of no-growth.[15] No-growth or "negative growth" is an objective of policy that is clearly unacceptable politically and, in any case, is recognized as an approach that, as one commentator put it, "is like [aiming to] burn down the house to cook the pig trapped inside" [Roberts, 1974, p. 123].

But the difficulty of such market-based schemes lies in their operational parameters: i.e. how can the market be made to work in a way that includes this "license-to-pollute" approach? One can take as representative of this school of thought the measures that William Ruckelshaus, former director of the United States Council of Environmental Quality (CEQ), advocates:

> (i) oblige consumers to pay the "full cost" of a resource use, that is, "internalizing the externalities" and thereby "bending the market system towards long-term sustainability;" and,
>
> (ii) introduce the notion of "environmental resources" as "capital" on the grounds that "[the refusal] to treat environmental resources as capital [induces one to] spend them as income."

---

[13]In the Marxian and Schumpeterian models -- and, as well, in the Keynesian model -- a capitalist market-driven economy cannot achieve a steady state since the inner dynamic of the system impels accumulation. Schumpeter [1952] calls this process "creative destruction." He sees this compulsive innate process as a major contributing cause for the eventual collapse or transformation of the capitalist system.

[14]Tietenberg cautions, however, that "transforming" an existing industrial structure to reposition it for the future will be an expensive proposition." For an excellent textbook, see Baumol and Oates [1988].

[15]There are very few who would advocate a "no-growth" objective as a desirable one. One articulate economist who espouses this view is E.J. Mishan. See, for example, Mishan [1980] and Mishan [1974].

There is unquestionably a usefulness, albeit limited, in the concept of internalizing those external diseconomies that are environmental and operationally trying to use incentive-based schemes such as the auctioning of tradable pollution permits that are set within a regulatory framework rather than relying on stringent regulations alone. Implicit in this approach are such concepts as "full cost of a resource use" and "the using-up of ecological capital" that are to be counted in setting the prices. The policy implications of these concepts are rarely clarified by a definition of what comprises such costs, nor by any operational guidelines as to how to measure and allocate them in the real world.

In line with this market-based approach, some economists have proposed inclusion of natural resources into the measurement of national accounts. See, for example, World Bank [1989]. Their proposal calls for incorporating natural resources into the concept of capital, as though there is not a critical distinction to be made between (i) those natural resources that, *in situ* or transformed yield an income flow or in certain uses (or non-use) prevent an income loss, and (ii) those that are valued for their environmental contribution in the sense that they are indispensable or irreplaceable and have no measurable market value or even a notional price. How, for example, does one measure the value of a resource that takes the form of a beautiful landscape, or of forests that provide watershed cover (thus regulating run-off and preventing floods) or act as carbon dioxide absorbers that have an influence on climate? Measurement of the concept of "ecological capital" poses serious operational problems for possible use in policymaking.

There are thus many questions to answer before this approach can be applied ***on a significant enough scale*** and taken seriously as a policy option:

- How are the permissible pollution levels to be set?
- How are the licensees to be regulated as to levels of compliance?
- How is the market to operate to set a price for units of the permitted quota when there are too few parties on either the supply or demand sides within a trading region?

Recognizing the limitations of market forces to achieve environmental objectives and recognizing the need for legislation to set regulatory bounds to limit environmental damage and for tax and subsidy policies to discourage environmentally deleterious activities and encourage environmentally good behavior, proponents of this approach must still contend with the difficulty of determining the limits at which the regulatory environmental constraints should be set and could be set (when account is taken of political realities) and of determining the costs and benefits associated with these environmental externalities.

Despite the lack of information, the uncertainties, and the constraints, however this approach can go part way to addressing some types of environmental problems. ***The more critical question is whether this goes far enough.*** Given the crisis nature of current environmental trends, there is a growing recognition that much more reliance must be placed on governmental intervention that goes beyond the imposition of strong regulatory standards and a host of measures to ensure compliance at both the national and the international levels of governance.

Unfortunately, placing an undue degree of trust in the "invisible hand" of the market place reinforces the inertia barrier to achieve the necessary changes. The tendency is then to set environmental objectives to accommodate the established order of things with its inherent bias to consumerism and accumulation that, while sometimes characterized as manifestations of the greed syndrome, constitute, in their essence, the motor driving the market system.

B. Risk Aversion as a Barrier to Change

Governments have had an understandable tendency to move very cautiously, if at all, in response to the urgings of those who have been advocating bold measures to prevent or slow down global warming and other forms of environmental deterioration. Given the stakes involved and the uncertainties on both the cost and benefit sides, the slowness of the response can be attributed to the factor of risk aversion.

The concepts of hazard, risk, and uncertainty are critically important in the process of policymaking. There is always a danger emanating from the phenomenon of "hazard" which is an inherent attribute of all systems that have the potential for the occurrence of an incident or series of events leading to a catastrophic outcome. The aspect of risk is the chance of such an undesirable event or progression of events happening in a certain time frame, but it can be defined to reflect the likelihood of occurrence of the unwanted events and their consequences whether in relation to routine operating conditions -- as applies to certain levels of emissions into the environment -- or in relation to exceptional happenings such as accidents like Bhopal or Chernobyl that emitted massive amounts of dangerous substances.

Uncertainty is inherent in all these aspects of risk, but the routine operations of a system, such as those that apply to trends in trade and capital movements and to trends in the use of energy and various forms of energy in the development of economies, provide a basis for assessing the probability and consequences of risks. The degree and scope of risk can, after all, be changed by altering policies and programs and by making changes in the prevailing institutional arrangements or systems if the alteration is significant enough.

There are several approaches to handling this factor of risk:

(i) Risk minimization with respect to the outcome by taking bold and prompt action early. In effect, this would "play it safe" ***at almost any cost*** on the grounds that there is great danger in ***not*** acting boldly when delay is likely to be incalculably costly. This applies particularly to the threat of irreversible environmental damage in which case the benefits of avoiding the feared outcome of delay is beyond measure. Accordingly, there is no need to count the cost. This "take-no-chances" view can be characterized as essentially an insurance or "no regrets" approach.

(ii) Risk minimization with regard to what has to be done now. That is, counting the costs and the benefits ***before*** taking that leap into a costly no regrets prevention program for which both the urgent need and the outcome are uncertain.

In either case, the key elements of risk assessment center on the degree of uncertainty with respect to available or obtainable information (scientific, economic, financial, as well as social, cultural, and political) and the costs and benefits that go beyond the financial aspects. These would include such factors as the inconvenience or convenience, discomfort or comfort, pain or enjoyment, etc., of making the necessary adjustments in structure and process.

There are many questions that need to be answered:

- Is there reliable evidence of long-term climatic change?

- Can changes in temperature ranges be attributed to specific causal factors?

- To what degree can the changes be attributed to the use of the various fossil fuels?

- What might be the physical consequences to life on earth of various ranges of temperature changes?

- What would be the likely financial and non-financial costs of various degrees of prevention?

- What would be the likely costs of adjusting to the temperature changes -- as calibrated by the various degrees of prevention?

- What are the relationships of costs and benefits in these various scenarios for both industrialized countries and developing countries?

- In any global agreement, what cost-sharing formula would be both equitable (assuming the cost/benefit aspects were to be the basis for the criteria) and feasible (having in mind comparative financial and other resources and capabilities, both technical and political)?

Without adequate scientific, economic, or financial, social or political information there is not a sufficiently solid basis on which to establish environment policy pertaining to the greenhouse effect of fossil fuel use. In dealing with an issue of this nature, policymakers have to contend with unknowns, immeasurables, and non-commensurables and attempt the trade-offs that are the very essence of policymaking. This is particularly so with respect to the environment where the trade-off is between a short-term sacrifice that is rather certain in financial terms and a long-term gain that is very uncertain, even with the best of knowable information and under the best of circumstances.

In devising programs linking carbon emissions and climate change policymakers thus face a wide range of uncertainties starting from the scientific knowledge of linkages from fossil fuel's carbon emissions at point of origin to the degree of radiative trapping or greenhouse effect in the upper atmosphere, from that effect to climate change, from that climate change to agricultural activities, sea levels, etc.[16]

In addition to the difficulties of handling the climatic and other uncertainties and of assessing the attendant risks of one course or another, there are some difficult policy questions that need to be asked and answered: How much prevention or what degree of climate change is acceptable, and at what cost for every increment of temperature change?

---

[16]See Miller [1992] for more details and United States Department of Energy [1990], pp. 144 & 149.

How does the answer to the second question influence the first one? Given the high cost of emission control technologies and programs to stabilize and then reduce CO_2 emissions, which in the United States alone is estimated to exceed US$1 trillion in dollars (in present value terms) over the next century, there is reason to pause for more information on the cost side before making irreversible decisions. Uncertainty with its associated risks is definitely "a pervasive characteristic of environmental problems." See Helm and Pearce [1990].

The problems are, of course, compounded by the fact that it takes not only scientific (and associated) talents and time, but a great deal of money just to firm up the knowledge base on which models are built. To this there must be added the costs of inventing, designing, and testing relevant technologies and standards, and the costs of implementing programs. The government of the United States reports that over $30 billion is being spent annually on emission control programs, an expenditure that is described as the "largest and strongest" research program in the energy/environment field [United States Department of Energy, 1990, p. 186]. Given the magnitude of the additional costs of doing a great deal more, as seems to be necessary, there is an additional complicating factor: if one country steps out too far in the lead there is a risk of being put at a cost disadvantage in the short-term *vis a vis* its competitors. Furthermore, there is a further risk in playing the role as pioneers in devising and applying costly environmentally desirable technologies. What if these costly programs prove to be ineffectual? This is a possibility that, in effect, would make such policies and their related programs even more expensive with commensurate costs in terms of its competitive position. This type of risk poses a formidable barrier that can only be overcome by global cooperation that spreads the risks both on the research side and in its application.

The element of uncertainty goes beyond the risks in not knowing what will be secured for the money spent to achieve specific emissions reduction targets, say, a 20 percent reduction over a decade that is often set as a target on the basis of round numbers and assessment of feasibility. Feasibility is a concept with scientific, technological, financial, economic, and socio-cultural dimensions, a complexity that adds more uncertainty with respect to what that target could be. This aspect of policymaking thus calls for a different type of information, namely, the financial and other adjustment costs of adapting to life with a range of targets of acceptable climate changes, i.e. the various total costs of preventing or slowing such change and the costs of alternative courses of action or inaction. Given the uncertainties and associated risks, it is hardly any wonder that the public and the policymakers often opt for a cautious approach of counting costs before they leap.

This reluctance to gamble is likely to be greater when those who bear the costs and those who reap the benefits are not within the same region or nation, or where they are in quite separate groups. This asymmetry between geographic areas or political jurisdictions and between groups is an aspect of the policy dilemma pertaining to risk that is of special significance for the developing countries. In the case of environmental issues such as carbon emission and global warming where the scope is global, the impacts on both the cost and benefit sides are bound to be very different as between industrialized and developing countries, and they are bound to be perceived differently as well. This asymmetric aspect is clearly evident with respect to the predicted impact that involves a range of possibilities or likelihoods of climate change and of such effects as rising ocean levels, altered cropping patterns and productivity, etc. The best estimates of the potential economic impact on national incomes are that the national incomes of the industrialized countries could be reduced by less than 1 percent over the next half-century, but would likely have a much more harmful impact on developing countries [Nordhaus, 1990].[17]

This asymmetry can be most dramatically illustrated by taking the case of fuelwood, the use of which has implications with respect to both energy and environment, but which is of vastly different significance for developing and industrialized countries. In the former, a very high percentage of energy is provided by fuelwood and other forms of biomass to meet the cooking and heating needs of their citizens while in the latter countries it remains an insignificant source of energy. Development of "stand-alone" energy technologies such as solar, wind, biogas, etc. (usually labeled renewable energy) would greatly benefit those living beyond the reach of the electrical grid networks by increasing their productivity and providing a range of amenities that would add to their well-being, but it would also be environmentally desirable from the point of view of preventing the ecological damage that stems from fuelwood dependency. It is, thus, quite clear that there is a large income and environmental bonus to be derived from conducting research focused on bringing down the costs and simplifying the design of such technologies so as to enable their widespread application as a substitute for fuelwood.

But this bonus from developing a substitute for fuelwood is not global in its benefits, and therein lies the difficulty. Fuelwood dependency and the ecological damage it creates are effects that are confined to limited regions of the globe, regions that are inhabited by the poor and powerless. Given the asymmetry of the costs and benefits associated with the development of stand-alone energy technologies and programs, donor countries are reluctant to incur the risks of funding such research no matter how large the potential benefit.[18] This is a case where the barrier of risk aversion combines with that of vested interests to impede the adoption of environmentally beneficial policies and programs.[19]

There is another dramatic case of asymmetry that confounds policymaking dealing with the global environmental issue: to cut or not to cut the large areas of tropical rainforest that are environmentally helpful to the global community in their role as an absorber of CO_2. The tropical rain forest issue is a contentious one pitting the vested interests of Brazil that stand to gain from clearing the rain forest against the planetary interest of reducing the net carbon emissions as much as possible. By pursuing a policy of cutting back on the exploitation of their rain forests, Brazilians incur a cost in terms of lower immediate revenues from a constrained policy in developing this frontier. They also enjoy a minor environmental benefit with the greater benefit accruing to the global community that does not have to forego any income from this policy. In this instance, there are uncertainties and commensurate risks due to lack of information as to the environmental effects of alternative ways of opening up the extensive tropical rain forest frontier area.

---

[17]These effects do not, however, take into account the random occurrence of catastrophic events. Only with some basis for establishing the probability of such events, is there an actuarial foundation for calculating what "climate insurance" should cost.

[18]Again, "vested interests" plays a role in addition to that of risk aversion as we shall see when we look at the research funds allocated to conventional energy technologies, particularly nuclear, as against the stand-alone energy technologies that are generally more environmentally benign.

[19]The 1981 United Nations Conference on New and Renewable Sources of Energy provides a case in point to illustrate the roles of both risk aversion and of vested interests. This is discussed further in the next section.

But vested interests pose the greater obstacle, as will be seen when considering possible courses of action. Handling this issue in an even-handed way poses an even greater challenge for governance at the global level.

C. Vested Interests as a Barrier to Change

1. The Systemic Nature of Vested Interests

The factor of vested interests is probably the most powerful barrier militating against change. From a global perspective, the major environmental culprits are to be found in the industrialized parts of the world where the environmental degradation is closely correlated to the modern energy and capital-intensive industrial processes and the related economic systems. One should expect opposition from those in this system who would expect to lose the most financially by assuming that they will be asked to bear the major part of the costs for environmentally sustainable policies without commensurate benefits.

In connection with the energy transition issue where multinationals are very involved, direct political pressure is exerted to assure both the weakest possible regulatory and fiscal framework that public reaction will permit, and one that is biased in favor of the firms associated with the major conventional energy sources of oil and gas, coal, and nuclear. Through lobbying for special tax or subsidy and tariff or quota provisions, the large multinationals and others in the establishment can gain a disproportionate degree of support for high-cost production and for exploration and research, support that enables them to be in a favorable position to capture the economic rent both from market restrictive practices and from improvements in existing energy technologies as well as from new technologies.

In the industrialized world, the group loosely characterized as "big oil" serves as a good example of how the vested interests factor can act as a barrier to change. The composition of this group extends across the whole energy supply spectrum from fossil fuels (oil, coal, and natural gas) to the hydro and nuclear power segments of the industry. This group has shown its ability to protect its vested interests in the conventional sources of energy as against those of new, alternative energy sources. They are all well-positioned with their exceptionally favorable capital position. As extractive industries relying on a depleting resource base, the oil, coal, and natural gas industries, enjoy exceptional depreciation and tax allowances which, together with retained earnings, enable them to invest heavily in both research and exploration, and maintain their energy market share. The implications of this disproportionate power for those who would maintain the *status quo* is especially important with regard to the relatively meager support given to research on alternate forms of energy.

Despite resistance by the private sector to environmental constraints in terms of additional costs, greater complexities and the threat of fines, and other penalties imposed to enforce their adherence to environmental standards, progress is being made with regard to control of emissions, effluents, and other deleterious by-products of industry. But it is a slow process, and the report cards for all industrialized countries still show failing grades. The spate of internationally and nationally legislated and proposed actions, is impressive -- until one looks more closely at their substantive measures in terms of enforceable arrangements and degrees of change implied or articulated with regard to the nature of the regulations, their levels, their timing, and their funding for implementation and enforcement.

One overwhelming reason for this dismal record relates to the costs if the programs are to be implemented in a way that has a high probability (but no certainty in light of the present state of knowledge). The governments and the business leaders in the industrialized countries have been busy counting the financial costs of living up to the various promises of achieving and maintaining an acceptable environment. As already noted, there is a large price tag for a full-scale emission control program that will stabilize and then reduce harmful carbon emissions to "acceptable" or tolerable levels. As these estimates of costs and the associated uncertainties have been toted up, the degree of enthusiasm has waned.

The business community is lobbying for versions of environmental legislation with milder levels of regulation and with more ample tax loopholes. While this is a straightforward way of exercising the power of vested interests, there is, as well, a broader, more subtle but no less important, interpretation of vested interests that should be considered, namely, the forces that work for the maintenance of the stability of the prevailing system on the basis of their own special advantage. These groups, in the exercise of their power in influencing policies, can be relied upon to constrain the political policymakers from making radical changes, that is, those changes that in their scale and scope have ramifications that are systemic. Since the nature of the challenge posed by environmental degradation is of a scale and scope that might well call for actions that correct systemic weakness or failure, an environmental action program is likely to be ambitious in its rhetoric and modest in its follow-through.

There are several systemic features that can be identified as contributing to this state of affairs.

- ***In the case of politicians***, a myopic condition prevails. They have great difficulty, as politicians facing near-term re-election, in taking a perspective beyond the time-horizon of their term in office and, as well, in taking a national or international perspective beyond immediate concerns of their constituents. Even were they to have the best of intentions with regard to the longer-term future, the politician and the policy advisers have to face the problem of how to assess the risks associated with alternative approaches when the environmental externalities are so uncertain and information so incomplete.

- ***In the case of management in the private sector***, the time-horizon is hardly longer. They are generally judged by quarterly returns or the annual bottom line and use a high discount rate as an investment criterion, especially when real interest rates are high. Furthermore, there is fear engendered by uncertainty about the financial ramifications should they be forced to internalize the environmental diseconomies or, in other words, be forced to assume environmental costs that might be of a magnitude that would contribute to down-scaling or bankruptcy.

Thus, policymaking in both the public and private sectors tends to be constrained by a short-term view that heavily discounts the future and by a parochial view that makes it difficult to handle issues that cut across sectoral and ministerial or organizational lines that are established to protect or promote those interests.

2. Poverty, the Greatest Polluter: Its Global Systemic Roots

The systemic aspect of vested interests manifests itself most dramatically in the case of those developing countries that take on obligations in good faith but are burdened with severe debt servicing obligations and, at the same time, are dependent on a narrow range of exports to earn the foreign exchange with which to meet these obligations. The pressured circumstances incline policymakers to take less account of environmental consequences that can only be felt over the longer-term such as the deterioration of a watershed by clearing forest cover and continued dependence on fuelwood which the rural populace relies upon for well over 50 percent of their energy requirements for cooking and heating and in some areas, as much as 90 percent. This is exacerbated by the fact that the governments of developing countries have collectively a small fraction of the capacity of the industrialized countries to undertake energy research, and in particular, research on those energy technologies that are most suitable for their needs and that are, at the same time, more environmentally desirable.

More importantly, even where there is an appreciation of this danger, the policymakers of countries in these straits find it extremely difficult, if not impossible, to diversify and thus break away from a pattern of trade involving the export of those primary commodities whose cultivation have an adverse environmental impact.[20] They may even welcome foreign investors in ventures involving pollution-intensive products when such investments are attracted to their shores by the promise of lower or laxly-enforced environmental standards. The temptation to turn a blind eye to environmental regulatory standards is greater when the need for foreign exchange earnings is great, as it is bound to be when their economic and financial plight is exacerbated by their debt servicing obligations.[21] The pressure on these countries has mounted as they and their creditors have been engaged in a ritualized process that can be best characterized as an exercise in brinkmanship that pushes debtors to the limit of their endurance. See Miller [1991].

Borrowers are being obliged to commit themselves to undertake structural adjustment as a condition for the creditors agreeing to adding the unpaid interest to the outstanding debt and, on occasion, coming forth with some additional loans.[22] One unintended result of the usual conditionality associated with these Structural Adjustment Loans (SALs) is a reduction in the budgetary allocations to such programs as research, health, education services and related infrastructure, as well as to programs involving the environment such as waste disposal, water and air pollution control, and other environmental protective measures that

---

[20] A recent study of the changing patterns of trade by I. Walter and J.H. Loudon, "Environmental Costs and the Patterns of North-South Trade," has shown that the products these developing countries have been exporting have tended to be characterized by "higher than average environmental and resource-damage costs." Cited in World Commission on Environment and Development [1987], p. 80.

[21] "By early 1985, UNCTAD's commodity price index was 30% below the 1980 average...These countries are turning the terms of trade against themselves, earning less while exporting more, (leading) to cases of unsustainable overuse of the natural resource base." World Commission on Environment and Development [1987]. While the commodity price index has since made a slight recovery, many of the exportable commodities on which the developing countries depend for their foreign exchange have not as yet recovered.

[22] The term "structural adjustment" embraces a range of policies that would open their economies to private investors, place greater reliance on market forces, privatize publicly-owned enterprises, devalue their currency, reduce real wages, and so forth. In effect, the prescription for salvation involves belt-tightening in various forms and by various means.

call for increased budgetary outlays but can not show a quick payoff in terms of improving the foreign trade balance.

In effect, what is being witnessed is the imposition of policies that entail living off or eating into the capital base of the debtors' economy both to expand exports to service debts and to meet immediate basic needs. One observer has aptly called this process "cannibalization." It is this process with its intense quality of stress that undoubtedly prompted Indira Gandhi to describe poverty as "the greatest polluter."

3. A Case in Point: The United Nations Conference on New and Renewable Sources of Energy

The manner in which the factor of vested interests works to block such environmental initiatives is clearly demonstrated in the case of the 1981 United Nations Conference on New and Renewable Sources of Energy (UNCNRE) held in Nairobi. The need for research in this area was recognized, as was the need for global cooperation to undertake programs to develop energy technologies that are low cost, sturdily designed, and simple to operate and maintain. The thirty workshops, background papers, and conference discussions confirmed the likelihood of both scientific and technological breakthroughs that would provide cheap, simple, and durable technologies with a payoff not only in terms of welfare for the rural populace (for digging deeper wells, obtaining running water and healthier sanitation facilities, releasing women and children from the fuelwood gathering chores, etc.) but also in terms of income through increased agricultural productivity and in terms of the environment through reducing the dependency on fuelwood with its adverse ecological consequences.

The conference was conceived as a response to the very dire circumstances of the indebted oil-importing developing countries. It was recognized that some action had to be taken to ease their dependency on oil and subsequently reduce their expenditure of scarce foreign exchange. There was a general acknowledgment that when the situation called for global cooperation each nation separately could not take effective measures. The Nairobi Conference was ostensibly conceived as a step towards such global cooperation in so far as its mandate was to identify the problem and recommend steps to meet it, including international-scale action. A Plan of Action emerged from the two years of preparatory work. The recommendations pertained to actions that were known *a priori*, as, for example:

> (i) governments should undertake ***surveys*** and ***assessment*** programs regarding alternatives to oil, gas, coal, and nuclear power, using the information as a basis for planning for the development of hydro and other environmentally-benign sources of energy;
>
> (ii) more ***research*** should be undertaken on alternative sources of energy, particularly as applied to poorer countries;
>
> (iii) the costs and risks of ***demonstrating*** new technologies should be shared so as to accelerate their application;
>
> (iv) more ***training*** should be provided for personnel involved in both policymaking and project preparation and in building, operating, and maintaining new components of their country's energy systems.

The conference could make little progress beyond exhortations to act when the resolutions in the so-called "Plan of Action" were devoid of funding or concrete program initiatives. The oil-importing countries that had sought the conference were unable to advance their cause for promoting non-conventional environmentally helpful energy sources; even though the energy problem was recognized to be a matter of priority and urgency for most of the developing countries, and, indeed, for the global community in terms of the environmental implications of failure to take effective measures. The failure of that conference to achieve an action program with the requisite financing is testimony to the large gap between lip service and follow-through even on issues of great import. The failure can be attributed largely to the factor of vested interests, but part of the failure should be attributed to the inertia factor that weakened the force of the intellectual appreciation of the desperate need for change that had prompted the conference in the first place.

III. Steps to Overcoming These Barriers

In the last two decades there has been a rapid increase in the number of non-governmental organizations (NGOs) that have articulated agendas with very ambitious environmental goals, both in terms of what is to be achieved and the speed of doing so. They range from analytic NGOs such as the Worldwatch Institute to more activist ones such as Greenpeace, and to so-called "green" parties contesting elections. To put pressure on policymakers, all of these NGOs paint a doomsday scenario if their environmental program goals are not met. But few NGOs can operationalize their general ideas in a realistic manner.

There are, however, environmental advocates who propose steps that appear to be more responsible, reasonable, and realistic. They set out national and global policy agendas with ambitious but, in their view, realizable targets that include specific measure as transitional steps.[23] Among this group are those who might be labeled the "new growth" advocates whose message has most concisely been encapsulated in the phrase "sustainable development." The words convey a clearly worthwhile concept: development, yes, but development with concern for the long-term.

However, the concept as enunciated has done little to suggest how their programs are to be implemented. Certainly, the newly-aroused concern for the environment does not negate the popular desire for the fruits of development. Given the projected trends in population growth alone, a growth that is expected to triple the world population from 5.3 billion to over 16 during the course of the next century, it is safe to assert that global growth in the output of goods and services is an imperative. This judgment holds for the long-term since (i) even the most conservative estimates envisage, at best, a levelling off of the population increase by mid-21st century at levels that are double present numbers, and (ii) the largest increase would occur in the developing countries where the aspirations for an improved living standards cannot be denied.

---

[23]See, Christopher Flavin's chapter entitled "Slowing Global Warming," in Worldwatch Institute [1990], for a concise, yet comprehensive, statement of the current state of knowledge of the global environmental condition and of the proposals which are extant on the "global warming" aspect of the environmental problem. See also Speth [1990]. To this list one might add the writings of Jim MacNeill, formerly secretary of the Brundtland Commission whose views are contained in World Commission on Environment and Development [1987], and, more succinctly, in an interview published in *New Environment* [1990].

For those living in the poorer developing countries, this prescription of "new growth" appears as a cruel joke. With 80 percent of the world's population, they utilize less than 20 percent of the available global supplies of energy and other resources. But beyond the aspect of equity, there is an even more formidable obstacle, namely, their very limited capability to design and use alternative technologies that would enable them to grow with lower resource inputs per unit of output. Inertia is forced on them by virtue of their poverty and their economic and social structure.

For those living in the richer industrialized countries, the deceptively simple answer is, as was noted earlier, to advocate changes in the present pattern or the traditional model of development so as to lower the requirements for environmentally-harmful forms of inputs, particularly of energy, and more particularly, of fossil fuels. It would be difficult enough in these countries to make the necessary profound changes in economic and social organization, in culture and in life-style that such a sustainable development policy calls for. But even here the sustainable development concept has thus come up against hard reality and there is, therefore, growing skepticism, a state of mind that has the effect of reinforcing inertia.

If the actions to address these concerns have not been commensurate with their recognition and seeming popular support, one may turn to an answer which identifies two serious shortcomings in the approach of the advocates who speak and write for the environmental movement:

(i) Failure to make clear the key distinctions between those who stand to gain and those who stand to lose from the changes called for in the recommended programs of action and, with respect to the programs of action themselves, between the categories of governance, that is, between the developing countries and the industrialized ones:

- account must be taken of both the willingness and the capability to make policies and implement programs that integrate the issues of environment into the political and economic decisionmaking process;

- given the nature of environment impacts that are transnational or global, the issue of governance at the international level is critically important for the resolution of this crisis - but it is clearly more difficult to achieve when the peoples of the industrialized and of the developing countries have different perception about the causes, the effects, and the urgency of action at the international level where action calls for a cooperative approach.

(ii) The loose manner in which environmental resources are defined which gives rise to a vague or non-existent distinction between depletion or degradation of natural resources that can safely be depleted without necessarily prejudicing future welfare -- a category one might call "transformable natural resources" -- and those that cannot be transformed from their natural state into products that are marketable. The latter category of resources are those that are valued for their own sake in the form and on the site that nature has provided: beautiful landscapes, serene atmosphere, the quality of the atmosphere in terms of such attributes as the thickness of the ozone layer and the range of climate change, etc. These resources are irreplaceable and priceless and, in some cases, indispensable for the continuance of life on earth for the human species.

All this suggests that, as a first step, it is imperative to operationalize the concepts associated with the growth-environmental objectives and that, to do so, it must be recognized that the challenge of achieving a "new growth" state of affairs is a political task in the most profound sense of the term. There is little chance of succeeding to attain any pattern of development that is sustainable without being clear about the necessary and sufficient conditions for that to happen. These necessary conditions can be identified in terms of what it takes to overcome the three basic barriers to change that impede their realization which, as elaborated in Section II are the following:

(i) the public's inertia -- with its ignorance, skepticism, fatalism, alienation, and other attributes;

(ii) the aversion to risk-taking exacerbated by the exceptional degree of uncertainty about environmental processes and implications; and,

(iii) the resistance to change by those having vested interests in the *status quo* or a slight but not sufficient modification thereof.

Few of the environmental advocates -- even when they recognize that the necessary conditions for achieving a new growth pattern call for fundamental change -- seem prepared to break their troubling silence about the role of vested interests in maintaining the *status quo.* It is becoming clear that it is not enough to remain in the eco-protest phase with only vague references to changing institutional arrangements, especially when the prevailing arrangements are skewed towards accumulation and profit-making on a short payback basis and other innate attributes that are inimical to environmental objectives.

In societies that are democratic a great measure of popular support is necessary to make the requisite changes. To overcome inertia, a sense of urgency is critical. Battles cannot be left to the run-of-the-mill politicians but to statesmen; that is, a type of politician who has a broader longer-term global view and the courage to follow the implications of their analysis to its logical conclusions. It would not be sufficient to win small victories in the political arena but then lose ground through heavy reliance on decisionmaking characterized by a narrow financial and parochial focus and by a short-term perspective. A slow incremental approach cannot be expected to suffice when there is a strong likelihood that the sense of danger about environmental degradation will grow dull with time -- until it is temporarily revived by some dramatic catastrophe that provides yet another warning.

There appears to be a window of opportunity already opened when the world's attention is focused on this issue and there is a global crisis with its more-than-incipient signs of breakdown [Young, 1989, pp. 230 & 194].[24] The inertia factor could work for change if the public's consciousness could be aroused to a more intense pitch and sustained for a time long enough to force some significant action, to go beyond the attitude of merely coping. The forces of vested interests will continue to work to dampen the public's anxiety and will

---

[24]The concept of "regimes" is defined as "sets of implicit or explicit principles, norms, rules and decision-making procedures around which actors' expectations converge in a given area of international relations." The heading of the relevant section in Young's book is aptly titled "Seize Opportunities." The environmental crisis would seem to make a good fit as a candidate.

accentuate the risk factor in terms of lost incomes and lost jobs that might be the consequences of any serious environmental action program, whether it be national or international in scope. It is difficult for a public with an inability to imagine future scenarios to see that the greater risk is on the side of inaction that is camouflaged by obfuscating rhetoric. To overcome this resistance, there is no escaping the need for political explicitness about the implications of sustainable development and "new growth."

"No gain without pain" might be a suggested motto since it is evident that the scope, scale, and speed of the actions required to achieve environmental-development objectives will not be in harmony with the traditional order of things and that resistance from those in the establishment has to be anticipated. The battles will not be fought over the technical aspects but played out on the political field, both nationally and internationally. There are many proposals that need not necessarily evoke a sharp political reaction and yet could be helpful - even though by no means sufficient. These might be put forward at the first phase since the barriers to change are then likely to be lower and on that account, the probability of making some gains is likely to be commensurably higher. The assessment of probabilities that would influence the strategy and tactics of the elements of an environmental action program is not amenable to generalization at the local, regional, or national level of governance. At these various levels of governance there are nuanced differences in the nature of inertia, risk, and vested interests and in the strength of these barriers to change.

Many of these proposals call for a far-reaching shift of social priorities and all that it implies. Many are advanced without spelling out these necessary conditions that would, in effect, mean radical institutional change. Though in some cases the objectives of the agenda of the proposers are spelled out and scheduling for a transitional period is articulated for a step-at-a-time approach, the implied threat to the established order of things is either not recognized or is consciously muted. The rhetoric is, however, likely to be very appealing.

There is a lot to be said for this pragmatic approach. It reflects a cautionary assessment that the quantum leap in the public's concern about the environment has not yet evoked a corresponding process of political action and of institutional adaptation. But the questions remain: Does this environmental program and its policy framework go far enough and fast enough? Are they sufficient and consistent with establishing the minimally necessary conditions to enable both industrialized and developing countries to maintain a reasonably rapid growth trajectory and, at the same time, doing so in an environmentally sensitive manner?

For the debt-burdened developing countries in particular the answer must be "no": so long as they are under extreme pressure to service their debt, the short-term will overwhelmingly dominate the longer-term in their policymaking and environmental concerns will take a back seat. Accordingly, the scope of the environmental battle plan must be widened to include debt relief measures of an across-the-board nature if it is to be substantial enough to make a real difference. Beyond this, it is necessary to take steps to launch a global structural adjustment program which addresses the factors that sustain inertia with its fast population growth and unsustainable patterns of development that are excessively and needlessly capital and energy-intensive.

This proposal can be said to be an environmental analogue to the Bretton Woods agreement of 1944 that for a quarter century set rules of the game for international trade and capital flows.[25] The environmental equivalent would be to establish an agreement under an international convention that sets environmental norms and provides for procedures to enforce a system of rewards and penalties to secure adherence to the agreed-upon environmental norms of good behavior and to discourage violations by suasion and fines. In this regard there should be a distinction made between industrialized and developing countries with respect to the norms and the system of penalties and incentives. In addition, the agreement would have to provide for capital and technical assistance and for a trading system that enables the developing countries to play their part in this global effort for assuring an environmentally desirable future. Unless and until these conditions are met the global economy will continue to be plagued by a festering condition that will frustrate efforts to build environmental sensitivity into debtor country policies and into global relations. It is this assessment of the global problem that has prompted calls by President François Mitterrand and others for a "new Bretton Woods," for policy reforms that would alter some key features of the prevailing global system of trade and capital movements. Environmental objectives cannot be realized without a congenial policy framework that is global in scope.

Nor can it be achieved without considering the financial aspect. There have been many proposals put forward that would dampen the demand for environmentally-damaging energy uses and lure demand towards alternative energy sources that are more environmentally-benign and, at the same time, raise revenues to meet the financial requirements of effective environmental programs. The most popular is a global carbon tax on the users of fossil fuels which at $50 per ton of carbon emission would yield annually in the United States alone about $28 billion if 10 percent of the revenues were allocated to environmental programs.[26] The auctioning of saleable pollution rights would be another source. For the Third World debtor nations, the financing proposals include reducing the debt burden by a vigorous program of converting their debt into entitlements for the creditors to establish nature preserves or debt-for-nature swaps. These swaps are helpful in reducing debt but they have a limited scope in relation to the magnitude of the debt problem that these countries face. All these sources would be helpful; however, even if their limitations were to be overcome and their full potential realized and allocated for environmental programs, there would still be a substantial shortfall.

---

[25] The most directly relevant reference with regard to this approach can be found in the Commonwealth Secretariat [1984].

[26] One of the most strongly promoted proposals is for a "carbon tax" to discourage the use of fossil fuel and other energy sources that are the large sources of carbon emissions, principally CO_2. For a succinct treatment of this tax issue, see Wallich and Corcoran [1990], p. 171. They quote sources critical of a study by the Congressional Budget Office that proposed a $28 per ton tax on carbon-containing fuels that would generate $163 billion or more between now and 1995 and reduce CO_2 emissions by 20% by the end of the century or soon after. The skeptics claim that a tax high enough to drive down carbon emissions would have to be at least $100 per ton of carbon which is not politically feasible in the U.S. on grounds of its inequitable impact on incomes and jobs. Some critics prefer setting permissible limits and establishing a market in emission permits, thus letting the market set the price. Can regulators know where to set the limits? Can we know how much the demand for carbon-emitting products would fall as their prices were increased - [the price and income elasticities of demand]? Can we be assured that there will be enough bidding and offering parties in the auction market for these emission permits? Christopher Flavin in Worldwatch Institute [1990], pp. 28-29, notes that "picking the correct tax is a complicated exercise...[but] a conservative estimate is that large-scale efforts will cost on average at least $50 per ton of carbon...Incorporated in the price of carbon-emitting fuels...[this tax can be regarded] as the cost of avoiding climate change."

This financial shortfall applies with special relevance for the Third World countries that would have to play a role in a global program to reduce carbon emissions, including foregoing financial returns by reducing the use of their tropical rain forests for their own benefit and that of the international community. Many of the governments of these countries hold different views as to what constitutes an environmental problem or as to their seriousness and the urgency of the need for remedial action; but, in any case, they weigh priorities differently if they do not have the requisite capability to take corrective action to tackle their part of these global environmental problems.

This raises a thorny problem related to the non-reciprocal benefits and costs from some global environmental measures such as those called for with respect to exploitation of the tropical rain forests of the Amazon Basin and other regions with vast forestry tracts. Since in the international realm cooperative solutions require binding agreements, there might well be a need for a *quid pro quo* that will entice the polluter to desist. This form of payment to developing countries could be troublesome since, as has been pointed out, this practice "can easily turn the morality of the 'polluter pays' principle upside down [to become] the 'victim pays' principle."[27]

There is, however, another way to look at the morality of this bargain: the richer industrialized nations, having in the course of their development used most of the pollutant quotient that the air and water can absorb and still maintain an acceptable quality, are now merely being obliged to pay their fair share for the *past* use of the "global commons" that has acted as a garbage dump with no authority established to charge dumping fees. Payment by the industrialized nations for past due fees that can be paid into a newly established environmental fund would be morally more palatable. Payments out of this fund could be made to those countries that need help in pursuing environmentally beneficial policies and programs; the list of recipients might then include those that desist from globally harmful activities.

This type of arrangement is likely to be the only basis for reaching international agreements to obtain the necessary cooperation for tackling the issue of global warming and other global-scale environmental problems. The idea, therefore, cannot be dismissed as unthinkable on grounds of high principle, especially as the issue of principle or morality cuts both ways. In any case, if the Third World countries are to play their part, they must be assisted with the financial wherewithal that will enable them to change their pattern of growth in line with the new global environmental ethic.

It is hardly enough to continue to wring hands in a paralysis of despair in the face of a big threat and challenge, nor to cry "wolf!" or adopt the tactics of what has been called,

---

[27]Helm and Pearce [1990] believe that "the issue of 'side payments' will dominate the 1992 United Nations Environment Conference in Brazil." The analysis rests heavily on the options and outcomes of the situation found in the "Prisoners' Dilemma" and in the "Problem of the Commons," (the atmosphere being a global commons measured by a quality index), both of which provide useful analytic analogues for identifying the trade-offs from cooperative and noncooperative actions and for judging the preferred outcomes. In another article in the same issue, D. Dasgupta writes on another aspect of the same issue: "The private cost to Brazil in pursuing a carbon dioxide depletion policy will be far less than the global cost...thus the idea of international compensation to the depleter for reducing the rate of depletion should no longer be regarded as far-fetched. Partial debt-relief for a lower rate of plunder of the Amazonian forest is something that will probably be on the agenda in the near future. This is a Pigovian subsidy. It is hard to imagine that there are many other options open to us." See Dasgupta [1990], p. 55.

"panicky eco-action." One of the essential first steps is the identification of what the "right thing" is that should and could be done, based on the best available knowledge while striving to improve that knowledge and narrow the range of uncertainty in both the scientific and socioeconomic realms. Concurrently, steps must be taken to identify the institutional obstacles to "doing the right thing," or, at least, to moving in the right direction which would include the acquisition of more knowledge through a global multi-faceted research effort.

On the basis of an understanding of what should and could be done and of the institutional barriers the next step could be taken with the requisite degree of confidence, namely, the articulation of policies, programs, and projects that are important and that are feasible, even in the light of the obstacles that lie in the path of forging such an effective environmental policy and program in the energy sector. In effect, this would be forging a global energy future to maintain a life-supporting environment quality. This is a mega issue involving, as Professor Fred Knelman put it, "a debate about politics, economics, culture, ethics, and equity." But above all, the issue is the fate of the global society or civilization. Professor Kenneth Boulding, an economist who has sometimes been described as a social philosopher with imagination and compassion, has framed the issue in appropriate terms [Boulding, 1966, p. 11]:

> This whole problem is linked up with the much larger one of the determinants of the morale, legitimacy and 'nerve' of a society, and there is a great deal of historical evidence to suggest that a society that loses its identity with posterity and which loses its positive image of the future loses also its capacity to deal with present problems, and soon falls apart....One can hope, therefore, that a succession of mounting crises, especially in pollution, arouse public opinion and mobilize support for the solution of the immediate problems, and that a learning process will be set in motion which will eventually lead to an appreciation of and perhaps solutions for the larger ones.

References

Baumol, W. and C. Oates [1988]. *The Theory of Environmental Policy.* Second Edition. New York: Cambridge University Press.

Boulding, Kenneth E. [1966]. "The Economics of the Coming Spaceship Earth." In H. Jarrett (editor), *Environmental Quality in the Growing Economy.* Washington, D.C.: Resources for the Future.

Chandler, William U. [1985]. *Energy Productivity: Key to Environmental Protection and Economic Progress.* Worldwatch Paper No. 63. Washington, D.C.: Worldwatch Institute, January.

Churchill, A. [1988]. "A Look Ahead to the Year 2010: Outlook for Energy and Supply Demand." *Bank's World* (World Bank), vol. 7 (October): 12-13.

Commonwealth Secretariat [1984]. *Towards a New Bretton Woods: Challenges for the World Financial and Trading Systems.* London: Commonwealth Secretariat.

Dasgupta, P. [1990]. "The Environment as a Commodity." *Oxford Review of Economic Policy*, vol. 6, no. 1.

The Economist [1988]. "Electricity in the Third World: A Dark Future." *The Economist* (May 7, 1988).

Hardin, G. [1968]. "The Tragedy of the Commons." *Science*, vol. 162.

Helm, D. and D. Pearce [1990]. "Assessment: Economic Policy Towards the Environment." *Oxford Review of Economic Policy*, vol. 6, no. 1.

Holdren, John [1990]. "Energy in Transition." *Scientific American, Special Issue: Energy for Planet Earth*, vol. 263, no. 3 (September): 156-63.

MacNeill, J. [1989]. "Strategies for Sustainable Economic Development." *Scientific American, Special Issue: Managing Planet Earth*, vol. 261 (September): 154-65.

Meadows, Daniella, Dennis Meadows, Jorgen Randers, and William Behrens [1972]. *The Limits to Growth.* New York: Universe Books.

Miller, M. [1991]. *Debt and the Environment: Converging Crises.* New York: United Nations Publications.

Miller, M. [1992]. *Sustainability and the Energy/Environment Connection: Overcoming Barriers to "Doing the Right Thing."* EDI Working Papers, Energy Series. Washington, D.C.: World Bank.

Mishan, E.J. [1974]. "Ills, Bads, and Disamenities: The Wages of Growth." *Daedalus Special Issue: The No-Growth Society* (Fall).

Mishan, E.J. [1980]. *The Costs of Economic Growth.* New York: Penguin.

New Environment [1990]. *New Environment*, Premier Issue (September).

Nordhaus, William D. [1990]. "Greenhouse Economics: Count Before You Leap." *The Economist*, vol. 316 (July 7-13): 21-24.

Roberts, Marc J. [1974]. "On Reforming Economic Growth." *Daedulus Special Issue: The No-Growth Society* (Fall).

Ruckelshaus, William [1989]. "Toward a Sustainable World." *Scientific American, Special Issue: Managing Planet Earth* (September).

Schumpeter, Joseph [1952]. *Capitalism, Socialism, and Democracy*. Fourth Edition. London: Allen & Unwin.

Speth, Gus [1992]. "Environmental Security for the 1990s in Six Not-So-Easy Steps." *WRI Issues and Ideas Newsletter*. Washington, D.C.: World Resources Institute, January.

Tietenberg, T. [1990]. "Using Economic Incentives to Maintain Our Environment." *Challenge* (March-April).

United Nations [1990a]. *Energy Statistics Yearbook*. New York: United Nations.

United Nations [1990b]. *Global Outlook 2000: An Economic, Social and Environmental Perspective*. New York: United Nations.

United Nations [1990c]. *National Accounts of the U.N. Statistical Office*. New York: United Nations.

United States Agency for International Development [1988]. *Power Shortage in Developing Countries*. Washington, D.C.: USAID.

United States Department of Energy [1990]. *National Energy Strategy Interim Report*. Washington, D.C.: United States Department of Energy, April.

Wallich, Paul and Elizabeth Corcoran [1990]. "Carbon Levies." *Scientific American Special Issue: Energy for Planet Earth* (September).

Walter, I. and J.H. Loudon. "Environmental Costs and the Patterns of North-South Trade."

World Bank [1989]. *Environmental Accounting for Sustainable Development*. Washington, D.C.: World Bank.

World Commission on Environment and Development [1987]. *Our Common Future*. New York: Oxford University Press.

Worldwatch Institute [1990]. *State of the World - 1990*. New York and London: W.W. Norton & Co.

Young, Oran [1989]. *International Cooperation: Building Regimes for Natural Resources and the Environment*. Ithaca, New York: Cornell University Press.

5

Indices for a Greenhouse Gas Control Regime: Incorporating Both Efficiency and Equity Goals

Kirk R. Smith, Environment and Policy Institute, East-West Center; Joel Swisher, Civil Engineering, Stanford University; Rebekah Kanter, Environment and Policy Institute, East-West Center; and Dilip R. Ahuja The Bruce Company, Washington, D.C.[1]

I. Introduction: Indices of Equity and Efficiency

Any successful program to slow or reverse the buildup of greenhouse gases in Earth's atmosphere will require cooperation among a wide range of nations. This is because the problem is truly global in character. The atmospheric lifetimes of most of the gases in question are so much longer than the time required for global mixing that, to a first approximation, emissions from any place on the planet have essentially similar impact on global climate as emissions from any other. In addition, the current emissions of no one nation or group of nations clearly dominate. The developed countries have generally emitted more greenhouse gases (GHGs) in the past, but most future emissions scenarios indicate a significantly rising proportion from developing countries. The developing countries are also likely to be more vulnerable to the effects of global warming, as they are to possible diversion of development funds [Gleick, 1989]. Furthermore, each greenhouse gas is emitted by its own particular mix of activities, e.g., fossil fuel use, air conditioning, agriculture, deforestation. Because the mixture of activities is so different in each country, there are significant differences among nations in their patterns of emissions, requiring negotiation from a number of viewpoints in the development of mitigation programs [Wirth and Lashof, 1990].

---

[1]This chapter is a revision of the original working paper by this title which was prepared for the Economic Development Institute's Energy Investments and the Environment Workshop held in Washington, D.C. in October 1990.

Those advocating creation of such a multilateral program are required to face, among other tasks, five categories of questions:

(i) Is there adequate theoretical and observational evidence of significant potential harm if nothing is done?

(ii) If so, then the following questions need to be addressed: Could a ***feasible program*** of GHG remediation[2] accomplish sufficient benefits to be justified?

(a) What part of this program is best devoted to reduction of GHG emissions or increases in GHG sinks (natural or anthropogenic processes that absorb GHGs from the atmosphere)?

(b) What part of this program is best devoted to reduction of human vulnerability to global warming through, for example, accelerated economic growth of certain kinds in poor countries?

(iii) Is there a rational and politically acceptable way of ***establishing priorities*** among potential remediation projects?

(iv) Is there a rational and politically acceptable way of ***allocating the costs*** for these projects?

(v) What kind of ***international institutional mechanisms*** are needed to facilitate the financing and implementation of such projects?

Although there is by no means universal agreement, many observers believe that the answers to questions (i) and (ii) are likely to be in the affirmative, i.e. there could be significant risk without action and significant reduction of risk with action. It is not the purpose of this chapter to directly address these issues. Rather, this study, will focus on the last three questions, with particular emphasis on (iii) and (iv), the means to decide both what needs to be done and who will pay. It will mainly address those remediation measures related to alterations of GHG flows (iia, above), but in Part III will briefly discuss the equally important issue of vulnerability reduction (iib).

First of all, the means used to choose and allocate the costs for remediation projects will need to be reflective of physical reality, i.e. they will have to identify (i) projects that actually accomplish remediation and (ii) nations that have sufficient resources to pay for them. They will have to be flexible, i.e. be able to take into account new scientific information and changing global conditions. Also, they will have to be efficient, i.e. low-cost to apply and

---

[2]Here remediation refers to a wide range of actions that may result in the reduction of net emissions from GHG sources, an increase in net GHG sequestering by GHG sinks, or decreases in the vulnerability of human populations to warming. Potentially there are also other ways to reduce the threat of climate change from greenhouse gas emissions, such as artificially blocking sufficient incoming sunlight from reaching the earth to balance increased GHG warming. At present, these options do not seem likely to be feasible, but should their prospects improve, they could be judged in the same type of indexing framework considered here.

result in the choice of projects that achieve the most possible marginal risk reduction for each dollar of each donor's contribution. Finally, they will have to be seen as objective and equitable, i.e. use criteria in the choice of project locations and donors that are understandable and justifiable to a diverse global audience [Bertram et al., 1989].

Furthermore, since the international transfers involved in such an effort potentially could become larger than any ever previously undertaken for environmental purposes, even rivalling total current international trade, such a scheme may be required to incorporate a number of additional criteria. These criteria could include promotion of general economic efficiency, sustainable use of resources, local environmental quality, and global resilience. Such a program may as well be expected to discourage certain undesirable activities by nations such as failing to stem rapid population growth and refusing to join into international GHG agreements.

A. Mechanisms

Much of the discussion about global GHG remediation programs has focused on question (v), the international mechanisms by which resources for GHG reduction could be moved [e.g.,Grubb, 1989]. These mechanisms fall into three major categories:

(i) Direct emissions constraints through national or sector targets, e.g., "emissions will be reduced 25% in each country [or in the coal industry or the automobile fleet] before 2010."

(ii) Recognition that the cost of control is quite different for different sources and potential sinks and that pursuing control options on the basis of marginal costs can potentially reduce the cost of achieving a given degree of overall emissions reductions compared to option (i) above. This efficiency can be captured in two generic ways:

(a) Through a command-and-control infrastructure where central authorities keep track of marginal costs and assign targets to each source or potential sink separately.

(b) Through tradeable permits, where, subject to a centrally chosen overall emission constraint, individual emissions sources can exchange permits in order to preferentially exploit low-cost options first. (This is analogous to the "emissions trading" procedure now used in some countries to reduce the cost of compliance with air pollutant regulations.)

(iii) Taxes on fuels and other sources of emissions (or, conversely, subsidies on emissions sinks or reduction measures) to create economic incentives that shift society away from GHG-emitting activities.

Other possibilities include auctioned quotas, a combination of options (i) and (ii), where high-cost-control countries could buy emission rights from low-cost-control countries before assigning them at a national level. Or, options (ii) and (iii) could be combined in a

"World Greenhouse Fund" that would collect funds centrally from sources (or groups of sources like countries) and distribute the proceeds to cost-effective sinks or control measures.

Note that each of these mechanisms applies to international exchanges, not necessarily to exchanges within the participating countries. For example, options (ii) or (iii) could be implemented alone, under a central authority that allocates permits to or collects taxes from individual sources in different countries. Or, these types of policy instruments could be applied at the national level by governments operating under option (i) at the international level. Finally, either permits or taxes could be exchanged both domestically or internationally under an international allocation of the responsibility to pay for, but not necessarily implement, emission reductions. In this case, the responsibility of the central authority would be greatly reduced compared to options (ii) or (iii) applied alone.

The task here is not to add to the considerable on-going discussion of the relative merits of these mechanisms, except to emphasize that they all share at least one critical requirement before they can be implemented: agreement on an indexing scheme. The operation of any of these mechanisms, for example, requires some way to compare different flows of different GHGs from different sources over time. Showing compliance with either overall targets (i) or those tailored to individual sources (ii) will require a means to assess the total impact of a set of projects that each reduce different amounts of different GHGs. Choosing the proper amount and distribution of taxes (iii) will require such an index as well. This kind of index is explored in Part II.

There are also, however, more complex tasks required of indices in the creation and evaluation of any of the global mechanisms being considered. For example, for determining the initial distribution of tradeable permits. These tasks are discussed in Parts III and IV in some detail before returning to the implications for particular mechanisms in Part V.

B. Indices

Deciding which projects to fund and who should pay implies the use of indices to weigh potential projects and donors against one another.[3] The indices should be composed of individual indicators that are deemed to be relevant according to the criteria mentioned above, particularly efficiency and equity [Munasinghe, 1990]. The application of the appropriate index should not only rank and prioritize, but preferably also give a quantitative indication of how much better one project is over another or how much more one country should pay than another.

Choosing indices, therefore, is the crux of efforts to decide which projects to fund by whom. Consider, for example, the widely reported claim that no matter whose estimates of deforestation are taken, Brazil ranks third or fourth in the world as an emitter of GHGs [World Resources Institute (WRI), 1990]. This might imply to some observers that Brazil could be held responsible for a good proportion of the present world problem and, on this basis, might be a good candidate as a significant donor to an international program. ***This would be an unfortunate interpretation, however, for the index used to create this ranking is inappropriate to the question at hand. In particular, responsibility is best judged on a per capita***

---

[3] "An 'index' is a single number derived from two or more indicators" [Ott, 1978].

and not on a per nation basis. Otherwise, quite perverse results can be obtained, for example that Hong Kong should have the same allotment as China until they merge in 1997, when their total allotment would drop by half. By only changing the WRI index (which also has other problems) to a per capita basis, Brazil drops to 7th, 17th, or 47th among nations, depending on which of three different estimates of deforestation is chosen [WRI, 1990]. This is a much more appropriate indication of Brazil's degree of responsibility for the present situation than is an index that ignores its population size [Smith et al., 1991].

On the other hand, the population size of a country could be one appropriate indicator for incorporation into an index designed to rank countries as to the potential for energy efficiency programs that could have the biggest effect on GHG emissions. In this case, governments of populous nations may well be able to achieve larger reductions. The point is that ***the index must be chosen with regard to the question being asked.*** There is no universal index capable of answering the range of questions listed above.

1. A Two-Nation, One-Pollutant Model

To illustrate further, consider a two-nation, one-pollutant model of the world: fossil-fuel carbon dioxide from India and the United States [Smith, 1989b]. (These are the second most populous developing nation and developed nation, respectively, each with about 22% of the population of its group.) Consider the seemingly straightforward question, "What will be their relative responsibilities for increasing GHG emissions over the next 35 years?"

Table 1 lists some of the relevant parameters for 1986 as well as projections for the year 2025 given United Nations (UN) population estimates and three possible future energy scenarios for the United States (annual per capita fossil fuel use grows at 0%, +0.5%, as it has in recent years, or -1.5%, which is what would be needed to reach a 30% reduction in total emissions by 2025). The sole scenario for India, 4.4% growth, was chosen because it is similar to recent rates and allows the average Indian in 2025 to achieve a rate of 1 ton carbon per capita, about the 1990 world average, or what the United States achieved before 1900. Presumably, however, advances in technology and its application by 2025 would allow much more benefit per unit of emissions than achieved by the United States at similar emission levels.

One possible index to answer the question of relative responsibility would be based on the expected change in national emission rates. Thus, India's annual emission rate in 1986 was 8.3 times less than the United States, but, at a United States growth rate of zero (the middle scenario), India would be emitting at the same rate in 2025. Over the period, however, the total responsibility might better be indicated by the cumulative total national emissions added since 1986, which shows 2.3 for the United States: India ratio. In other words, this might be considered their relative responsibility over the period to be used, for example, to allocate costs of international programs. (Higher ratios indicate that more responsibility would fall on the United States.)

Since per capita indices are generally more suitable for questions of responsibility, however, the table reveals that the ratio of per capita emission rates will change from 27 to 5.0.

It is argued here, however, that the best index for determining responsibility is per capita cumulative emissions. This is based on the physical reality that the most critical single

Table 1: Emissions Indices: Carbon as carbon dioxide from fossil fuels and cement, India versus the United States

		1986		1950-86			2025	1950-2025	1987-2025
	Population (10)	Emissions Capita (ton)	Emissions Nation (10 ton)	Cumulative Capita (10 ton)	Population (10)	Emissions Capita (ton)	Emissions Nation (10 ton)	Cumulative Capita (ton)	Incremental Cumulative Nation (10 ton)
United States (+0.5%)	242	5.0	1210	155	301	6.1	1830	376	60
United States (0%)	242	5.0	1210	155	301	5.0	1500	355	54
United States (-1.5%)	242	5.0	1210	155	301	2.8	834	308	40
India (4.4%)	781	0.19	150	2.8	1450	1.0	1450	22	23
Ratio United States/India	0.31	27	8.3	55	0.21	6.1 5.0 2.8	1.3 1.0 0.58	17 16 14	2.6 2.3 1.7

Source: Basic data from Marland et al. [1988].

Notes: Percentages shown in parentheses are the growth rates in per capita carbon emissions assumed for this scenario.
Population inputs are medium-case estimates from United Nations [1988].
The three ratios shown in these columns correspond to the three per capita United States carbon emission growth rates (+0.5%, 0%, -1.5%).

parameter for determining the global warming at any one time is the cumulative amount of the GHG in the atmosphere. As shown in Table 1, the amount placed into the atmosphere since 1950 as part of the United States industrialization process is equivalent to about 155 tons per person in 1986, about 50 times that of the average Indian, at 2.8 tons.

According to the scenarios in Table 1, the Indian per capita cumulative contribution would increase by a factor of 8 over the period, while the United States contribution would only double. Because of the large difference in initial values, however, during these 39 years, the Indian's contribution would increase by 19 tons, while the average United States citizen's contribution would rise more than 10 times as much, i.e. 200 tons. The ratio of total cumulative amounts at the end of the period would, at 16, be lower than what it was in 1986 (55), but still high. At that point, the average Indian would still be responsible for only a minor part of the total atmospheric accumulation, less than 6% that of the average United States resident.

2. Indices Do Matter

Table 2 shows a summary of the various values in the two-nation model and illustrates the wide range of answers that could be derived from use of indices that vary only in two parameters--present versus cumulative and per nation versus per capita. It is useful to note that these values are much more sensitive to the index chosen, than to the particular emissions scenario used. Assume, for example, that the United States was able to reduce its per capita carbon emissions use by 1.5% each year for the 39-year period, reaching a total emission rate more than 30% below that of 1986 (and the per capita emissions down by more than 40%). How much difference would this rather heroic effort make in the final ratios? It would make very little difference for cumulative per capita indices. As shown in the table, the difference in ratios for cumulative atmospheric carbon would be less than 15% (14 versus 16). Conversely, if the United States were to continue to expand its fossil fuel use by 0.5%, as it did during the late 1980s, the ratio would only rise to 17 by 2025.

As will be discussed in detail in later sections, there are many other possibilities to vary indices to reflect the real world of multiple criteria, greenhouse gases, and nations. What is emphasized here is that the index does indeed make a difference, sometimes a very large difference, and thus must be chosen with care.

C. An Index Framework

In considering a negotiated reduction in global GHG emissions, both equity and economic efficiency must be pursued. Nations can reach an agreement only if each participant is satisfied that the goals of the agreement are fair, and that the responsibility for implementing (or paying for) the agreement is assigned equitably. There are equity concerns not only across nations and generations (i.e. time periods) but also within nations, as well [Siddiqi, 1990]. Economic efficiency is essential to minimize the total implementation cost and make the agreement less painful to each participant. Efficiency requires that available resources be combined with the least expensive opportunities to achieve the agreed-upon reductions.

Table 2: Ratio of Responsibilities: United States/India

	Current Emissions		Cumulative Emissions		
	1986	2025	1986	2025	1987-2025 Increment
Per Nation	8.3	1.0	16	3.6	2.3
Per Capita	27	5.0	55	16	10

Source: Authors. Based on data in Table 1, no-emissions-growth scenario for the United States.

Note: Shown are a number of indices that might be used to compare relative responsibilities for greenhouse gas emissions. Here are recommended Natural Debt indices, i.e. those three in the lower right quadrant that are based on cumulative emissions per capita. Carbon dioxide (CO_2) emissions are from fossil fuels and cement production.

An agreement based on the principles of equality and efficiency requires the definition of negotiating criteria to measure each country's contribution. These principles suggest several different criteria, each of which address different questions and may occupy different stages of the negotiation process.

Typically, discussions of agreements to limit greenhouse gas emissions consider only one criterion at a time. This may be a mistake, because it is difficult to define a criterion for which many countries would be willing to be held to the same standard as all other countries. Proposals for allocations of emission rights have included those simply based on population, as well as on equal percentage reductions, similar to the Montreal Protocol limiting emissions of chlorofluorocarbons (CFCs). (See Appendix A.)

Other proposals vary in complexity and emphasis. Most, however, mix equity and efficiency goals into the same index. Krause et al. [1989], for example, advocate on the basis of simplicity an equal share of emission rights to developed and developing countries over the next century. Westing [1989] proposes a "Law of the Air," in which emission rights are based on each nation's land area. Following the structure of the Montreal Protocol, Chapman and Drennen [1990] discuss a range of emission allocations, which all implicitly assume that a country's share of the emission reduction responsibility must be accomplished by measures to reduce its own emissions, resulting in insoluble trade-offs between equity and efficiency goals. Similarly, Wirth and Lashof [1990] try to balance equity and efficiency in an emission allocation scheme based on a combination of population and wealth.

Although these proposals are somewhat more sophisticated than the percent-reduction basis of the Montreal Protocol, they share the disadvantage of being unable to reconcile equity and efficiency goals. These goals, and the interests of different countries, could be weighed against one another in increasing detail until each country's individual allocation becomes the matter of debate, rather than the criteria for the allocation. Negotiations at this level, however, create more incentives for finding excuses not to agree to reductions than for finding emission reduction opportunities [Grubb, 1989].

It may be easier to find a point of agreement by separating the negotiating criteria, and the indices to measure them, according to the two general questions set out to be addressed [numbers (iii) and (iv) listed in the beginning of Part I]. Using this approach, one can consider the competing goals of equity and efficiency, while maintaining a rational (but still negotiable) basis for assigning allocations at the national level.

The basic negotiating criteria are categorized in terms of the following questions:

To determine the best projects, these questions must be addressed:

(i) What are the goals (globally, and who should do what)?
(ii) What are the best opportunities (who can do what)?

To determine who will pay, these questions must be addressed:

(iii) Where are the needed resources (who can pay)?
(iv) Who has responsibility for the problem (who should pay)?

These four questions are shown, together with some of the information flows needed to address them, in Figure 1.

Figure 1: Typology and Indices for Allocating Greenhouse Gas Emission Reductions

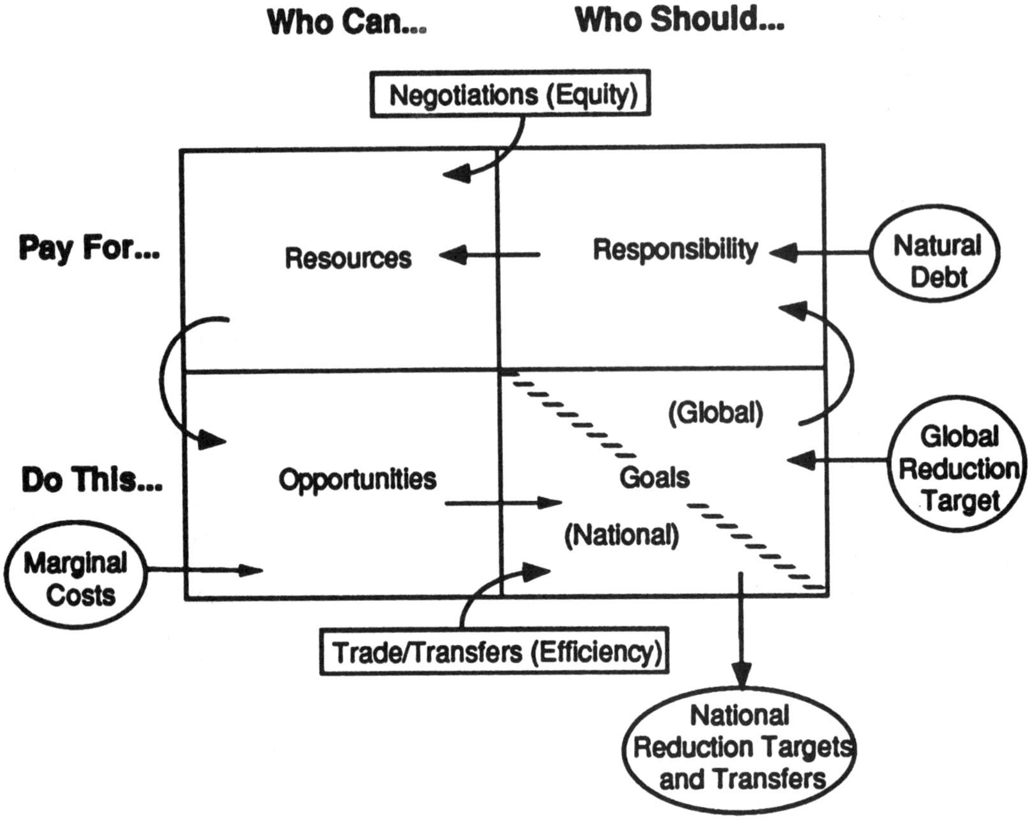

Source: Authors.

Note: This figure shows a framework for creating indices to address the two principal questions: (i) What are the best remediation projects?, and (ii) Who will pay for them?

The "Who can..."questions in the left column are addressed by criteria that can be measured according to physical and financial quantities, and the "Who should..."questions in the right column are addressed by criteria that, while they can be quantified, must involve a large degree of value judgement. The "Pay for..."questions in the top row involve equity criteria, based on past and present activities, while the "Do this..."questions in the bottom row involve efficiency criteria, based on present and proposed future action.

The starting point of a negotiating process is considered to be the global level goal for emission reductions, based on a perceived common vulnerability to climate change. This goal may be the result of any combination of scientific, economic, and political considerations (questions (i) and (ii), above).

Once the general goal is set, each country's share of the responsibility for causing the problem can be determined, based on its past and present contribution to the source of the problem, namely carbon dioxide and other greenhouse gas emissions. As discussed in the two-nation illustration above, one measure of a nation's responsibility is cumulative per capita emissions. Smith [1989 and 1990a] has termed this the "Natural Debt," which, in analog to the national debt, is the assimilative capacity of the atmosphere that a country has borrowed in order to build its wealth. However measured, a country's share of responsibility for the problem is considered to be a measure of how much of the cost of emission reductions the country should pay. Note that this quantity may well be different from how much emission reduction a country should implement itself, which depends on the size and cost of its emission reduction opportunities, while responsibility depends on the size of the Natural Debt. (See Appendix Table B-1 for an international comparison of Natural Debts.)

Responsibility is a useful but incomplete measure of a country's contribution to a fund for emission reductions. A negotiated solution must also consider countries' resources with which to pay. This criterion addresses two issues, one practical and one ethical. The practical consideration is simply that a solution to the problem is more likely if those countries which have greater resources are willing to pay relatively more of the total cost. The ethical issue is that those countries with less resources have a relatively greater need to save resources to reduce their future vulnerability to climate change impacts.

Quantitative indices will later be suggested to estimate both responsibility and resources at the national level. It will also be suggested how these indices can be combined to measure a country's allocation of the cost of emission reductions. This step, however, is somewhat more arbitrary than the direct estimation of responsibility and resources, and may be best left to the negotiation process to reconcile each country's allocation.

Given the national allocation for paying the cost of emission reductions, one can compare this allocation with the national distribution of opportunities for emission reductions. Clearly, one does not expect the opportunities to be distributed among countries in the same way. Some countries will have a relatively high concentration of opportunities, while others will have a relatively large allocation of the obligation to pay for emission reductions.

As the costs of various emission reduction strategies become known, this information can be used to estimate the quantity of emission reduction opportunities that can be exploited below a given cost level. Economic efficiency requires that the selection of these opportunities should minimize total cost, and that the marginal costs (the cost of the most expensive measures implemented) of emission reductions in each country and each sector should be equal [Baumol and Oates, 1988].

Thus, the costs of emission reduction measures alone indicate which reduction opportunities should be exploited in which countries to achieve maximum efficiency. This efficient allocation of opportunities, matched with the cost allocation (based on equity) described above, indicates national goals, for both the funding and the implementation of emission reductions, that are consistent with the global goal, and with both equity and economic efficiency.

Because a country's allocation of responsibility ("who pays") and opportunity ("who acts") for emission reductions will not be the same, our criteria require some mechanisms to reconcile them, i.e. to transfer resources from the countries with excess unfulfilled responsibility to those with excess unexploited opportunities. More simply, the rich countries would help fund the poor countries to help reduce global emissions of greenhouse gases. The final result, as shown in Figure 1, is the national target for emission reductions and payments or transfers to accomplish the reductions.

This type of transfer has been proposed in various forms for various reasons. The authors find that some form of trade or transfer of funding for emission reductions is essential to satisfy all of the negotiating criteria. Any solution that prohibits such transfers implies that each country's share of the cost of emission reductions must equal its share of the reduction opportunities to be exploited. This requirement makes it impossible to achieve both equity and efficiency. To do so, the separation of responsibility from opportunity, and a mechanism for reconciling them through international transfers, is necessary, although certainly not sufficient. A discussion of mechanisms is found in Part V.

As will be seen later in this chapter, many of the indices that can be applied in the four categories shown in Figure 1 contain the structure of "greenhouse gases per unit," where the unit could be nation, population, income, energy use, etc., depending on the intended use. Parts III and IV, below, focus on the justifications and implications of choosing among these various index denominators. Before starting this discussion, however, it is necessary to carefully choose the appropriate numerator, i.e. the index by which the different greenhouse gases are aggregated. This is the task of Part II.

II. Greenhouse Gas Indices

As late as 1983, policy discussions of global warming induced by greenhouse gases focused almost entirely on carbon dioxide, with relatively little discussion of other gases (7 of 496 pages, for example, in National Academy of Sciences (NAS) [1983]). Since then, however, it has become well recognized that the other greenhouse gases play important roles. Indeed, present conventional wisdom is that, in total, these other gases account for about an equal amount of radiative forcing as CO_2, and, consequently, greatly shorten the time until an effective doubling of atmospheric CO_2 content occurs (from 2075 to 2030, for example, in WRI [1990].) Figure 2a duplicates one of the most commonly reproduced illustrations of the current relative contributions of the different gases. (Originally from Hansen et al. [1989], but spread widely by the United States Environmental Protection Agency (USEPA) [1989] and popularized in such places as *The New York Times* [see Passell, 1989].)

Understanding the relative contribution of the different gases is vital to the development of an appropriate index for answering any of the questions listed in Part I. This is because the different gases are produced in different relative amounts by different activities,

Figure 2a:
Estimated Current Contributions of Different Gases to Increased Radiative Forcing

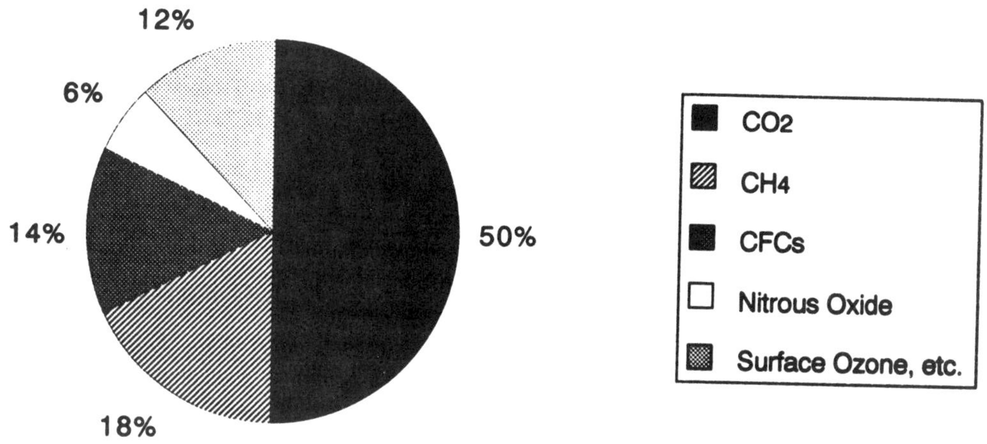

Source: Authors.

Note: Relative global warming potentials of current mix of global greenhouse gas emissions as frequently represented.

Legend: CO_2 = carbon dioxide
CH_4 = methane
CFCs = chlorofluorocarbons

Figure 2b: Activities Contributing to Global Warming

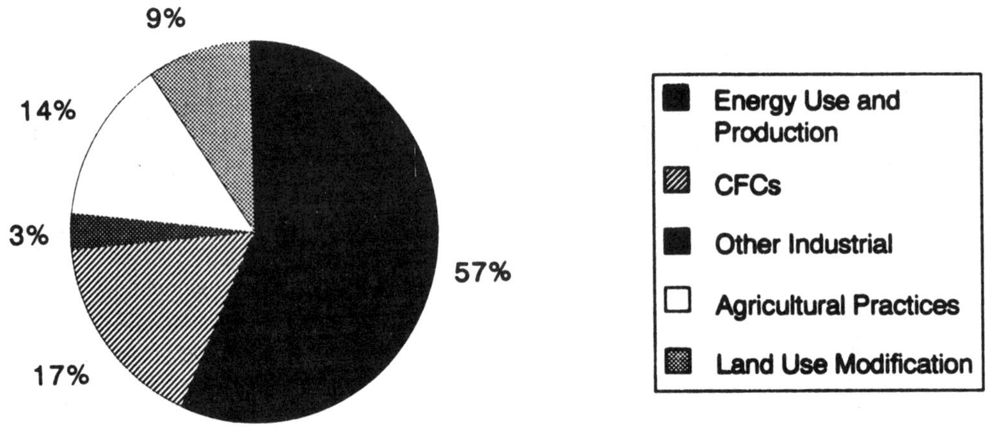

Source: Authors.

Note: Based on Figure 2a, this figure shows the relative contribution of the different gas-producing activities.

Legend: CFCs = chlorofluorocarbons

Figure 2c: Regional Shares of Present Greenhouse Gas Emissions

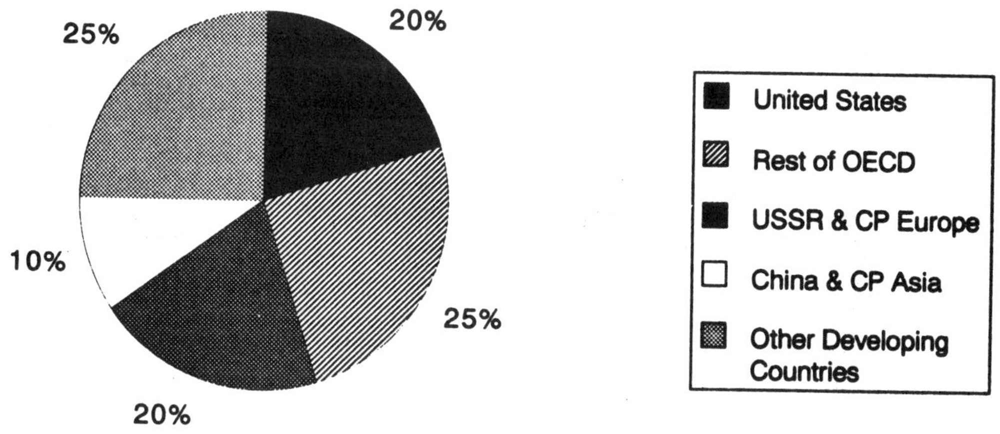

Source: Authors.

Notes: Based on Figure 2b, the relative contributions of different groups of nations.

These are all based on an instantaneous index, which is probably not appropriate for most policy questions.

Legend: OECD = Organization for Economic Cooperation and Development
USSR = Union of Soviet Socialist Republics
CP = centrally planned (economies)

which are in turn undertaken in different degrees by different countries. This can be seen in Figures 2b and 2c, which are commonly reproduced illustrations of the relative importance of different activities and countries implied by the greenhouse gas weightings of Figure 2a.

Agreeing on the relative importance of the gases is a crucial first step in determining national accountabilities and the relative value of different greenhouse-gas reduction projects. Carbon dioxide, for example, is released mainly by fossil fuel use, while methane to a great extent seems to be released by livestock and wetland agriculture. An index that weighted methane more heavily, therefore, would tend to make more attractive those projects addressing emission reductions within these agricultural activities and, conversely, make more accountable those countries that have traditionally engaged in more of such activities, i.e. developing countries. An index weighting CO_2 more heavily, on the other hand, would tend to focus attention on fossil fuel combustion, the bulk of which occurs in developed countries.

Unfortunately, however, until quite recently [Arrhenius and Waltz, 1990; Lashof and Ahuja, 1990; Rodhe, 1990], there has been little effort to carefully choose the indexing system by which the different gases are aggregated so that it is consistent both with physical reality and the needs of policy [Smith and Ahuja, 1990]. In addition, because of the complexity of the problem, there have been some false starts, in which indices were proposed that do not reflect physical reality [e.g., Ellington and Meo, 1990; Hammond et al., 1990]. As a result, much of the discussion of policy alternatives has been biased by indices that give a distorted view of the relative importance of the different gases, activities, and nations.

A. Greenhouse Gas Indices: The Radioactivity Analogy

The release of a GHG results in increased warming because of what is called the "radiative forcing" of the gas molecules in the atmosphere. To quite varying degrees, the different GHG molecules act to make the atmosphere retain additional amounts of reradiated solar energy, thereby leading to warming. Relative to CO_2, for example, a methane molecule in the atmosphere has a radiative forcing about 21 times higher and that for a molecule of CFC-12 is nearly 800 times higher still. Clearly, with such widely ranging radiative forcings, the total weight or number of molecules in a GHG mixture is not a good index of relative importance.

The relative radiative forcings, as shown in the second column of Table 3 for the most important GHGs, are commonly used to index GHGs, for example being the basis by which Figure 2 was created. Used this way, they portray the total and relative radiative forcings of the GHG at any one moment. If all the GHGs acted the same in the atmosphere, e.g., were removed at the same rate, then the relative radiative forcings would also be appropriate measures of their relative total impacts. This, however, is not the case. Two other factors also need to be considered: atmospheric residence times and chemical interactions.

Consider, for analogy, two containers of nuclear waste containing different mixtures of radioactive substances. Just as with GHGs, the total weight would not be a good index of relative hazard, since some substances are much more radioactive than others. The amount of radioactive disintegrations per second measured in curies or becquerels is, in radiation, the

Table 3: Parameters for Important Greenhouse Gases[a]

Trace Gases	Estimated Atmospheric Residence Times	Radiative Forcing Relative to CO_2	Global Warming Potentials: Direct, Integration Time Horizon, years: 20	100	500	Direct + Indirect[c], Integration Time Horizon, years: 20	100	500
1. CO_2	[120][b]	1 [1]	1 [1]	1 [1]	1 [1]	1 [1]	1 [1]	1 [1]
2. CH_4	10	58 [21]	26 [9.5]	6 [2.2]	2 [0.73]	63 [23]	21 [7.6]	9 [3.2]
3. CFC-11	60	4,000 [12,000]	3,700 [11,000]	2,900 [8,600]	2,030 [6,100]	4,500 [13,500]	3,500 [10,500]	1,500 [4,500]
4. CFC-12	130	5,700 [16,000]	5,740 [16,100]	5,900 [16,500]	6,140 [17,200]	7,100 [20,000]	7,300 [20,500]	4,500 [12,600]
5. N_2O	150	210 [210]	213 [213]	225 [225]	260 [260]	270 [280]	290 [300]	190 [200]
			Conversion to CO_2					
1. CH_4	--	<1>[c]	2.8 [1]	2.8 [1]	2.8 [1]	See Above See Above	See Above See Above	See Above See Above
2. CO	--	<1>[c]	1.6 [1]	1.6 [1]	1.6 [1]	7 [4.5]	3 [1.9]	2 [1.3]
3. NO_x	--	--	--	--	--	150 [130]	40 [35]	14 [12]
4. NMHC	--	<1>[c]	2.6 [1]	2.6 [1]	2.6 [1]	31 [12]	11 [4.1]	6 [2.3]

Source: Shine et al. [1990].

Notes: [a] Estimated lifetimes (years), radiative forcings relative to CO_2, and direct and indirect Global Warming Potential Indices for three time periods. Numbers refer to ratios by weight; numbers in brackets refer to ratios by molecule (or carbon atom for NMHC)

[b] The duration of an increase in CO_2 in the atmosphere is described only approximately by a single exponential decay (1/e) time of 120 years. The integrated value (infinite integration time) results in a period equivalent to about 320 years. See Siegenthaler [1983].

[c] Their atmospheric chemical interactions related to tropospheric ozone (O_3) and stratospheric water (H_2O) are taken into account here.

Legend: NMHC = non-methane hydrocarbon
CO_2 = carbon dioxide
CH_4 = methane
CFC-11 = chlorofluorocarbon-11
CFC-12 = chlorofluorocarbon-12
CO = carbon oxide
NO_x = nitrogen oxide
N_2O = nitrous oxide
-- = information not available

rough equivalent to radiative forcing as an index to compare the immediate relative hazard of radioactive mixtures.

To compare the total or long-term hazard of such nuclear waste mixtures also requires knowledge about the half-lives of the different radioactive substances and whether they may change into still other radioactive substances (daughter products) as they decay [Morgan et al., 1964]. One mixture could have a high initial radioactivity but be composed mainly of iodine-131, which has a half-life of 8 days. The other, however, might contain significant amounts of cesium-137 and plutonium-238, which decay with half lives of 30 and 24,000 years, respectively. Clearly the total hazard would not be well represented by radioactivity alone, which ignores that the iodine-131 would be essentially gone in a few months while the others would be nearly unchanged.

The same is true with GHGs. Some are removed from the atmosphere in a few years, while others take hundreds of years. Thus, to compare different GHG mixtures, e.g., those emitted from different countries, it is important to consider the atmospheric lifetimes (or half-lives). These are listed in column 1 of Table 3.

Figure 3 shows that the relative importance of different GHGs can change dramatically over time. Here, the curves start from the relative radiative forcings of current global CO_2 and methane concentrations (above pre-human background), shown on the vertical axis where t = 0. This is the instantaneous index, i.e. one not considering lifetimes, where total methane is about 40% as important as CO_2 (as in Figure 2). This is based solely on radiative forcing at the moment of release. The downward sloping curves after this point represent the change in relative radiative forcing that occurs as the GHGs are removed from the atmosphere over time. Because methane has such a short lifetime compared to CO_2, its relative importance decreases quickly. After 20 years, the methane released at the beginning of the period has become less than 10% as important as the CO_2. After 100 years, less than one in ten-thousand of the methane molecules is left, while about half the CO_2 remains. From most perspectives, the relative impact of current atmospheric methane concentrations is much less than the 40% indicated by an instantaneous index.

It is not exactly true to say that an instantaneous index is wrong, for it does represent a systematic means to compare mixtures, albeit with a peculiar time horizon. It is hard to think of a policy question that such an index is suitable for addressing, however. Societal concern about GHGs clearly extends beyond the immediate year that emissions occurred and an index should be chosen accordingly.

1. Time Horizons

There are various forms that the time horizon could take:

(i) ***Index years***. As shown in Figure 4, present GHG mixtures could be weighted on the basis of their relative impact on radiative forcing in a particular future year, e.g., in 2050.

(ii) ***Index periods***. Instead of a particular year, a particular period could be chosen, e.g., the relative forcing in the 50th year after release.

Figure 3: Relative Decay of Carbon Dioxide and Methane

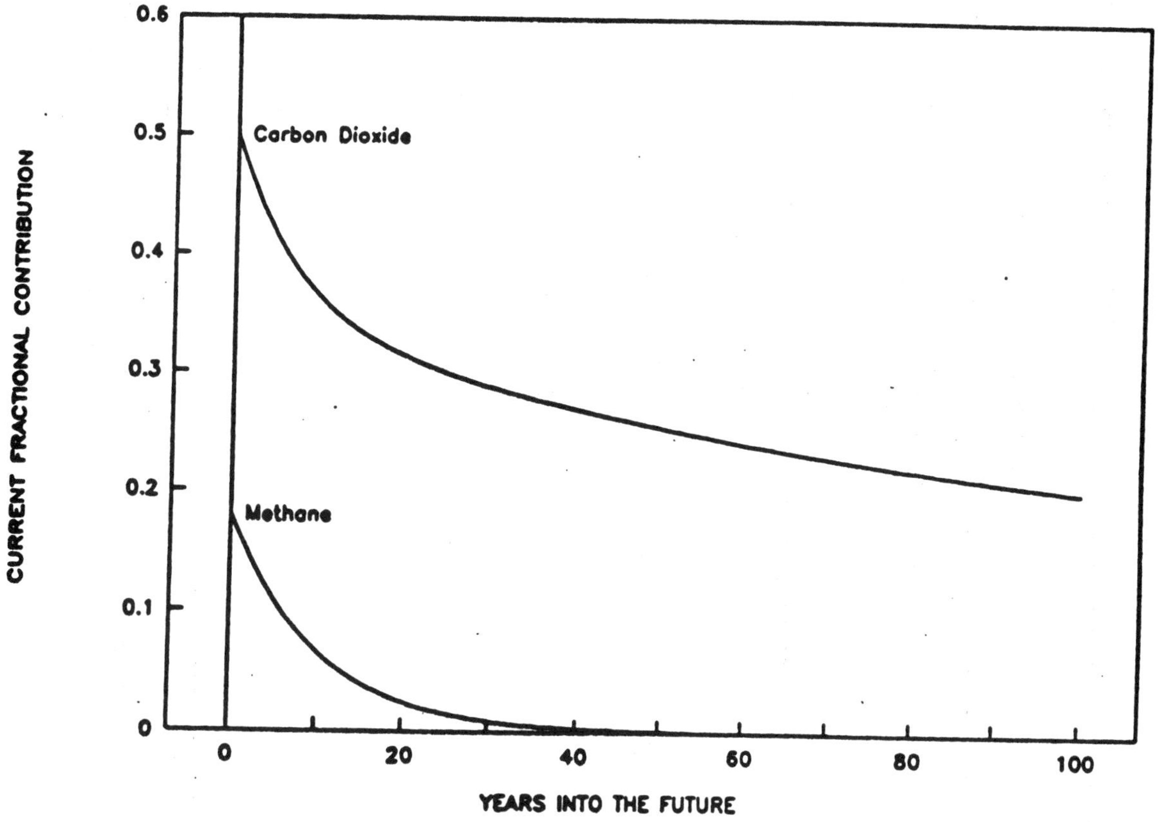

Source: Authors.

Note: Taking the starting values equal to those in Figure 2a, this figure shows how quickly methane (CH_4) is removed from the atmosphere compared to carbon dioxide (CO_2). It illustrates that a comparison at any year other than zero (instantaneous) would show methane to be substantially less important than is indicated by the initial 50:18 ratio.

Figure 4: Comparison of Four Time Horizons for Indexing Greenhouse Gases

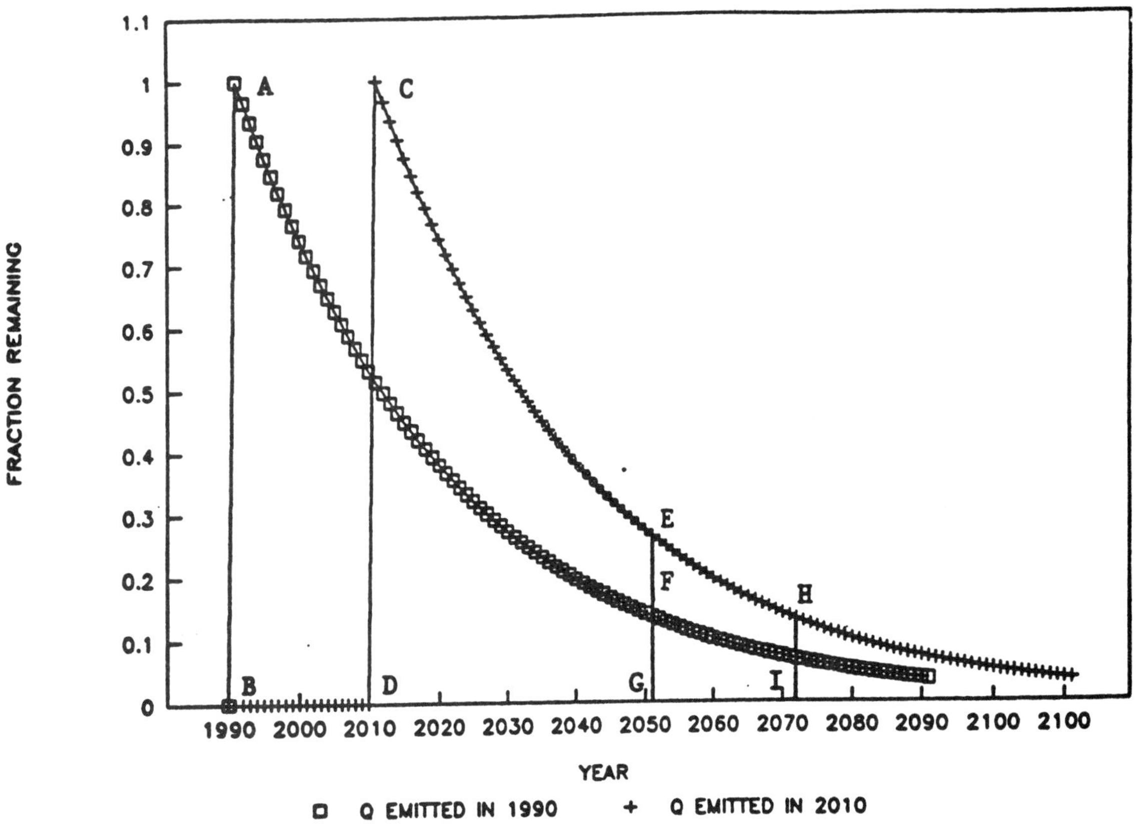

Source: Authors.

Note: Using a hypothetical gas with a residence time of 30 years, this figure illustrates four ways in which time horizons might be applied to emissions from two sample years, 1990 and 2010:

(i) ***Index year***, where the impact is taken as the amount of warming left at a certain year, i.e. if the index year were 2050, 1990 emissions would be indexed as the distance FG and 2010 emissions as EG.

(ii) ***Index period***, where the impact is taken at a specific future year, i.e. if the period were 60 years, 1990 emissions would again be weighted as FG, but 2010 emissions would be weighted as the distance HI.

(iii) ***Year cutoff***, where the ***area*** under the curve up to a particular year is used as an index, i.e. for 2050, the area under the 1990 curve between AB and FG, and the area under the 2010 curve between CD and EG.

(iv) ***Period cutoff***, where the area under the curve is taken for a fixed period after emissions, i.e. for 60 years, again the area under the 1990 curve between AB and FG, but under the 2010 curve between CD and HI.

Please note that there will be little difference among these options when one pollutant is overwhelmingly dominant. The last index is the one chosen for use here.

(iii) ***Year cutoffs***. Mixtures could be weighted according to the total radiative forcing from the date of emissions through to the year of cut off, e.g.,2050. This is represented by the entire area under the curves to the left of the chosen year in Figure 4.

(iv) ***Period cutoffs***. Instead of a particular year, a particular period could be chosen, e.g.,the integrated radiative forcing for 50 years beyond the year of emissions.

(v) ***Discounting***. Radiative forcings in future years could be weighted according to how distant they are from the present, as is standard in economics for comparing monetary flows over time. As shown in Figure 5, at a 5% discount rate, radiative forcings next year would only count about 95% as heavily as those this year. The radiative forcing due to this year's emissions in the 20th year would count less than 40% as much. (A 5% discount rate for CO_2 is roughly equivalent to an 18.6-year time horizon.) The discount factor is applied in addition to the decay factor due to GHG removal from the atmosphere over time.[4]

2. Focus on Period Cutoffs

Although there are arguments for other choices, the authors focus on period cutoffs in this chapter, which is consistent with the report of the Intergovernmental Panel on Climate Change (IPCC) [1990]. The relative global warming potential (GWP) of the important gases are shown for several time horizons in Table 3. Except for CO_2, the gases have atmospheric lifetimes less than 150 years and, thus, the longest period shown, 500 years, gives nearly the same value as would complete integration (an infinite time horizon). Because some proportion of CO_2 releases is thought to have a rather long residence time (at least 800 years), however, a 500-year time horizon may only account for something like half of what would be indicated by a complete integration (Seigenthaler 1983; Lashof and Ahuja, 1990).

In addition to radiative forcing and lifetime, chemical reactions create additional complications in constructing accurate indexing schemes. Several types of chemical interactions are important:

(i) Some GHGs and non-GHGs change into other GHGs, as methane (a GHG) and carbon monoxide (a non-GHG) change eventually into CO_2. (A rough analog to radioactive daughter products.)

(ii) Some non-GHGs act to increase the lifetime of GHGs, as carbon monoxide does for methane, giving them a GHG equivalence even though not being GHGs themselves.

(iii) Some GHGs as well as non-GHGs affect the creation of tropospheric (lower atmosphere) ozone, a powerful GHG.

---

[4]Although discount rates are usually taken to be positive, i.e. impacts far in the future are weighted less than those near the present, there are occasions when negative discount rates seem to apply, i.e. when happenings in the future are weighted more heavily than those in the present.

Figure 5: Effect of Discounting on Carbon Dioxide (CO_2) Decay

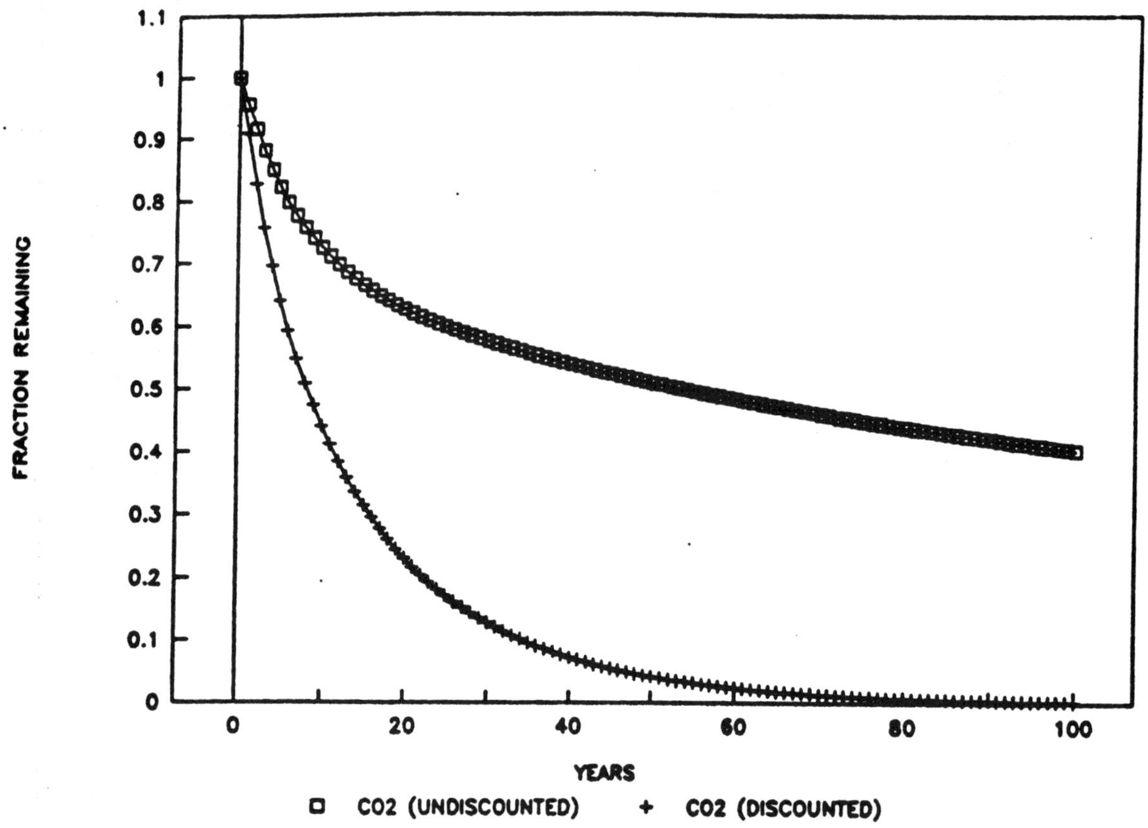

Source: Authors.

Note: This figure shows the relative area under the undiscounted and discounted decay curves of carbon dioxide (CO_2) concentration in the atmosphere. At a 5% discount rate, the ratios of the two areas are 1.5 at 20 years, 3.8 at 100 years, and 11.4 at 500 years. The ratio at infinite integration is about 22.6, but the ratio only reaches 22 at a time horizon of about 3000 years.

This is not the place to discuss these interactions in detail, partly because knowledge is still rapidly developing. For the purposes of this chapter current estimates of these important indirect effects are listed in Table 3, again by cutoff period.

The indirect effects are known with much less confidence than lifetimes, which, in turn, are less well understood than radiative forcing. In addition, local conditions have the largest influence on indirect effects, intermediate on lifetimes, and least on radiative forcing. Also, to a much greater extent than radiative forcing, which can simply be added together, indirect effects also depend in detail on the actual concentration trends of individual gases [Penner et al., 1989]. Consequently, as more research is done, the magnitude of changes in estimates of these parameters can be expected to be roughly according to these relative uncertainties.

B. A Two-Nation, Two-Pollutant Model

To illustrate the importance of time horizon, the two-nation model presented in Part I can be upgraded to two pollutants: CO_2 and methane. United States and Indian emissions for 1987 are shown in Table 4. Note that, by the instantaneous index (time horizon = 0), the United States produces only 3.0 times as much GHG as India when methane (CH_4) is included. This is clearly much less of a responsibility than the factor of 7.9 for CO_2 alone. Thus, it is not surprising that United States negotiators tend to argue for including gases such as methane that are produced in relatively greater amounts by developing countries [Stewart and Weiner, 1990].

On the other hand, on a 500-year basis, the ratio rises to 5.7 or 6.7 (depending on whether indirect effects are included), effectively doubling relative United States responsibility. A completely integrated index (an infinite time horizon) would result in a ratio of 7.3. Note also that inclusion of indirect effects tends to penalize nations such as India with relatively high methane production, i.e. the United States/India ratio decreases. Thus, negotiators for the United States could be expected to argue for the inclusion of indirect effects, for shorter rather than longer time horizons, and, perhaps, for applying a discount rate as well.

Figure 6 provides further evidence of the sensitivity to choice of time horizon. It compares the impact of time horizon on the ratio between the 1987 emissions of the United States and India compared to the ratio between the United States and the Federal Republic of Germany. Note that with an instantaneous index, the ratios are quite different, but that with a time horizon of about 565 years, the two match, i.e. emissions of the United States are 6.9 times either those of Germany and India, which, therefore, have equal weightings. At an infinite time horizon, however, the two are different again.

C. Which Time Horizon?

Before proceeding to discussions of indices for accountability and action, it remains to choose the time horizon to use in this chapter. As with nuclear waste, there is no unassailably objective way to choose the appropriate time horizon for GHGs. It is not just a technical question, but one also related to social and moral values and conventions as well

Table 4: Greenhouse Gas Indices According to Time Horizon for India and the United States[a]

	1987 Emissions			Total CO_2 Equivalents By Time Horizon (years)			
	Million tons C as CO_2	Million tons C as CH_4	0 (10^6 tons)	20 (10^9 ton-y)	100 (10^9 ton-y)	500 (10^9 ton-y)	Infinite (10^9 ton-y)
United States	1200	32	1900	29 [24]	79 [73]	210 [200]	[400]
India	150	23	630	10 [6.5]	18 [13]	37 [30]	[54]
Ratio United States/ India	7.9	1.4	3	2.9 [3.7]	4.4 [5.6]	5.7 [6.9]	[7.3]

Source: Authors. Based on coefficients in Table 3 and current emissions in WRI [1990], Table 24.1.

Notes: [a] Direct plus indirect warming.

Note that including methane and using short time horizons tend to make the United States contributions seem relatively smaller, i.e. the ratio goes down.
CO_2 emissions are from fossil fuels and cement production only.
Numbers in brackets refer to direct warming only (no indirect effects). See Table 3.

Legend: CO_2 = carbon dioxide
C = carbon
CH_4 = methane
ton-y = tons per year

Figure 6: Effect of Time Horizon on Relative National Emissions

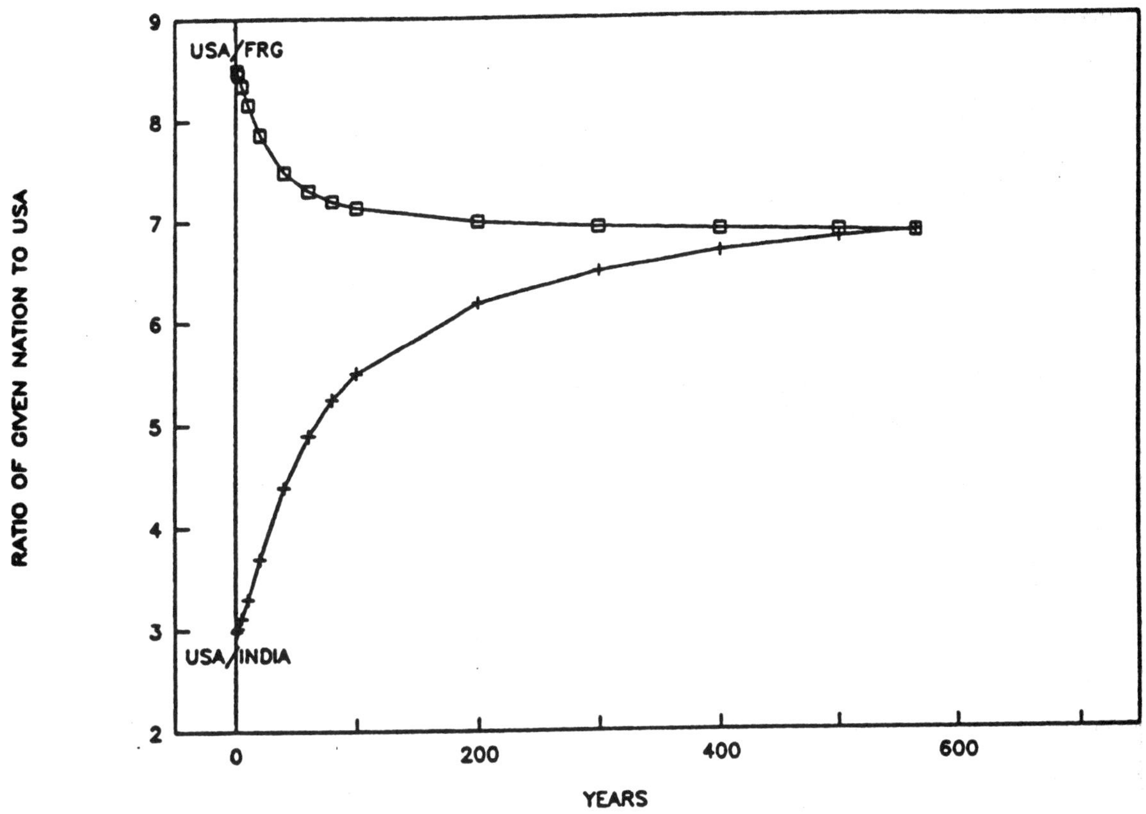

Source: Authors.

Note: This figure shows the sensitivity of Global Warming Potential to time horizon. The lower curve plots the points listed in Table 4, i.e. the United States (USA)/India ratio for 1987 emissions of carbon dioxide (CO_2) and methane (CH_4). The upper curve plots the same kind of data for the United States/Federal Republic of Germany (FRG) ratio. Note that, compared to the United States, a longer time horizon tends to make India ***less*** accountable while making the Federal Republic of Germany ***more*** accountable. Note also that, relative to the United States, an instantaneous index (time horizon of 0) shows India much more accountable than the Federal Republic of Germany (a ratio of 3.0 compared to 8.5), but at a time horizon of 565 years, the two ratios cross at about 6.9. Not shown are the ratios beyond 565 years.

as to the particular policy issue being addressed. Because the principal interest in this chapter is index denominators (Parts III-IV), only one time horizon, 100 years, has been looked at as a reasonable representation of the period over which most of the policy debate seems to have centered. (For CO_2, this is roughly equivalent to a discount rate of 0.84%.) This can be justified on the basis that society clearly has concerns extending beyond a few years and yet is not likely to feel obligated to make large sacrifices to protect generations hundreds of years into the future, the capacities and needs of which are so uncertain today. Intermediate time horizons thus seem most logical, but there is nothing sacred about the precise figure of 100 years.

A larger study would also examine the implications of choosing a range of time horizon forms and magnitudes. In addition, as pointed out by the IPCC [1990], each type of potential impact from global warming has its own time scale. General warming might be most appropriately indicated by a 500-year horizon, sea-level rise by 100 years, and rates of temperature change by 20 years, for illustration. Thus, gases that have different atmospheric residence times will tend to have a different pattern of influence on the impacts of concern.

D. Past, Current, and Future Emissions

The discussion above focused on GHG releases from a single year. Often, however, emissions over a number of years will need to be considered. Figure 7 shows how the individual contributions from single years combine together in what look to be a pile of annual "warming worms." Although each warming worm has a 100-year cutoff, the cumulation has no cutoff. At any year, the total radiative forcing is due to the total contribution remaining that year from each of the past 100 warming worms. Between now and any point in the future, the total radiative impact is the area under all the warming worms from now until that year.

With a 100-year period time horizons, past emissions are composed of two segments:

(i) With a 100-year horizon, no present effect is attributed to emissions previous to 100 years ago.

(ii) For emissions during the last 100 years, the radiative forcing impact could be indexed in three ways:

(a) That expressed to date,

(b) That committed out to 100 years after the original emissions, but not yet expressed, or

(c) The total of (a) and (b).

These periods are illustrated in Figure 8. There is not enough space to compare the results of using these different indices, and therefore (c) has been relied on in the Natural Debt

Figure 7: Incremental Warming from Annual Emissions

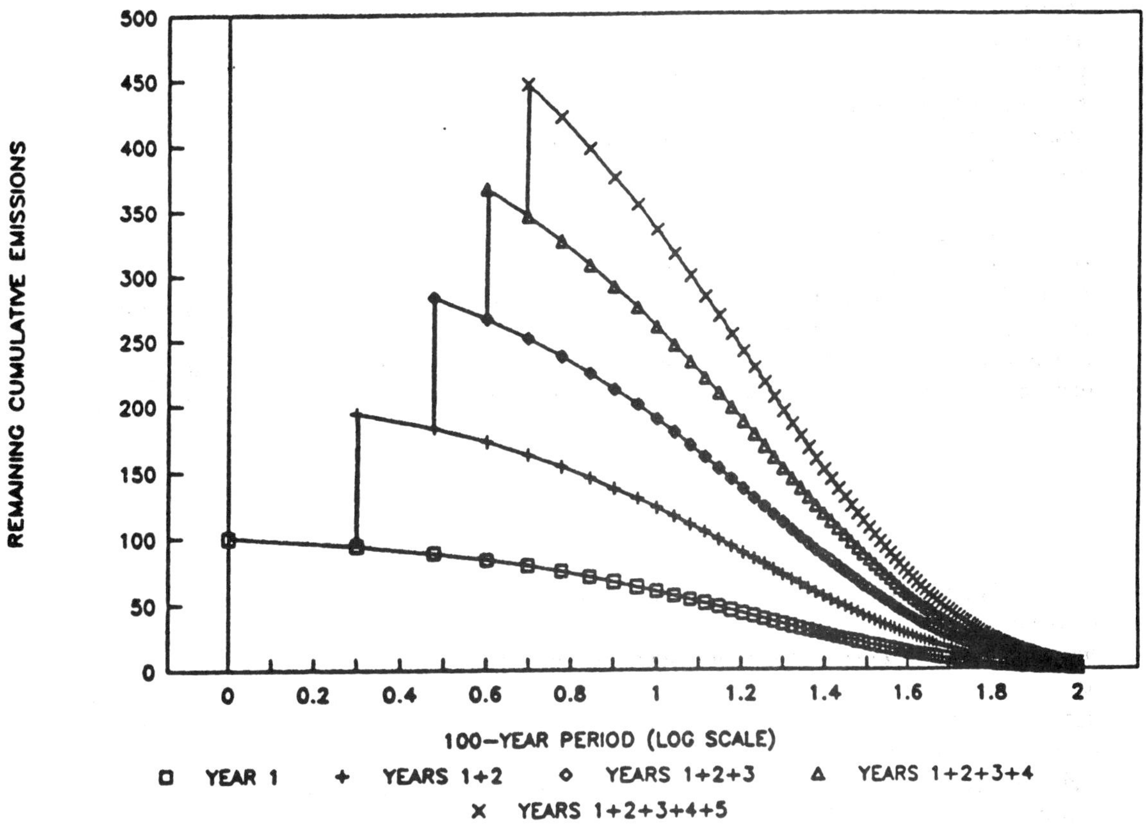

Source: Authors.

Note: This figure illustrates the interaction of the incremental warming added year by year (for 5 years only). The area within each year's warming increment represents the total contribution of that year to global warming, here set to 100. The warming in any particular year is the total of the remaining warming from all of the previous years. Note the log scale on the horizontal axis, which is needed to fit the curves onto one legible graph.

Figure 8: Alternatives for Indexing Past Emissions

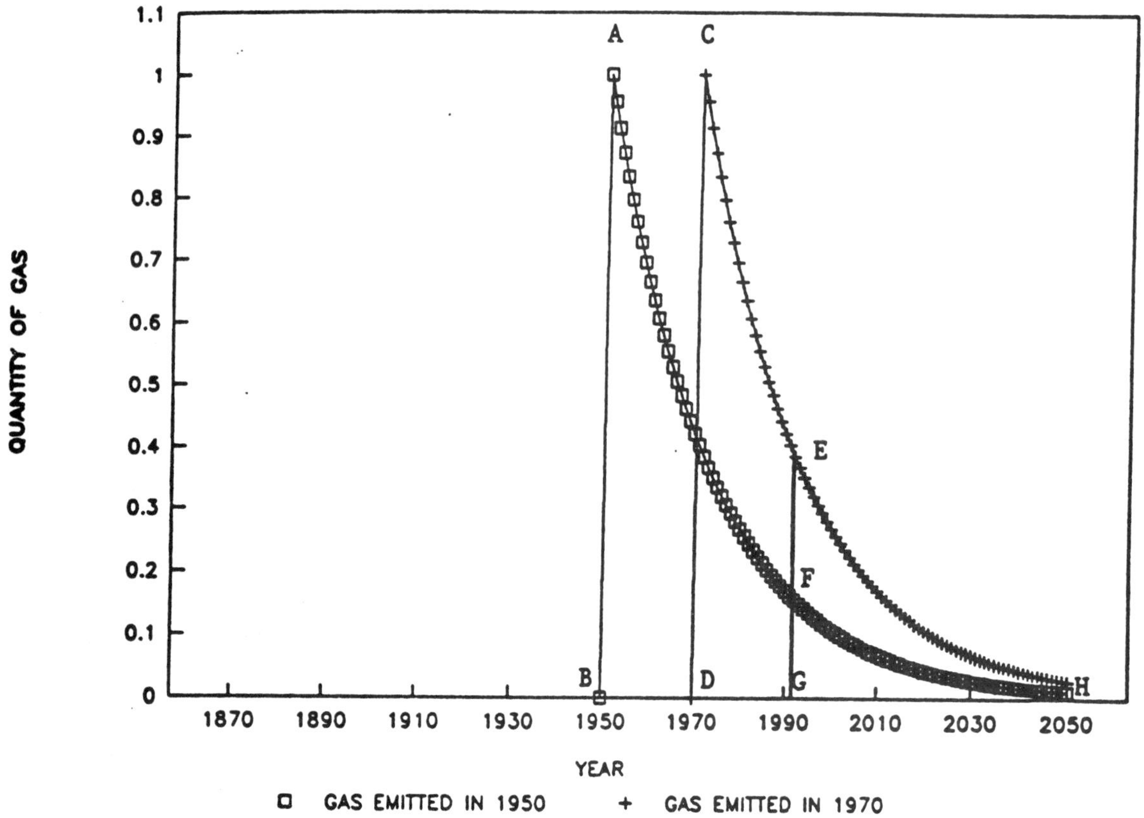

Source: Authors.

Note: With a 100-year time horizon, emissions previous to 1890 are no longer considered to be affecting present decisions. Emissions in the last 100 years can be counted in three ways as illustrated in the figure, which shows emissions from two sample years, 1950 and 1970. The choices are:

(i) Count only the warming up to the present, i.e. the area under the 1950 curve between AB and FG, and the area under the 1970 curve between CD and EG.

(ii) Count only the warming under the curves in the future, i.e. under the 1950 curve between EG and H and under the 1970 curve from FG to 2050 (not shown).

(iii) The sum of (i) and (ii).

Here option (iii) has been adopted.

calculations, which seems most consistent with the choice for present and future emissions, i.e. period cutoffs.[5] (See Appendix Table B-1.)

E. Data Limitations

Although emissions databases are being improved, there are still important gaps. Since the purpose is mainly to explore the implications of various indices for addressing the issues organized in Figure 1, it has not been attempted to expand upon the available emissions data bases. The authors wish, however, to make clear what is included and what is not.

1. Non-CO_2 GHGs

There seem to be few reliable historical data for non-CO_2 GHG emissions. As a result, these gases are not included in indices involving cumulations of past emissions. Current emissions of methane and chlorofluorocarbons were based on the compilations of the World Resources Institute [1990].[6] Although there are global estimates, it was not attempted to derive national emissions of other greenhouse-related gases, such as carbon monoxide (CO) and nitrogen oxides (NOX). The inclusion of these gases, which are already regulated in many countries to prevent ill-health, would greatly complicate international negotiations.

2. CO_2

CO_2 emission sources are divided into two principal categories: ***industrial*** and ***biogenic***. Industrial emissions, which are relatively well characterized, largely derive from the fuel cycles of coal, oil, and natural gas. The Oak Ridge Database [Marland et al., 1989] provided for historical fossil fuel CO_2 emissions back to 1950 since access was not available to a longer time series [see, however, Subat, 1990].

Biogenic emissions result basically from land use changes, such as deforestation, that cause a net decrease in the standing stock of carbon in vegetation and soil [Houghton et al., 1987]. Biogenic emissions in Parts III and IV have not been incorporated because they are

---

[5]Alternative GHG-emitting actions will also have different temporal patterns, e.g., cutting down a forest will result in CO_2 emissions immediately from material burned on site, on an intermediate scale, e.g., loss of coil carbon, and over the long term, e.g., decay of lumber made from the trees. Thus, some method will also have to be developed to compare emissions committed but not yet expressed by actions today.

[6]The World Resources Institute "Greenhouse Index" used in their report [WRI, 1990; Hammond et al., 1990] is not used, however, because it fails to explicitly consider GHG lifetimes, chemical interactions, past GHG cumulations, or national population sizes and has the perverse characteristic of giving lower levels of national responsibilities, the higher the current GHG concentration becomes in the atmosphere. Unfortunately, due to the widespread distribution of this report, the already turbid GG waters have been additionally muddied [Smith et al., 1991], a point noted by other observers as well [Pachauri, 1990; United States Agency for International Development (USAID), 1990]. The result is a distortion of relative national contributions in the WRI report, at least for most policy questions of interest.

not adequately understood both because of gaps in the present and historical data, and also because of tricky conceptual issues having to do with defining a baseline and determining the difference between gross and net emissions (CO_2 can be taken up by land areas that are not apparently undergoing changes in use).

With more time, estimates for historical emissions of methane, CFCs, carbon monoxide (CO), and, possibly, other GHGs could be made using existing international data, as could estimates of fossil fuel CO_2 emissions prior to 1950. It will not be so simple to sort out the problems in estimating biogenic emissions.

3. Nations

For ease in illustrating the issues, it was chosen to limit discussion only to the 62 countries that had at least 10 million people in 1986. These contain substantially more than 90% of the world's population.

In summary, Table 5 shows the rather limited set of data which was chosen to be used here to illustrate issues related to indexing. With these choices among the various ways to index greenhouse gases and to deal with data gaps, the first set of questions in Figure 1 [(i) Who should pay? (ii) Who can pay?] is now addressed.

III. Who Pays (To Solve the Problem) and How Much?

Given complete information on historic emissions of all greenhouse gases and their transformations in the atmosphere, one could calculate the contribution of each country to increases in the current concentrations from emissions of greenhouse gases since pre-industrial times, and require that remedial action by each country be proportional to that contribution. This follows the familiar "polluter pays" principle where responsibility for clean-up lies with those who caused the problem. Yet, simple as it may seem, this approach to solving the greenhouse issue is unworkable for several reasons.

- The approach as stated does not consider the populations of countries.
- Data on emissions of most gases become unreliable the farther back in time one goes. Country-specific data on many non-CO_2, non-CFC greenhouse gases are not known even for recent years.
- Shifting political boundaries and dominion of one country over another makes problematic any assignments before 1950, even for gases such as CO_2 for which data may be available.
- Though one may be able to calculate historic responsibilities, a country's current ability to allocate resources for the problem's amelioration may be limited or vice versa, i.e. past emissions may be low where current wealth is high.

For these reasons, the question of responsibility is separated from the resources a country has to help solve the global climate problem. As discussed in Part II, the calculation of

Table 5: Data Sources Tapped for Constructing Greenhouse Gas Indices in This Chapter

Emissions	Non-CO_2 Gases	CO_2	
		Industrial	Biotic
Cumulative (Part III)	None	Yes[a]	No
	CH_4[b]		
Current (Part IV)	CFC-11[b] CFC-12[b]	Yes[c]	Yes[d]

Sources: Authors.

Notes: [a] 1950-1986 emissions [Marland et al., 1988].
[b] WRI [1990].
[c] Mean 1980-1986 annual emissions [Marland et al., 1988].
[d] Houghton et al. [1987].

Legend: CO_2 = carbon dioxide
CH_4 = methane
CFC-11 = chlorofluorocarbon-11
CFC-12 = chlorofluorocarbon-12

responsibility to CO_2 emissions from fossil fuels (and cement) is limited to after 1950, although recognizing that further efforts could push the year backward [Subak, 1990] and bring more gases into consideration.

A. Indices of Responsibility and Ability to Pay: A Brief Review

Several investigators in the last two years have attempted to allocate the global carbon budget based on exogenous considerations of the maximum acceptable warming or its rate of increase [Solomon and Ahuja, 1990].

Dividing emissions rights equally among countries, coupled with the ability to sell or lease those rights, is the simplest scheme. Yet it is fraught with inequities because it does not link emissions to human beings or activities. Thus it has few, if any, proponents.

The second easy basis for allocating rights is land area [Westing, 1989]. Since 1950, national boundaries have not changed much. Its stability as a measure, the ease of measurement, the avoidance of monitoring and verification difficulties are what recommend it. (It is quite difficult to cheat.) There was a time, according to Grubb [1989], when the United States was arguing informally in international fora that its continental land mass necessitated enormous energy expenditures in having to move goods and people. Ultimately, with the possible exceptions of those countries with large wastelands (e.g., Mongolia), land area is a measure of natural resources. Using it as an index to allocate emission rights, however, favors large but sparsely populated nations (e.g., Australia) and discriminates against small densely populated nations (e.g., Japan).

The third suggestion requires cuts, say 20%, of each country's emissions regardless of cost or the efficiency with which the emissions are "used," i.e. result from benefit producing activities. It is similar to the approach followed in the Montreal Protocol where the original signatory nations agreed to cut production of selected compounds by 50% by a specified time. By "grandfathering" currently inefficient emissions, this scheme penalizes those countries, like Japan, that have been able to develop economies that already emit less per unit of economic output [Study Group on Policy Options for Moderating Global Warming, 1990].

Most important, equal reductions based on current emissions would be clearly unacceptable to developing countries as it would not allow the growth required to meet development needs.

If it is accepted that every person has an equal right to atmospheric resources, the ultimate global commons, then the most obvious and equitable basis is to distribute emissions permits in proportion to national populations [Princeton University, 1988]. If rights in subsequent years continue to be proportional to contemporaneous populations, this may be an incentive for population growth. For this reason, and to make his scheme more palatable to industrialized countries, Grubb [1989] has suggested that allocations be based on adult populations. This would have the effect of reducing net transfers from countries with rectangular age distributions to developing countries with pyramidal age structures, but could be seen as discrimination against children. Depending on the definition of "adult," it would provide a 15-21 year delay between births and receiving the allotment, and thus reduce the pro-natalist incentive.

An alternate incentive for population stabilization could be built into the scheme by pegging the allotment to the entire population in a recent year and not increase future allotments. Compared to an index based on adult population, this would seem to represent less discrimination against children in the first years of an international protocol and no more discrimination in later years.

In this chapter, it has been argued that repayments to natural debt should be proportional to the amounts borrowed [see also Smith, 1990a]. Thus the appropriate index for establishing responsibility is the one that measures historic emissions integrated over time divided by population integrated over time (see below Section D). Grubb [1989] objects to this scheme on the grounds of ***impracticality*** (i.e. industrial countries would not agree) and ***ignorance*** (countries in the past were unaware that they were depleting a finite resource).

Arguing in a similar vein to Grubb that any index based on per capita emissions alone would require unacceptably huge reductions in industrial countries (up to 75%) or entail massive transfer payments to developing countries, Wirth and Lashof [1990] have proposed apportionment on per capita and per gross domestic product (GDP) bases of 50 percent each, i.e.

$$0.5\ (\text{emissions/population}) + 0.5\ (\text{emissions/GDP})$$

with all the quantities being for the current or a recent year.

Solomon and Ahuja [1990] have proposed a similar index that is directly proportional to emissions and inversely proportional to both GDP and population, the ratio being integrated over time. It is not clear, however, if GDP should find a place in an index for responsibility since countries would have already benefitted from that economic activity.

B. Responsibility vs. Ability to Pay

As there are several concerns that need to be addressed in any allocation scheme, the primacy given to such criteria as simplicity, equity, efficiency, the perceived ease of reaching agreements, etc., leads to different indices for allocating carbon budgets. Yet, it seems preferable, and perhaps easier to obtain agreements as well, if the indices for different objectives are kept separate (and reconciled later in the process) than to assert that they are measures of something that they do not measure. This is the course that is explored here.

C. Ability To Pay

In spite of its well known difficulties, gross national product (GNP) is accepted widely as an index of national economic resources. With a few modifications, to account for a country's debt situation, a country's GNP is used to determine its contribution to the UN system, for example. As explained in Appendix A, with certain modifications, the international fund set up under the Montreal Protocol also relies on the UN scale to calculate a country's contribution to be used for technology transfer and financial assistance to signatory developing countries to use safer substitutes for CFCs.

There are a few methodological problems with international comparisons of GNP statistics, arising from the presence of large informal sectors in some economies, the vagaries of fluctuating exchange rates, and the differences in purchasing power. To some degree, adjustments can be made to correct for these problems, for example in the development of Purchasing Power Parity (PPP) statistics [Summers and Heston, 1988].

There is one drawback to using GNP, even if corrected for purchasing power, as an index of payments into a fund for the mitigation of the climate change problem. This is that no allowance is made for "disposable national income," so that poor countries like Indonesia and rich ones like Sweden would be expected to make similar contributions because their population ratio happens to be approximately equal to the inverse of their ratio of per capita GNP. To determine a country's ability to pay (ATP), it seems obvious that some measure of wealth based on per capita income is required.

One way to define an ability to pay would be to subtract from the GNP, some threshold of "basic need." In the case of the global fund set up under the amendments to the Montreal Protocol, countries that emit less than 300 grams of CFCs/person-year are exempted from contributing. The cut-off defines who will and who will not be contributors to an international fund. One such cut-off that could be used, for example, would be one of the "poverty line" estimates discussed in the 1990 *World Development Report* [World Bank, 1990].

One argument for using such a cut-off is that countries below this level require all the resources they have to bring their populations up to a minimum acceptable income. A rationale related directly to climate change is that countries below this limit are more vulnerable to the effects of adverse climate change and should devote most of their resources to reduce this vulnerability.

Many would argue, however, that the poverty line is not a sufficiently high goal, and yet it is difficult to define some other income level as an acceptable minimum. Here, the authors take the somewhat different approach of choosing an income that seems to be capable of achieving a minimum "quality of life" based on the past ability of countries to achieve adequate levels of infant mortality, life expectancy, and literacy. These are combined in the Physical Quality of Life Index (PQLI) developed by Morris [1979].

The 1986 per capita income ($1800) which is the average income of nations with a Physical Quality of Life Index of 80-90 is used here as a cut-off. This represents the approximate inflection point in the relationship of PQLI and GNP (see Figure 9a). Below this point, small changes in income often lead to large increases in PQLI, while above it, large increases in GNP only produce modest increases in PQLI.

Thus, a country's ability to pay can be defined as being:

$$\text{ATP} = \text{GNP} - [\text{population} \times (\text{GNP/capita})_{\text{threshold PQLI}}]$$

See Appendix Table B-2, which shows this index calculated both with GNP and with GNP corrected for Purchasing Power Parity (PPP). In the latter case, the cutoff in 1980 was $3400 (see Figure 9b). The table shows that the United States ATP changes by only 10% (36.7% to 40.3%) if GNP is changed to PPP, but that other countries' ATPs can change dramatically. The ATP of the Union of Soviet Socialist Republics, for example, changes from 18% to 12% (of the world total), while that of Mexico increases by a factor of 18 and Romania goes down by almost a factor of five.

Figure 9a: Per Capita Gross National Product and Physical Quality of Life Index (1986)

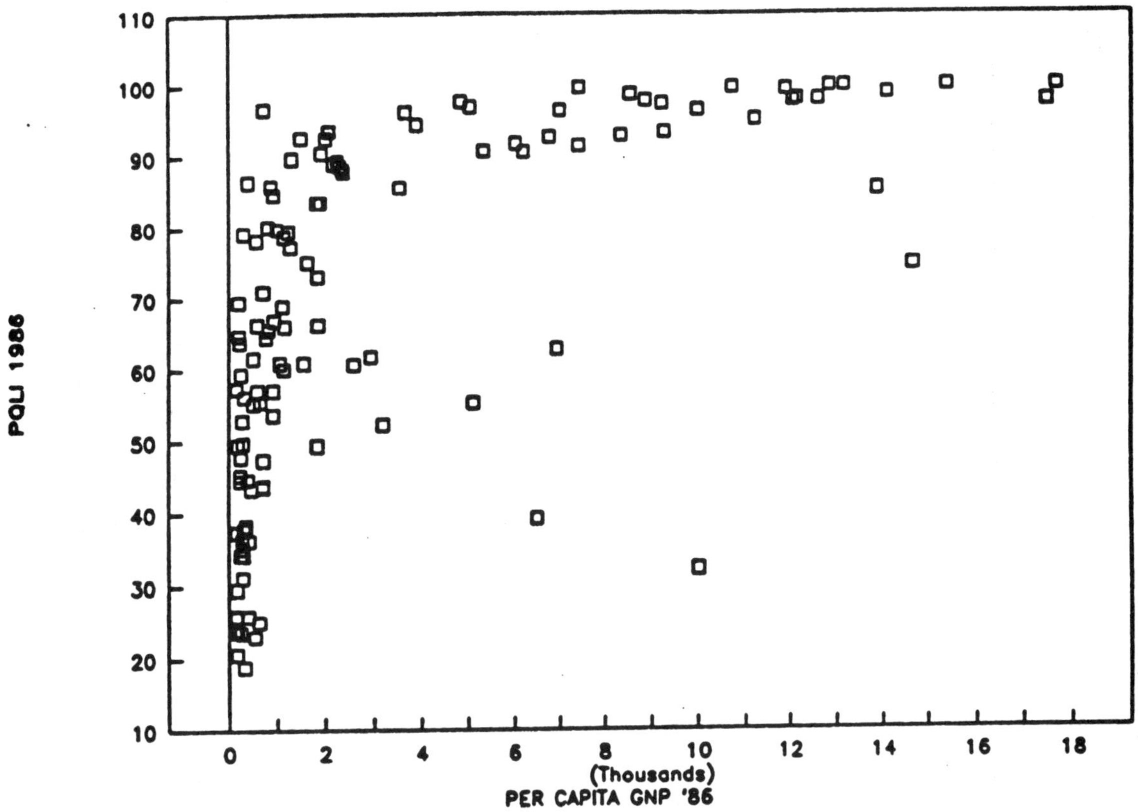

Source: Authors.

Note: Figures 9a and 9b show the international relationship of Physical Quality of Life Index (PQLI) and per capita income using (a) 1986 gross national product (GNP), and (b) 1980 gross domestic product (GDP) adjusted for purchasing power parity (PPP). Discernible in both, but more striking in (a), is the inflection point at a PQLI of approximately 90. Compared to nations above that level, a unit of additional income in nations below 90 generally results in a significantly larger increase in PQLI.

Figure 9b: Physical Quality of Life Index and Per Capita Gross Domestic Product (1980) Adjusted for Purchasing Power Parity

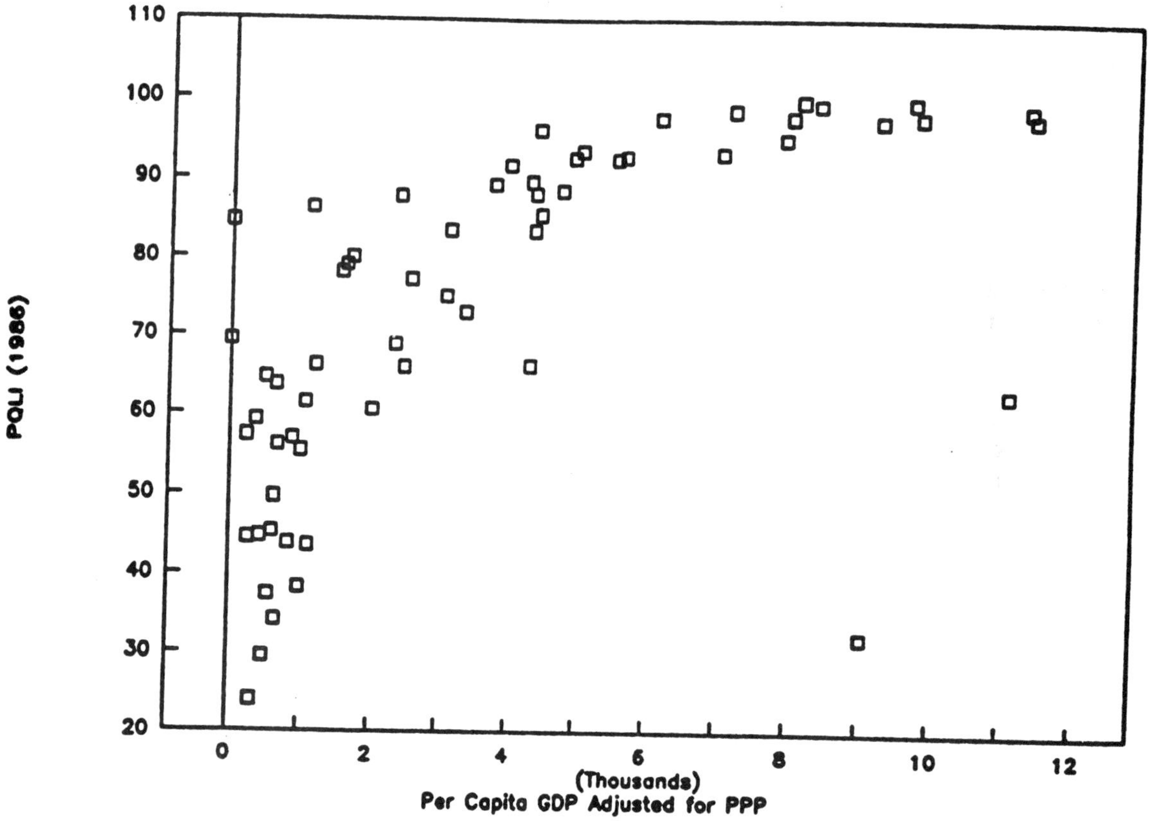

Source: Authors.

Note: Figures 9a and 9b show the international relationship of Physical Quality of Life Index (PQLI) and per capita income using (a) 1986 gross national product (GNP), and (b) 1980 gross domestic product (GDP) adjusted for purchasing power parity (PPP). Discernible in both, but more striking in (a), is the inflection point at a PQLI of approximately 90. Compared to nations above that level, a unit of additional income in nations below 90 generally results in a significantly larger increase in PQLI.

D. Responsibility

Indices of ability to pay, do not take into account the responsibility of a country for having caused the problem. Responsibility itself can be measured in different ways. The two main ways are to directly measure historic (including current) contributions to causing the problem and the other tries to address how efficiently a country has been using its resources. As with ATP, the formulation presented allows both to be addressed separately.

International agreements to limit climate change will be easier to negotiate if they are perceived to be equitable. Hence, they must begin with the premise that every human being has the same equal right to atmospheric resources [Grubb, 1989]. As shown in the reference list, many recent attempts have been made to allocate responsibility for present global warming according to current emissions of greenhouse gases and responsibility for mitigation based on anticipated growth rates.

Comparisons according to present national emissions are not generally applicable, because no allowance is made for population size [Smith, 1990a]. Similarly, as shown in Part I, comparisons based on growth rates alone are misleading because absolute additions are ignored. (Such analyses, however, are essential for indicating where potentials for reduction lie.)

The contribution of a gas to global warming is a result of the earth's exposure to the gas, which in turn is a function both of atmospheric concentration and residence times [Smith and Ahuja, 1990]. This argues that the responsibility of countries for the present situation is best indicated by total historical per capita emissions integrated over time, i.e. Natural Debt (ND). From the standpoint of physical reality, this is a better measure of responsibility than current emissions or growth rates, because integrated emissions directly drive climate warming.

The most direct, unambiguous and accurate reflection of a country's contribution to the greenhouse problem is then given by:

$$\sum_t \sum_g \text{emissions}$$

where g refers to the greenhouse gases that need to be included (on a CO_2-equivalent basis) and t to the years over which the emissions need to be summed. As discussed in Part II, deciding on which gases and time periods to incorporate will be a matter for negotiations.

The responsibility for causation needs to be tempered by the number of people for which these emissions were caused. Thus responsibility for causation is proportional to the Natural Debt (ND):

$$\text{ND-1:} \quad \sum_t \sum_g \text{emissions} / \sum_t \text{population}$$

Alternative ways of calculating this index are

$$\text{ND-2:} \quad \sum_t \left[\sum_g \text{emissions/population}\right]$$

or,

$$\text{ND-3:} \quad \sum_t \sum_g \text{emissions/current population}$$

For a stable population, all three formulations are identical, but for both increasing and declining populations, the three yield different answers and only the first gives CO_2-equivalent emissions for a person-year of population during the time emissions were taking place. Indices ND-1 and ND-3 based on 1950-86 emissions and populations are shown in Appendix Table B-1.

In parallel to the ATP index, therefore the final form for determining responsibility (RESP) becomes:

$$RESP = \sum_t \sum_g \text{emissions} - [\text{population} \times (\text{ND threshold})]$$

It remains, then, to choose a threshold ND. A number of ways to do this exist: e.g., based on PQLI, as with ATP; based on that needed for stable global GHG concentration; or based on global averages. (These are not attempted here.)

Appendix Table B-3 compares RESP using both ND-3 and three different thresholds: 5, 10, and 20 tons per capita. Note that lower thresholds tend to decrease the relative responsibilities of developed countries, such as the United States, Germany, and the United Kingdom, but increase those of developing countries. Only with the lowest threshold does China have any responsibility and India's responsibility remains is zero for all the thresholds shown.

E. Allocated Payments by Nation

It now remains to combine resources (ATP) and responsibility (RESP) into an overall Assigned Allocation index --RR-- that is transparent in formulation so that it can be easily manipulated in the course of negotiations. In parallel with Wirth and Lashof [1990], the combination could be a simple sum:

$$RR = a(ATP)^x + b(RESP)^y$$

or, in line with Solomon and Ahuja [1990], it could be a product:

$$RR = k\left((ATP)^x\right) x \left((RESP)^y\right)$$

The second combination (product) implies that if either ATP or RESP is zero, payments are zero.

It could be argued, however, that responsibility for a debt does not disappear just because the borrower is unable to pay now. This supports the first formulation where RR will always be more than zero for a larger group of countries.

The two indicators of concern, ATP and RESP, can be given different weights, by changing the exponents, x and y, and/or the scalar multipliers, a and b. In practice, these values would be subject to negotiation.

Appendix Table B-4 compares the additive version of this Assigned Allocation index using equal weighting for both ATP and RESP and showing also the effect of varying the natural debt threshold and income measure (GNP or PPP). The result is more stable than either the ATP or RESP index by itself. The United States allocation remains at about 37%, for example. China still retains a small allocation in three scenarios, but India's RR remains zero for all combinations.

Appendix Table B-5 compares the multiplicative version of the Assigned Allocation index using equal weights for the two indicators, showing both types of income indicators and two different natural debt thresholds. Note that the United States contribution is above 69% in all cases, undoubtedly a politically unacceptable result. Most developing countries, on the other hand, have RR = 0.

F. Conclusion

It is widely held, although by no means universally so, that, to paraphrase Lord Keynes, economic growth by itself is only a means to certain ends, and that, after an agreeable quality of life has been thereby achieved, society should consider placing its emphasis elsewhere. More explicitly, after reaching some, admittedly difficult-to-define, level of adequate physical well-being, individuals should no longer expect special assistance by the broader society to bring them further. This can be seen also as being consistent with physical reality inherent in a finite world, i.e. there should be incentives to use finite physical resources in ways that lead to quicker achievement of these minimum levels by humanity at large.

One aspect of this approach that has not been well explored is what it implies for the measures of efficiency (indices) that should be used to judge various human activities. Rather than such indicators as income or energy use, which are open ended, it implies the use of thresholds or indicators that actually have fixed ranges, i.e. have a maximum corresponding to achievement of the level of adequacy.

It is thus no accident that the indices both for ability to pay (ATP) and for responsibility contain indicators with thresholds and that ATP is based on an indicator with finite extent, i.e. PQLI. Implicit in the use of PQLI is acceptance that the object of development assistance and policy should be an improvement in the quality of life. It has long been recognized that there exists a strongly positive relationship between PQLI, one measure of quality of life, and GNP. Nevertheless, it can be argued, a simple increase in per capita income should not be taken as the ends, however, but as the means to improving the quality of life. In particular, although there is a strong overall correlation, the ratios are quite different for different countries, an important consideration in indices designed to assign international responsibilities and costs.

Indices of both responsibility and resources to determine the relative allocation of costs for a global program have been looked at separately in Figure 1. Ways to combine the two together would be determined by direct negotiation in international fora. It remains now to move to the next line of the figure, i.e. to decide what ought to be done and where.

IV. Emission Reduction Opportunities and National Goals

As developed in the Part III, the numerator of the resources/responsibility (RR) index encompasses only present accumulations of past CO_2 emissions from fossil fuel use. In addressing opportunities and goals, however, it is possible and advisable to enlarge the numerator to include other sources of CO_2 and other gases. Here, as summarized in Table 5, methane, CFCs, and biotic CO_2 have been included in numerators dealing with the question of "who acts?" More detailed studies would add the other gases listed in Table 3.

This is appropriate because there is better data about the current emissions of these gases. The uncertainty about natural and human-influenced cycles for many of these gases creates less of a problem for indices relating to the question of "Who acts," i.e. where are the best emissions reductions projects. For most projects, it should be possible to set up system boundaries for analysis that allow for calculation of the net change in emissions that might result for a range of GHGs. Because it is believed that the impact of the non-CO_2 gases can be high, this comprehensive approach seems best.

A. Emission Reduction Measures and Their Costs

There are many potential measures that can be used to reduce the emissions of greenhouse gases. Carbon dioxide emissions, in particular, can be reduced through increased efficiency of fossil fuel conversion facilities and all types of energy end-use equipment; fuel switching from coal and oil to natural gas and further to non-carbon sources such as hydro, geothermal, nuclear, solar and other renewable energy sources; and removal of CO_2 from combustion gases. Also, the long-term photosynthetic sink for carbon can be increased by reversing tropical deforestation and accelerating reforestation. Methane emissions can be reduced by burning solid wastes before they decompose to methane and by capturing and burning methane produced by the wastes; and by managing livestock populations and feeding patterns to reduce methane production. Emissions of nitrous oxide and the gases that lead indirectly to the formation of ozone and other greenhouse gases are more difficult to isolate, although a significant amount is related to the same processes that release carbon dioxide and thus can be controlled by the same measures. Finally, strict measures to curtail the emissions of CFCs are expected to be implemented in the near future under the Montreal Protocol and subsequent agreements, and these efforts are not considered here.

Each of the measures suggested above has some cost, which depends on where it is applied and the extent to which emission reductions are achieved. At each level of implementation, the total emission reduction can be divided by the total cost to determine the average cost of that level of reduction, or the incremental emission reduction and cost can be used to determine the marginal cost at that level of reduction. The efficient least-cost approach would be to rank each measure according to marginal cost, from least to most expensive. Then, the reductions available at a given marginal cost level can be summed to estimate the total emission reductions available at that level, creating an aggregate marginal cost curve (Figure 10a). With sufficient information, a global marginal cost curve could be constructed for measures available worldwide (Figure 10b).

Existing information, especially in developing countries, is clearly insufficient to accurately construct such a cost curve, although some recent analyses have made estimates

Figures 10a-10e

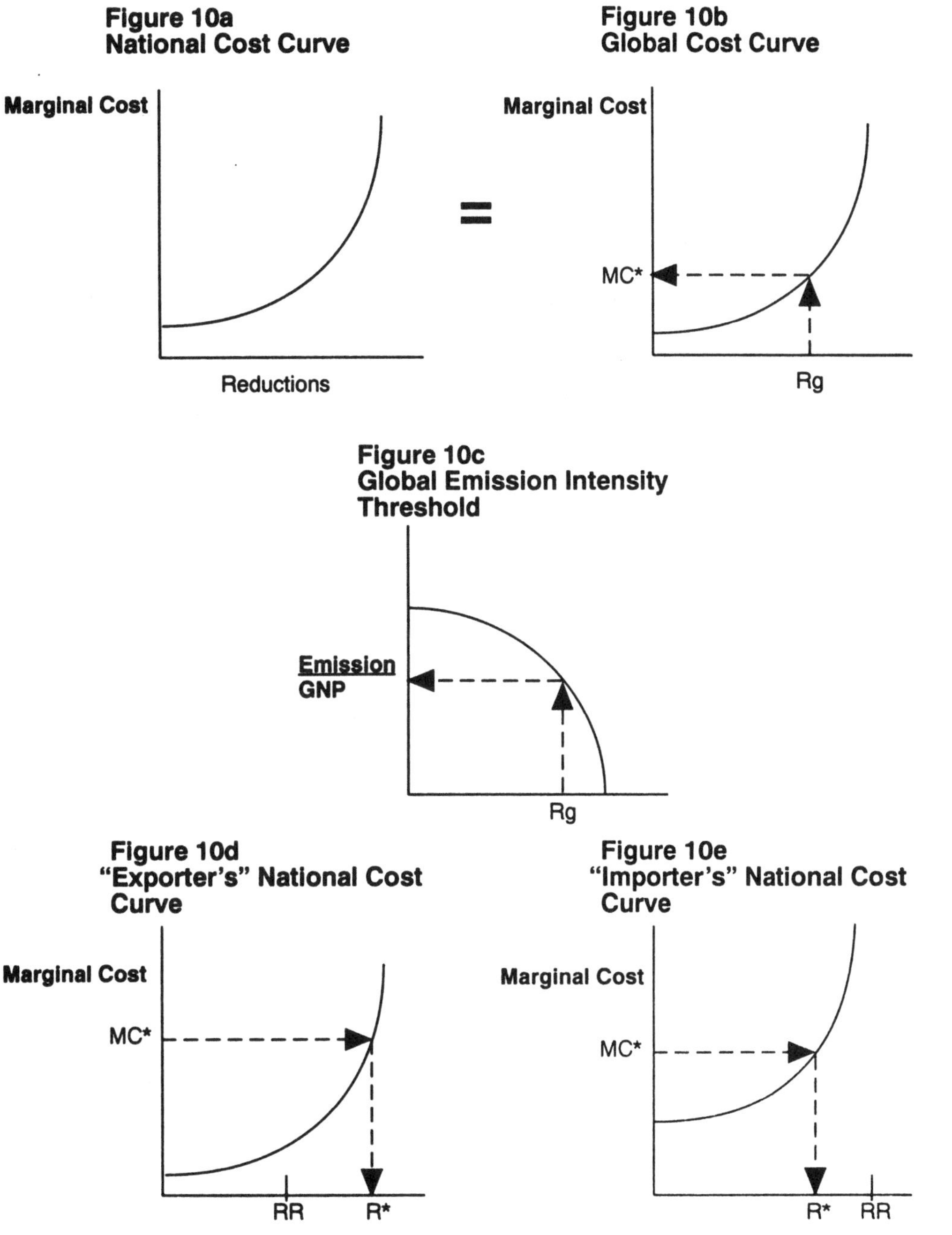

Source: Authors.

of representative cost curves [McKinsey and Co., 1989]. Even without complete information, the marginal cost curve as shown in Figure 10b is a useful conceptual tool for this discussion. It shows that, for a given level of emission reductions, there is a marginal cost threshold that represents the least-cost approach to achieving that level of reductions. Conversely, for a given cost threshold, there is a maximum level of reductions that can be achieved. Furthermore, one can imagine a global cost curve that, for a given marginal cost value, represents the summation of the national emission reduction measures.

If it is assumed that the global goal for emission reductions is to be achieved efficiently, i.e. at minimum cost, the global cost curve indicates the marginal cost threshold below which emission reduction measures should be implemented. Applying this same cost threshold to the cost curve at the national level indicates the cost-effective opportunities for reduction in a given country. Clearly, the distribution of such opportunities will not match the distribution of responsibility discussed in the previous section. At the global level, however, the total of all countries' emission reduction opportunities must match the total responsibility in order to achieve the global goal for emission reductions.

$$\sum(OP) = \sum(RR) = \sum[E(0)] - Eg = Rg$$

where

OP = national emission reduction opportunity
RR = national responsibility/resources
E (0) = emissions without reduction measures
Eg = global emissions goal
Rg = global emissions reduction goal

Another measure of emission reduction opportunities is the emission intensity of the global or national economy. The total reductions to be achieved must equal the reduction in emission intensity of the global economy, from the initial value to a lower threshold value. This emission intensity threshold value thus depends on the level of total emission reductions.

$$\sum(RR) = [\sum GNP] \; [\; Eg/GNP\ (0) - Eg/GNP\ (T)\;] = \sum (OP)$$

$$= \sum \{\; GNP\ [E/GNP\ (0) - E/GNP\ (T)\;]\; \}$$

where Eg/GNP (0) = global emission intensity without reductions
Eg/GNP (T) = global emission intensity reduction threshold
E/GNP (0) = national emission intensity without reductions
E/GNP (T) = national emission intensity reduction threshold

Note that the national intensity threshold that is needed to achieve a given global emission intensity threshold is not the same as the global threshold. This is because some countries' initial intensity may already be below the threshold intensity, bringing the global intensity lower than the threshold.

Thus, for a given level of total reductions, there is a global emission intensity threshold that must be reached. As the level of reductions increases, the threshold must decrease, corresponding to the increasing marginal cost threshold for further emission reduction measures. Thus, a given value of the global emission intensity threshold corresponds to a value for the global marginal cost threshold, assuming there is an efficient least-cost approach to emission reductions. This relationship is shown in Figures 10b and 10c.

At the national level, equity issues of responsibility (Natural Debt) and resources, discussed in Part III, indicate a country's share of the obligation to reduce emissions. This is shown in Figure 1 as "who pays." As the global emission reduction goal increases, the individual national obligations increase as well.

Thus, for an individual country: $RR = \%RR \sum(RR)$
where %RR = national share of emission reduction obligation

A country's opportunities to reduce emissions can be approximated by its emission intensity, compared to the global emission intensity threshold, Eg/GNP (T), or, more precisely, to the national emission intensity threshold, E/GNP (T), needed to achieve Eg/GNP (T).

$$E/GNP\ (T) = f\ (MC^*)$$

$$OP = GNP\ [\ E/GNP\ (0) - E/GNP\ (T)\ ] = f\ (MC^*)$$

To the extent that the emission intensity threshold indicates the least-cost goal for emissions reductions, this expression provides a reasonable estimate of the national emission reduction opportunity, and is therefore useful as an index for emission reduction opportunities. A more precise treatment is to consider the country's share of the global marginal cost curve for emission reductions.

The opportunity for emission reduction at the national level is a function of the global marginal cost threshold, as shown in Figures 10d and 10e. This relationship is consistent with the expressions shown above because each value of the emission intensity threshold corresponds to a certain marginal cost value. The marginal cost threshold is taken from the global marginal cost curve, Figure 10b. This value indicates the emission reductions available in a given country at a cost less than the threshold. This is the efficient level of reductions, and it may be greater or less than the emission reduction obligation of a given country, as shown by the two cases in Figures 10d and 10e.

$$R^* = f\ (MC^*)$$

Thus, $RR - R^* = PR = f\ (MC^*)$
and, $sum\ (R^*) = sum\ (RR) = sum\ (OP)$
where, R^* = emission reduction at marginal cost threshold
PR = excess emission reduction obligation
Define, $E(EP=0) = E(0) - RR$
and, $E^* = E(0) - R^*$
Thus, $PR = E(0) - E(PR=0) - R^*$
$PR = E^* - E(PR=0)$
$E^* = E(PR=0) + PR$

Where, E(0) = emissions without reduction measures;
E(PR=0) = emissions less reduction obligation (no transfers to/from other countries);
E* = emissions after reductions and transfers;

As suggested earlier, there may be a difference between a country's emission reduction obligation (RR), based on equity considerations, and its available emission reduction opportunities (OP or R*), at the efficient marginal cost threshold. This difference indicates the quantity of emission reductions that the country should pay to implement in other countries. These other countries are ones where the cost-effective emission reduction opportunities exceed the emission reduction obligation (i.e. where PR is negative as in Figure 10d). As shown above, such a payment raises the level of emission from that allowed by a country's obligation to reduce emissions {E(PR=0)} to the efficient level (E*), consistent with a least-cost approach to emission reductions.

Thus, the national-level goals, as shown in Figure 1, include both the emission reductions (R*) in a country and the excess emissions transferred (PR) to or from the country. The payment or receipt of an international transfer of resources can thus allow a country to fulfill its responsibility for emission reductions without pursuing measures that cost more than the efficient marginal cost threshold, or to exploit cost-effective opportunities without having to pay for emission reductions beyond its level of responsibility. Such transfers make it possible to reconcile equity (in "who pays") and efficiency (in "who acts").

B. Reconciling Responsibility and Opportunity

It is clear that equity and efficiency criteria will not lead to the same international distribution of emission reductions, and that some type of trade or transfer payments would be necessary to satisfy both basic criteria. Several mechanisms have been proposed to accomplish such transfers, and these will be discussed later.

Figure 10f shows another national-level marginal cost curve, intersected by the country's emission reduction obligation. If the country exploits the opportunities up to the marginal cost level at this intersection, there is no need for any international transfer. If less expensive reduction opportunities are available in other countries, however, the least-cost approach would be to pay for these opportunities according to the "demand" curve shown by the lower half of Figure 10g. Similarly, more expensive opportunities can be exploited through payment from other countries as shown by the "supply" curve in the upper half of Figure 10g. Depending on the international "price" of emission reduction transfers, the country could either "import" or "export" these services.

Summing the national-level "supply" and "demand" curve segments gives an international "market," shown in Figure 10h. The efficient, or "market-clearing" price, where the total of emission reduction opportunities exploited equals the total reduction goal, is the global marginal cost threshold. As shown in Figures 10d and 10e, this threshold determines whether a country should be an "exporter" or an "importer" of emission reduction services. These idealized representations of the transfer of emission reduction services assume that transaction costs are negligible and that no individual participant exercises market power to influence the price or quantity of trades conducted by others.

These transfers could be accomplished through a variety of institutional mechanisms. The key point is that, if an economically efficient least-cost approach is used, the quantities of emissions reduction services transferred would be those described above. Regardless of the institutional framework, the efficient allocation is the same. Because this allocation is unlikely to match the agreed-upon allocation of emission reduction obligations (based on resources and responsibility), some form of transfers are necessary to reconcile efficiency and equity.

Figures 10f-10h

Figure 10f
National Cost Curve and Required Reduction

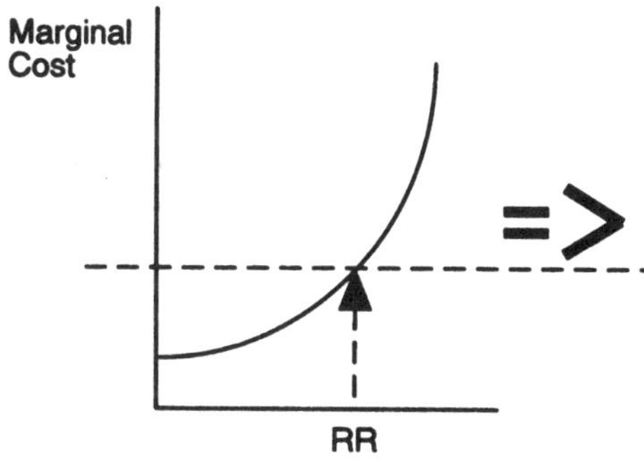

Figure 10g
National Supply and Demand for Emission Transfers

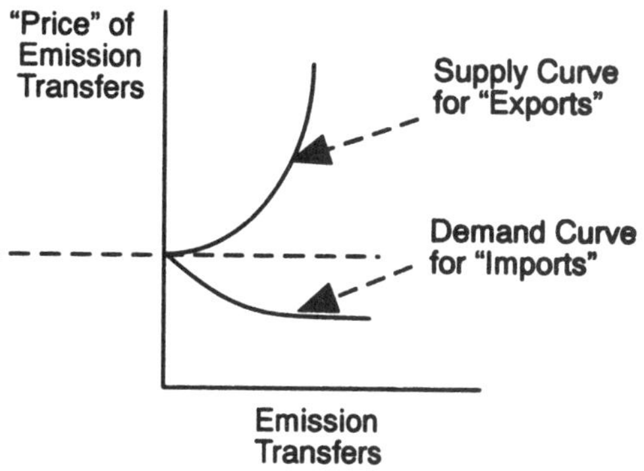

Figure 10h
Global Supply and Demand for Emission Transfers

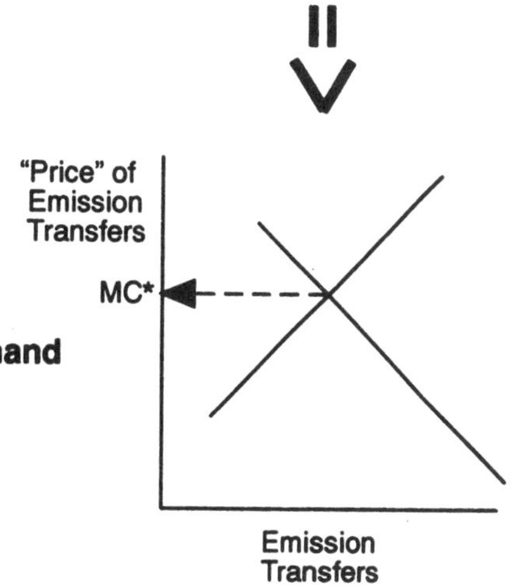

Source: Authors.

The idea of transferring financial resources in exchange for environmental services, through any type of economic mechanism, raises some fundamental questions. From the perspective of the industrialized countries that would be "buyers" of such services, why should they agree to pay large sums to developing countries to fulfill their responsibility for emission reductions? It is true that some countries could choose not to allow purchases of emission reduction services and instead pursue further reductions within their own borders. This, too, would meet their international obligations with regard to emissions reductions.

This option, however, is no different from practicing protectionism in regard to any other commodity or service. Restricting imports, of automobiles or environmental services, raises the cost of meeting the demand and hurts the efficiency of the international market. Basic international trade theory shows that buying from a foreign country with comparative advantage in the particular goods or service provides the foreign country with the foreign exchange to buy goods or services in which the first country has comparative advantage, and thus both are better off. This theory is supported by many international agreements and institutions, including the General Agreement on Trade and Tariffs (GATT).

From the perspective of developing countries that would be "sellers," a frequent question is whether these countries should be bribed to help clean up environmental problems caused by the industrialized countries. By separating the assignment of responsibility from the identification of cost-effective opportunities, the authors provide for the explicit recognition of the industrialized countries' responsibility for the problem and resources with which to solve it. This responsibility is best expressed by the obligation of these countries to pay for the bulk of emission reductions. Of course, if the developing countries follow in the wasteful development path of the industrialized countries, they will soon take on a significant degree of responsibility for themselves.

Given an equitable assignment of responsibility, the developing countries need not contribute to emission reductions beyond their (presumably small) level of responsibility, especially if such measures would compromise economic development. While agreeing to install a renewable energy project or replant a forest may impose an opportunity cost and constrain some future options, the same is true of the development of any export product. Exporting bananas, for example, requires the planting and maintenance of banana plantations to the exclusion of other options. The key question is whether the income from the emission reduction trade, together with the benefits inherent in the reduction measure itself, more than compensates for the opportunity cost of the measure.

The option of selling emission reduction services thus provides a chance for economic gain, rather than a penalty, provided that the seller selects worthwhile projects and receives sufficient compensation for the extra costs of achieving emission reductions in these projects. Since many developing countries would have a comparative advantage in exporting emission reduction services, they could profit from such transactions and use the income to finance other development activities. Refusing to sell emission reduction services, on the other hand, is another form of protectionism that, as discussed above, is inefficient and undermines the benefits of free trade.

Moreover, the ethical questions raised by proposed transactions where rich countries pay poor countries to dispose of toxic wastes do not apply to carbon emission reduction projects, such as energy efficiency and reforestation, that also foster goals of sustainable development.

C. The Emission Reduction Opportunities Index

A simple index is needed to estimate in advance the distribution of emission reduction opportunities, depending on the global level of emission reductions, and the differences between the levels of opportunity and responsibility in different countries. Using the emission intensity threshold is suggested for this purpose, because it does not depend on global marginal cost curves, which cannot be known accurately in advance. Because an increase in the marginal cost threshold corresponds to a decrease in the emission intensity threshold, these two measures should reveal differences in the distribution of national emission reduction opportunities in similar ways, without requiring or revealing the detail of the marginal cost information. (In other words, this is an attempt to estimate OP without yet knowing R*, which is the precise measure of OP.)

An estimate of national emission reduction opportunities, based on the emission intensity threshold, begins with an estimate of the country's and the world's gross product and emissions in the absence of reductions. Then, the global emission reduction goal indicates the fraction by which the global emission intensity must be reduced (Figure 10c). This is the global emission intensity threshold, Eg/GNP (T).

$$\sum (RR) = (\sum GNP) \; [\; Eg/GNP\ (0) - Eg/GNP\ (T) \;] = \sum (OP)$$

For a given level of global emission reductions, the national emission intensity threshold, E/GNP (T), can be obtained by solving the second equation above using totals for all countries. Finally, a country's reduction opportunity is the difference between its emissions without reductions and the product of its GNP and the national emission intensity threshold.

Thus there are three ways to determine the threshold for efficient emission reductions and the resulting distribution of emission reduction opportunities:

(i) Start by selecting a threshold, based on, for example, technical limitations;

(ii) Select a maximum marginal cost limit, which would reduce emissions to a certain emission intensity threshold level; and

(iii) Select the total emission reduction target (the left side of the above equations) and then set the national emission reduction threshold to satisfy this goal, (i.e. the value of E/GNP(T) that balances the equation).

This last approach is a compromise between simplicity and accuracy.

$$OP = GNP \; [\; E/GNP\ (0) - E/GNP\ (T) \;] = F\ (MC^*)$$

Similarly, $$R^* = f\ (MC^*)$$

The difficulty with this formulation is that these values must be estimated for future dates, since it is primarily future emissions that will be controlled. Under an actual emission reduction regime, the global goals and national obligations would have to be updated periodically, and the transfer mechanism, or "market," would be in continuous activity.

To estimate future emission reduction opportunities for individual countries, based on the emission intensity threshold, emissions/GNP and GNP/capita are projected forward using historic rates from 1970-1986 and use population projections from the Population Reference Bureau (PRB) are used [Marland et al., 1989; WRI, 1988; PRB, 1988]. The results for 2000 and 2020 are shown, as fractions of the world total, in the first two columns of Appendix Table B-6. Without emission controls, global CO_2 emissions would rise, according to our projections, from about 6 Gt-C in 1986 to 9 Gt-C in 2000 and 16 Gt-C in 2020.

Thus, accomplishing the internationally proposed goal of stabilizing emissions below current levels by 2000 would require emission reductions of about 30 percent compared to the no-control case [Netherlands Ministry of Environment, 1989]. In 2020, a reduction of 75 percent from the base emissions rate is necessary to reach a goal of two-thirds of current emissions, and almost 90 percent reductions are necessary to reach a goal of one-third of current emissions, as required for stabilization of the atmospheric concentration of CO_2 [USEPA, 1989].

The remaining columns of the last table (Appendix Table B-6) show, in MT-Carbon and fraction of the world total, the emission reductions that result from reducing each country's emission intensity to a given threshold, chosen to meet a goal for global emission reductions. Countries whose projected emissions are already below the threshold do not show any reductions. The goals are:

(i) for the year 2000, stabilization of emissions at levels of the 1980s;

(ii) the same emission intensity threshold as the previous case, applied to the year 2020;

(iii) emissions reductions in 2020 to one-third below current emissions; and

(iv) emissions reductions in 2020 to two-thirds below current emissions.

In light of the already proposed goal of 20 percent emissions reductions below current levels by 2005, a possible goal for 2020 might be a one-third reduction [World Conference on the Changing Atmosphere et al., 1988]. As mentioned above, however, actually stabilizing the CO_2 concentration would require a two-third reduction in emissions.

For a given level of global emission reductions, the global emission intensity goal can be obtained by solving the above equation using totals for all countries. The emission intensity threshold needed to accomplish this goal must be lower than the global intensity if some countries' emission intensities, without reductions, are already below the goal. The emission intensity thresholds used to calculate the values shown in Appendix Table B-6 are given at the top of each of the four columns, and the resulting global emission intensity is given at the bottom.

The emission intensity threshold necessary to reach stabilization of emissions in 2000 is only slightly below the world average, and above the current level for many countries. To the extent that the emission intensity threshold corresponds to a marginal cost threshold, this result suggests that measures to reduce emissions in countries with emission intensities greater than the threshold should be relatively inexpensive. These inexpensive opportunities represent the low opportunity costs of reducing deforestation in many tropical countries and the low marginal cost of improving energy efficiencies in countries, such as China and the Union of Soviet Socialist Republics, where current efficiencies are very low.

Many of these opportunities are in developing countries, where emission reduction measures such as forestry and energy conservation are cost-effective for their own sake, but are limited by capital constraints. Thus, the availability of modest amounts of foreign capital, through a transfer mechanism that satisfies the richer countries' emission reduction responsibilities, could assist the implementation of inexpensive emission reduction opportunities in developing countries and meet worthwhile development needs at the same time.

For 2020, maintaining global emission intensity at the same level as 2000, and thus at the same or perhaps a slightly lower marginal cost threshold, would not even maintain stable emissions due to population and GNP growth, let alone stabilize atmospheric CO_2 concentration. A one-third global emission reduction goal would lower the emission intensity threshold (and raise the marginal cost threshold) substantially. Many industrialized nations, including the United States, would then show significant emission reduction opportunities. Many developing countries, such as China and India, would still show proportionally larger opportunities, indicating that international transfers would still be useful to reconcile responsibility and opportunity. Some carbon efficient countries, such as France and Japan, would still show little emission reduction opportunities at this emission intensity threshold, which is only slightly less than their current level of emission intensity.

A two-thirds reduction goal would require even more expensive measures to further reduce the emission intensity threshold. Because the necessary reductions are so close to 100 percent of projected emissions, the emission reduction opportunities are distributed among countries in a similar pattern as the projected emissions. This distribution of opportunities is more similar than the previous cases to the distribution of responsibility, but there are still significant differences because of the wide range of efficiencies and the varying shares of current emissions in the cumulative emission total. The remaining differences between the national shares of responsibility and opportunity indicate that a transfer mechanism would still be needed to achieve this ambitious reduction goal. Because of the large quantities of emission reductions and the money they represent, such a transfer mechanism may be especially important in achieving an efficient least-cost result.

V. Conclusion

There are two important remaining questions from the list at the beginning of Part I, which can be discussed only briefly. Here they are restated thus:

(iib) How should resources be divided between vulnerability reduction and net emission reduction? and

(v) How would any allocation scheme actually be implemented?

A. Vulnerability

Since the earth is already committed to some amount of warming because of present and past emissions, it might be prudent for countries to spread the expenditures they set aside for responding to the threat of climate change between mitigation and adaptation projects.

Mitigation strategies are those that reduce future net emissions of greenhouse gases and slow the rate of climate change; adaptation strategies reduce the vulnerability of people to climate change, by such projects as building coastal defenses and developing heat resistent crops [Smith, 1990b].

Working Group II of the IPCC, on the Potential Impacts of Climate Change, has identified the most vulnerable human settlements as those especially exposed to natural hazards, e.g.,coastal or riverine flooding, droughts, landslides, wind storms, storm-driven wave surges, and tropical cyclones. The most vulnerable populations are in developing countries, particularly in the lower income groups--subsistence farmers, slum dwellers, islanders, and those living in coastal lowlands and semi-arid grasslands. Major health impacts might also be expected due to changes in the availability of food and water and in the habitats for disease vectors [IPCC, 1990].

On the basis of both limited resources and possible future diminution as a consequence of reduced crop-water availability, the Working Group has identified two broad regions that appear particularly vulnerable:

(i) some semi-arid tropical and sub-tropical regions, such as western Arabia, the Mahgreb, western West Africa, the Horn of Africa, southern Africa, and eastern Brazil; and

(ii) some humid tropical and equatorial regions, such as Southeast Asia and Central America.

There is a growing body of evidence that modern disasters tend to kill predominantly the poorest people in poor countries. Even when events occur that are similar to those elsewhere, the consequences are vastly different in different areas. The San Fernando earthquake in California in 1971 caused 62 deaths, while a smaller one in Managua, Nicaragua, the following year killed tens of thousands [Wildavsky, 1988]. Smith [1989b] provides similar examples wherein tropical cyclones of the size that may kill 10 people in Florida today might have killed many more people there early in the century and might kill thousands in Bangladesh even today. Thus it is clear from both cross-sectional and longitudinal studies that a country's vulnerability to natural disasters, and by extension to climate change, is, in general, inversely proportional to its level of economic development. Besides the evidence relating vulnerability to natural disasters, studies within and across income groups, not surprisingly, have found increasing vulnerability with decreased income.

All this argues that a developing country would be justified in attempting to accelerate those aspects of development that will assist its poorest and most vulnerable groups in attaining higher levels of income, health, education, and resilience that will allow them to cope with all sorts of environmental stresses, including those related to climate change [Smith, 1989b]. It was for this reason that the 1989 New Delhi International Conference on Global Warming and Climate Change (ICGWCC), one of the first held in a developing country, recommended [ICGWCC, 1989]:

> the developing countries' response to the Greenhouse challenge should be carried out in a way that enhances rather than diminishes development prospects. Where these are in conflict, priority should be given to development.

Although the question of how to divide resources between programs to reduce emissions and vulnerability will be settled differently in each country, a case could be made that some of the transfers from "responsible" industrialized countries should be used for increasing resilience. These transfers could be inversely proportional to income, general vulnerability (perhaps indicated by PQLI), and the presence of special conditions, as listed by the IPCC Working Group. (Tyler and Smith [1990] have proposed an index based on response to natural disasters in general as an overall vulnerability to environmental stress.)

There is a strong economic argument that economic efficiency cannot be maximized, unless victim avoidance and other adaption measures are considered along with emission reductions. Particularly in developing countries, the marginal cost effectiveness of vulnerability reduction measures may be much higher than for emission reductions. As in other cases involving environmental damage, however, finding an acceptable common metric to compare damage costs with control costs will be difficult.

B. Mechanisms to Transfer Emission Reduction Services

It appears essential for the success of international climate protection negotiations to separate the assignment of responsibility for climate protection (who pays for it) from the opportunities to reduce or prevent emissions (who does it). This separation requires a mechanism to transfer resources, when necessary, from nations with unfulfilled responsibility to those with unexploited opportunities. If such a mechanism exists, it would be less painful for nations to agree to an emission reduction goal and to accept their share of the responsibility for meeting the goal.

Before returning to the discussion of mechanisms started in Part I, the relationship between such mechanisms and the indices developed in the previous parts should be noted. The indices for resources and responsibility relate directly to the allocation among nations of the obligation to pay for emission reduction measures, although not necessarily to execute such measures in the same countries. Thus, these indices quantify the demand for emission reductions. As shown in Appendix B, responsibility and ability-to-pay (resources) can be combined in several ways, or these combinations can be a subject of negotiation. Because these two indices show relatively similar allocations among nations, the differences to be reconciled by negotiation would be small and therefore should not be difficult to reach.

The supply of emission reductions comes from the opportunities that have been quantified with another index. As was shown in Part III, the amount of opportunities depends on how far one is willing to push the emission reduction technologies, their marginal costs, and the global target for reductions. As the target becomes more ambitious, it requires more difficult technologies, which cost more.

The emission intensity threshold was used to create a simple index of opportunities, which can be calculated using available data. This simple index substitutes for the far more complex process of determining national and global marginal cost functions for emission reduction measures. Because decreasing emission intensity thresholds correspond to increasing marginal costs of emission reductions, our simple index indicates the relative amount of opportunities available as the marginal cost increases, without having to know the exact cost values.

The emission reduction opportunity index can thus be used in the near-term, before full cost performance data are available for emission reductions, to estimate the relative amounts of emission reduction opportunities for different countries that correspond to the chosen global target. Comparing the opportunities to each country's level of responsibility indicates the relative size of the emission reductions that would have to be funded through an international transfer in order to fulfill both equity and efficiency goals. As shown by the indices in Appendix B, the distribution of opportunities among countries is quite different from the distribution of responsibility, ability-to-pay (resources), or any combination of these two indices.

The implementation of a real transfer mechanism would require each participant to determine their own cost values and to seek to fulfill their level of responsibility at least cost, or perhaps at a profit. A great deal of information not currently available would come from such an effort. In the meantime, this simple index can provide a guide for designing an appropriate mechanism for the necessary transfers.

Referring back to the three generic categories of international mechanisms introduced in Part I, the use of indices depends somewhat on the type of mechanism used. The categories are (i) direct national or sector targets, (ii) centralized or market allocation of emission rights, and (iii) emission taxes or subsidies.

Under option (i), the assignment of responsibility to pay for emission reductions and the selection of where reductions will be implemented are combined. Thus, the indices for emission reduction opportunities and combined responsibility and ability-to-pay could be used to indicate each country's position in negotiating a combined allocation. As discussed earlier, the indices for these quantities indicate that there are great differences in the national distributions of these quantities. Thus, it would be difficult and unlikely to reach an agreement on the combined allocation.

Under option (ii), the key index at the international level is the negotiated or calculated combination or responsibility and ability-to-pay (resources). This index quantifies a country's obligation to pay for emission reductions. In the case of tradeable permits, the national allocation of emission permits is the difference between the uncontrolled emissions and the emission reduction obligation.

$$E = E(0) - RR$$

where E = E(0) = emissions without reduction measures
RR = national responsibility/resources

The objective of someone who must select emission reduction, either a central authority or an emitter looking to buy permits, is to find the least-cost opportunities, based on the marginal cost of emission reductions. As discussed earlier, the information is not currently available to simulate this process in order to determine total emission opportunities for every country. Thus, the emission opportunity index can now be used to make a preliminary estimate of the national allocation of emission reduction opportunities. In the case of tradeable permits, this index then indicates the quantity of emission permits that must be purchased by one country from another.

$$PR = RR - R^*$$

where R^* = emission reduction at efficient marginal cost threshold

A negative value of PR indicates that a country would be a seller of emission permits, or a recipient of international transfers to accomplish emission reductions in that country.

Under option (iii), an emission tax would normally be based on the rate of current emissions. This is a relatively simple measure for industrial CO_2 sources, but it becomes more complex when biogenic carbon emissions or other GHGs are considered. Note that if an emission tax had been in place throughout history, the total assessment would now be approximately proportional to the Natural Debt. Future taxes, however, would be based only on future emissions.

The distribution of tax revenues, if intended for GHG reduction efforts, would have to be allocated in some way. An economic efficiency criterion, as under option (ii), would be to fund measures with the lowest marginal costs. Thus, the emission opportunity could be used to make a preliminary estimate of the national allocation of emission reduction opportunities funded by emission tax proceeds or subsidies. This index would then indicate the net quantity of emission reductions that would be funded by one country with payments to others.

$$TR = ET - R^*$$

where ET = emission taxes paid

A negative value of TR indicates that a country would be a net recipient of international transfers from emission tax proceeds or subsidies to accomplish emission reductions in that country.

In summary, the indices of responsibility and ability-to-pay (resources) address the national obligation to pay for emission reductions, and the opportunity index provides a preliminary estimate of the availability of cost-effective emission reduction measures. The difference between these quantities suggests the potential for transfers via some type of international mechanism. Below a range of proposed international mechanisms are discussed, some of which conform to the three generic categories listed above, and others of which are hybrids. As mentioned earlier, a more complete and accurate accounting of reduction opportunities as a function of cost must await further information on the marginal costs of reduction measures in different countries.

One school of economic theory indicates that least-cost emission reductions can be achieved via emission charges or taxes. Polluters would be willing to pay up to the emission charge for measures to reduce emissions by whatever means [Baumol and Oates, 1988]. The additional flexibility of this scheme encourages innovation to find efficient technologies that may not otherwise be available to the regulated firm. One difficulty is finding the right level of emission charges to achieve the desired reduction in pollution. Ideally, this level would be equivalent to the marginal value of the environmental damage caused or avoided, but such values are very difficult to estimate.

Regarding CO_2, the World Conference on the Changing Atmosphere in 1988 called for a world fund for atmospheric stabilization, financed in part by taxes on fossil fuel use in industrialized nations, to promote conservation in developing nations [World Conference on the Changing Atmosphere et al., 1988]. This was the first of several such proposals for international funds to finance greenhouse gas reduction projects [WRI, 1989].

Recognizing that equity can only be achieved in the financial, rather than the physical, allocation of emission rights, Krause et al. [1989] proposes a 1:1 split of emission rights between the industrialized and developing worlds, with a per capita allocation within the two groups. Transfers between nations are to be accomplished through an international fund that would collect and distribute funds, based on proposals solicited for various types of worthy projects [Krause et al., 1989]. A related approach is an international carbon tax, the proceeds of which would be used to fund emission reductions through energy efficiency and forest management in developing countries [Goldemberg, 1990].

The carbon tax and world fund approaches are variations on option (iii) above, in which an emission tax is distributed to deserving emission reduction projects, presumably with marginal cost of emission reductions as a major selection criterion. The emission reduction opportunity index would give a preliminary estimate of the distribution of these funds.

McKinsey and Co. [1989] do not consider the allocation of responsibility or emission rights, but propose instead that the first stages of an international emission reduction agreement would be implemented through unilateral action. This proposal does stress, however, the need for international transfers to achieve economic efficiency, recommending an international clearinghouse mechanism to collect and distribute funds to the most cost-effective emission reduction measures.

Although the world fund or clearinghouse approach appears inherently fair and efficient, it may be difficult to implement. Defining the operating rules and enforcement procedures would require a high degree of consensus among nations, some of whom would have a great deal at stake, and achieving such consensus could be very time-consuming.

Moreover, it is difficult to imagine a preliminary version of such a system, as there would be little incentive for one nation to contribute until its trading partners did so. A CO_2 limitation agreement would constitute a major commitment by numerous nations, and one cannot imagine them entering such a commitment fully and simultaneously. Instead there should be a mechanism that allows gradual implementation, beginning perhaps voluntarily with one or more nations. The initial implementation of unilateral measures would likely achieve the most immediate results available, while later efforts would require a transition to multilateral action to improve the efficiency of the overall effort [McKinsey and Co., 1989].

Emission permits provide a market-based approach to achieving a given level of emission reduction. The number of permits issued can be selected to achieve the desired reductions, and market trading of these permits will achieve the minimum-cost outcome, assuming perfect competition, regardless of how the permits are initially allocated [Hahn and Noll, 1982]. Although the information burden is shifted from the regulator to the polluter under this scheme, there are many potential distortions in such a market for "bads" (as opposed to the conventional market for "goods," see Hahn and Hester [1987]).

Applied to global carbon emissions, tradeable emission permits would achieve the needed separation between the responsibilities and the opportunities for reducing emissions. As an example of an international emission permit system, Grubb [1989] recommends a per capita allocation of emission rights based on adult population. Emission permits would be awarded to and traded by governments, who would be subject to international enforcement procedures [Grubb, 1989]. Alternatively, negotiations based on the issues discussed earlier could achieve an allocation of responsibility, and a market for emission permits would achieve the implementation of the most cost-effective opportunities for reducing emissions.

These proposals are variations on option (ii) above, under which indices for responsibility and ability-to-pay (resources) could be used to allocate permits or obligation-to-pay. The differences between the allocation of these indices and the opportunity index would identify the directions and relative magnitudes of the international transfers that would be needed for emission permit "market clearing," under a tradeable permit system or under a more flexible international mechanism, as described below.

Both a "World Fund" and a global system of national emission permits are difficult to conceive without the presence of a global agency so strong as to have government-like characteristics, and any proposal dependent on the formation of a world government is likely to be dismissed. This position is often reached in discussions of arms control and disarmament [Schell, 1985]. It is consistent with the results of UN discussions of the global environment, in which world government instruments such as automatic global tax levies are not taken seriously [Laurenti and Lyman, 1990]. Considering that the United States does not pay its full UN dues and has withdrawn from UNESCO and FAO, this position appears rather sound.

Also, either of these systems would essentially dictate to individual nations the type of domestic pollution policy they would have to use in order to participate in the agreed-upon system. Some governments might endorse a pollution tax and some might favor tradeable permits, but neither approach allows flexibility in choosing domestic policy instruments. This is a serious issue because implementation at the national level has been the most difficult step in most international environmental actions [Caldwell, 1988]. In order to facilitate this difficult process, an international agreement should allow flexibility at the national level in the design of policy instruments to implement the agreement. This approach was an important element in the success of negotiations toward the Montreal Protocol on ozone-depleting gases [Benedict, 1988].

Another similar market-based approach is to use an international agreement to allocate the responsibility for investments in reducing emissions, but leave the choice of national implementation policies to the individual governments, as suggested by the Montreal Protocol. The decoupling of national responsibility and opportunities for reducing emissions could be reconciled by creating a currency for investing in carbon-saving services as a way to comply with national policies to reduce emissions [Swisher and Masters, 1989]. For example, the opportunity to sell such services as International Carbon Emission Offsets (ICEOs), or to trade them for debt relief, would give the developing nations a tangible economic incentive to use clean energy technologies and to protect their forests, rather than to deplete them.

A system of tradeable ICEOs would not require that individual nations use tradeable permits to enforce their own emission reduction policies. Different nations could use any performance-based or market-based approach, including an emission ceiling (regulating the quantity emitted), a carbon tax (regulating the cost of emissions), or other policy instruments. The essential prerequisite for an ICEO system is that individual nations allow investments that reduce carbon emissions in other countries to comply with their own national policies. The selection of technologies and programs to reduce emissions, and the decision whether to use domestic measures or buy ICEOs, would be left to firms and other entities who must comply with the national policy, thus decentralizing these decisions.

ICEOs are not meant to allocate international rights to emit CO_2, such as through an auction process proposed for some regional emission offset programs [Hahn and Noll, 1982]. This approach, applied internationally, would create immense market power for either buyers or sellers, and no international body would be capable of enforcing such a system. It is assumed that only international negotiation can accomplish the allocation, and that ICEOs would be used to supplement national policies to achieve the agreed-upon allocation. ICEOs would, however, provide a mechanism that can be gradually implemented, to allow the separation of the opportunities for reducing emissions from the responsibility to do so. By making a climate protection agreement easier to implement, this mechanism could make an agreement easier to reach.

C. Conclusion

There are two extremes to answering the questions posed in Part I, i.e. who acts and who pays. At one extreme lie those who suggest uniform cuts in some particular year's emission rates or simple allocations based per nation or group of nations. Because of their simplicity and apparent equity, such approaches have much to recommend them [Nitze, 1990].

At the other extreme lie approaches that attempt to right all the world's perceived wrongs by choosing GHG indices that include incentives to, inter alia, reduce population growth, enhance renewable energy sources for their own sake, and address intranational income equity. To do so is tempting because of the potentially large amount of resource reallocation that could be involved. It would seem, however, that the very importance of these other goals would argue against their inclusion in an index primarily designed for another purpose, i.e. remediation of global warming. Rather, these other issues should be addressed directly in their own right with measures that are designed to equitably and efficiently achieve the goals tailored to them.

This chapter has taken a middle path. It has developed a framework that allows some of the major criteria to be addressed separately, e.g., equity and efficiency and responsibility and resources, but does not attempt, at the same time, to address issues outside those that directly relate to greenhouse gases. On the other hand, these indices should not create perverse incentives that go against other important societal goals, such as limiting population growth. No matter what mechanism is used to transfer resources, such indices will be needed to monitor and evaluate the results.

References

Arrhenius, E. and T.W. Waltz [1990]. *The Greenhouse Effect: Implications for Economic Development*. Discussion Paper No. 78. Washington, D.C.: World Bank.

Baumol, W.J. and W.E. Oates [1988]. *The Theory of Environmental Policy*. Second Edition. New York: New Cambridge University Press.

Benedict, Richard [1988]. "A Landmark Global Treaty at Montreal." *Natural Resources Journal*, vol. 28: 427-429.

Bertram, I.G., R.J. Stephens, and C.C. Wallace [1989]. *The Relevance of Economic Instruments for Tackling the Greenhouse Effect*. A Report to the Ministry for the Environment, New Zealand.

Brown, L. et al. [1989]. *State of the World 1989*. New York: W.W. Norton.

Caldwell, L.K. [1988]. "Beyond Environmental Diplomacy: The Changing Institutional Structure of International Cooperation." In J.E. Carroll (editor), *International Environmental Diplomacy*. Cambridge, United Kingdom: Cambridge University Press.

Chapman, D. and T. Drennen [1990]. "Equity and Effectiveness of Possible CO_2 Treaty Proposals." *Contemporary Policy Issues* , vol. 8 (July): 16-28.

Dickinson, R. and R. Cicerone [1986]. "Future Global Warming from Atmospheric Trace Gases." *Nature*, vol. 319: 109-115.

Ellington, R.T. and M. Meo [1990]. "Development of a Greenhouse Gas Emissions Index." *Chemical Engineering Progress* (July): 58-63.

Gleick, P.H. [1989]. "Climate Change and International Politics: Problems Facing Developing Countries." *A Journal of the Human Environment*, vol.18, no. 6: 333-339.

Goldemberg, J. [1990]. "How to Stop Global Warming." *Technology Review*, vol. 93, no. 8: 24-31.

Goreau, T.J. [1990]. "Balancing Atmospheric Carbon." *Ambio*, vol. 19, no. 5: 230-236.

Grubb, M. [1989]. *The Greenhouse Effect: Negotiating Targets*. London: Royal Institute of International Affairs.

Hahn, R. and G. Hester [1987]. "The Market for Bads." *Regulation*, vol. 3: 48-53.

Hahn, R., and R. Noll [1982]. "Designing a Market for Tradeable Emissions Permits." In T. Magat (editor), *Reform of Environmental Regulation*. Cambridge, Massachusetts: Ballinger.

Hammond, A.L., E. Rodenburg, and W. Moomaw [1990]. "Accountability in the Greenhouse." *Nature*, vol. 347: 705-706.

Hansen, J., A. Lacis, and M. Prather [1989]. "Greenhouse-Effect of Chlorofluorocarbons and Other Trace Bases." *Journal of Geophysical Research-Atmospheres*, vol. 94, no. D13: 16417-16421.

Hardin, G. [1968]. "The Tragedy of the Commons." *Science*, vol. 162: 1243-1248.

Houghton, R. A. et al. [1987]. "The Flux of Carbon from Terrestrial Ecosystems to the Atmosphere in 1980 Due to Changes in Land Use: Geographic Distribution of the Global Flux." *Tellus*, vol. 39B: 122-139.

International Conference on Global Warming and Climate Change (ICGWCC) [1989]. *Conference Statement*. New Delhi: Tata Energy Research Institute.

Intergovernmental Panel on Climate Change (IPCC) [1990]. *Climate Change: The IPCC Scientific Assessment*. Cambridge, United Kingdom: Cambridge University Press.

Koehler, J. and S.A. Hajost [1990]. "The Montreal Protocol: A Dynamic Agreement for Protecting the Ozone Layer." *Ambio*, vol. 19: 82-86.

Krause, F., W. Bach, and J. Kooney [1989]. *Energy Policy in the Greenhouse*. El Cerrito, California: International Project for Sustainable Energy Paths.

Lashof, D.A. and D.R. Ahuja [1990]. "Relative Contributions of Greenhouse Gas Emissions to Global Warming." *Nature*, vol. 344: 529-531.

Laurenti, J. and F. Lyman [1990]. *One Earth, Many Nations: The International System and Problems of the Global Environment*. New York: United Nations Association of the United States.

Marland, G. et al. [1989]. *Estimates of CO_2 Emissions from Fossil Fuels Burning and Cement Manufacturing*. Report No. ORNL/CDIAC-25;NDP-030. Oak Ridge, Tennessee: Oak Ridge National Laboratory, May.

McKinsey and Co. [1989]. *Protecting the Global Atmosphere: Funding Mechanisms*. Report to the Steering Committee for the Ministerial Conference on Atmospheric Pollution and Climate Change. Noordwijk, Netherlands: Steering Committee for the Ministerial Conference on Atmospheric Pollution and Climate Change.

Mintzer, I. [1987]. *A Matter of Degrees*. Washington, D.C.: World Resources Institute.

Morgan, K.Z., W.S. Snyder, and M.R. Ford [1964]. "Relative Hazard of the Various Radioactive Materials." *Health Physics*, vol. 10: 151-169.

Morris, M. [1979]. *Measuring the Condition of the World's Poor: The Physical Quality of Life*. New York: Pergamon Press (for the Overseas Development Council).

Munasinghe, M. [1990]. "The Challenge Facing the Developing World." *EPA Journal* (March/April).

National Academy of Sciences (NAS) [1983]. *Changing Climate*. Report of the Carbon Dioxide Assessment Committee. Washington, D.C.: National Academy of Sciences.

Netherlands Ministry of Environment [1989]. *Noordwijk Declaration on Atmospheric Pollution and Climatic Change*. The Hague, Netherlands: Netherlands Ministry of Environment, November.

Nitze, W.A. [1990]. "A Proposed Structure for an International Convention on Climate Change." *Science*, vol. 249: 607-608.

Ott, W. [1978]. *Environmental Indices, Theory and Practice*. Ann Arbor, Michigan: Ann Arbor Science.

Pachauri, R.K. [1990]. *Emissions of Greenhouse Gases in the Developing Countries: Abatement Strategies and Perspectives*. Environment Division. Washington, D.C.: World Bank.

Passell, Peter [1989]. "Cure for greenhouse effect: the costs will be staggering." *The New York Times*, vol. 139, section 1, col. 5, p.1(N), p.1(L) (November 19).

Penner, J.E., P.S. Connell, D.J. Wuebbles, and C.C. Covey [1989]. "Climate Change and Its Interactions with Air Chemistry: Perspectives and Research Needs." In United States Environmental Protection Agency, *The Potential Effects of Global Climate Change on the United States: Appendix F - Air Quality*. Office of Policy, Planning and Evaluation. Washington, D.C.: United States Environmental Protection Agency, May.

Population Reference Bureau [1988]. "World Population Data Sheet." Washington, D.C.: Population Reference Bureau.

Post, W.M., T. Peng, W.R. Emanuel et al. [1990]. "The Global Carbon Cycle." *American Scientist*, vol. 78: 30-326.

Princeton University [1988]. *Princeton Protocol on Factors that Contribute to Global Warming*. Woodrow Wilson School of Public and International Affairs. Princeton, New Jersey: Princeton University Press, Fall.

Rodhe, H. [1990]. "A Comparison of the Contribution of Various Gases to the Greenhouse Effect." *Science*, vol. 248: 1217-1219.

Rotty, R. and C. Masters [1984]. *Past and Future Releases of Carbon Dioxide from Fossil Fuel Combustion*. Oak Ridge, Tennessee: Institute for Energy Analysis.

Sathaye, J., A. Ghirardi, and L. Schipper [1987]. "Energy Demand in Developing Countries." *Annual Review of Energy*, vol. 12: 253-282.

Schneider, S.H. [1989]. "The Changing Climate." *Scientific American* (September): 70-79.

Schell, J. [1985]. *The Abolition*. New York: Random House.

Second Meeting of the Parties to the Montreal Protocol on Substances that Deplete the Ozone Layer [1990a]. "Annex II, Article 1: Amendment." London: Montreal Protocol on Substances that Deplete the Ozone Layer.

Second Meeting of the Parties to the Montreal Protocol on Substances that Deplete the Ozone Layer [1990b]. "Annex IV, Appendix I." London: Montreal Protocol on Substances that Deplete the Ozone Layer.

Second Meeting of the Parties to the Montreal Protocol on Substances that Deplete the Ozone Layer [1990c]. "Report of the Second Meeting of the Parties to the Montreal Protocol on Substances that Deplete the Ozone Layer." Agenda Item No. 7. London: Montreal Protocol on Substances that Deplete the Ozone Layer.

Seigenthaler, U. [1983]. "Uptake of Excess CO_2 by an Outcrop-Difffusion Model of the Ocean." *Journal of Geophysical Research*, vol. 88, no. C6 (April): 3599-3608.

Shine, K.P., R.G. Derwent, D.J. Wuebbles, and J-J. Morcrette [1990]. "Radiative Forcing of Climate." Chapter 2 in Intergovernmental Panel on Climate Change (IPCC), *Climate Change: The IPCC Scientific Assessment*. Cambridge, United Kingdom: Cambridge University Press.

Siddiqi, T.A. [1990]. "Energy and Equity Issues in Global Climate Change Negotiations." UNCSTD Conference on Energy in Climate and Development: Policy Issues and Technological Options held in Saarbrucken, Federal Republic of Germany.

Smith, J. and D. Tirpak [1989]. *Potential Effects of Global Climate Change in the U.S.* Washington, D.C.: United States Environmental Protection Agency.

Smith, K.R. [1989a]. *Have You Paid Your Natural Debt*. Environment and Policy Institute. Honolulu, Hawaii: East-West Center.

Smith, K.R. [1989b]. "Developing Countries and Climate Change: Implications for Risk Management." In D. Street and T. Siddiqi (editors), *Proceedings of the Workshop on Responding to the Threat of Global Warming: Options for the Pacific and Asia*. Honolulu, Hawaii: Argonne National Laboratory and East-West Center: 2-37 - 2-41.

Smith, K.R. [1990a]. "Allocating Responsibility for Global Warming: The Natural Debt Index." *Ambio*, vol. 19, no. 8.

Smith, K.R. [1990b]. "Climate Change and the Risk Transition." *ASCE Energy Journal* (December).

Smith, K.R. and D.R. Ahuja [1990]. "Toward A Greenhouse Equivalence Index: The Total Exposure Analogy." *Climatic Change*, vol. 17: 1-7.

Smith, K.R. et al. [1991]. "Commentaries the WRI Greenhouse Gas Index." *Environment*, vol. 33, no. 2: 2-5, 42-44.

Solomon, B.D. and D.R. Ahuja [1990]. "An Equitable Approach to International Reductions of Greenhouse Gas Emissions." Annual Meeting of the American Association of Geographers held in Toronto.

Stewart, R.B. and J.B. Weiner [1990]. "A Comprehensive Approach to Climate Change." *American Enterprise* (November/December): 75-80.

Study Group on Policy Options for Moderating Global Warming [1990]. *Interim Report*. Tsukuba, Japan: Environmental Research Center.

Subak, S. [1990]. "Accountability for Climate Change." Draft research memorandum. Boston: Stockholm Environment Institute.

Summers, R. and A. Heston [1988]. "A New Set of Internation al Comparisons of Real Product and Prices: Estimates for 130 Countries, 1950-1985." *Journal of the International Association for Research Income and Wealth*, vol. 34, no. 1: 1-26.

Swisher, J. and G. Masters [1989]. *International Carbon Emission Offsets: A Tradeable Currency for Climate Protection Services*. Technical Paper No. 309, Civil Engineering Department. Stanford, CA: Stanford University.

Tietenburg, T.H. [1985]. *Emissions Trading*. Washington, D.C.: Resources for the Future.

Tyler, M. and K.R. Smith [1990]. "Vulnerability and Climate Change: A Natural Disaster Index." Environment and Policy Institute. Draft. Honolulu, Hawaii: East-West Center.

United Nations [1988]. *World Population Prospects, 1988*. Report No. E.88.XIII.7. Department of International Economic and Social Affairs. New York: United Nations.

United Nations General Assembly [1989]. "Evolution of the Methodology for the Scale of Assessments and Its Current Application." A/CN.2/R.532, Committee on Contributions. New York: United Nations.

United States Agency for International Development [1990]. "Greenhouse Gas Emissions and the Developing Countries: Strategic Options and the USAID Response." A report to Congress. Washington, D.C.: USAID.

United States Environmental Protection Agency [1989]. "Policy Options for Stabilizing Global Climate." Draft report to Congress, Vol. II: Chapters VII-IX. Washington, D.C.: UEPEA, February.

Westing, A.H. [1989]. "Law of the Air." *Environment*, vol. 31, no. 3: 3-4.

Wildavsky, A. [1988]. *Searching for Safety*. New Brunswick, Canada: Transaction Press.

Wirth, D.A. and D.A. Lashof [1990]. "Beyond Vienna and Montreal, Multilateral Agreements on Greenhouse Gases." *AMBIO*, vol. 19, no. 6-7: 305-310.

World Conference on the Changing Atmosphere: Implications for Global Security, Government of Canada, United Nations Environment Programme, and the World Meteorological Organizations [1988]. *Conference Proceedings: The Changing Atmosphere: Implications for Global Security, Toronto, Canada, June 27-30, 1988*. Geneva: Secretariat of the World Meterological Organization.

World Commission on Environment and Development [1987]. *Our Common Future* New York: Oxford University Press.

World Bank [1990]. *World Development Report*. New York: Oxford University Press (for the World Bank).

World Resources Institute [1988]. *World Resources 1988-89*. New York: Basic Books.

World Resources Institute [1989]. *Natural Endowments: Financing Resource Conservation for Development*. Washington, D.C.: WRI.

World Resources Institute [1990]. *World Resources 1990-91*. New York: Oxford University Press.

Appendix A

I. Summary
"Evolution of the Methodology for the Scale of Assessments and Its Current Application"[1]

The original guidelines regarding the apportionment of the Organization's expenses are contained in the terms of reference of the Committee on Contributions which were adopted by the General Assembly on 13 February 1946.

> ...Those guidelines identify the underlying principle and the basic elements of the scale methodology, namely the capacity to pay, the use of national income as its basic indicator, the low per capita national income allowance formula for a reflection of the relationship between national income and population size, and the notion of (implicit) ceiling and floor rates and their link with the capacity to pay. Additional factors to be taken into consideration included the temporary dislocation of national economies resulting from the Second World War and the ability of Member States to secure foreign currency. The period of scale applicability was also indicated...

Since the second half of the 1960s, discussion pertaining to possible changes in the methodology and scale of assessments has centered around their equity and fairness. Specific concerns which surfaced and resurfaced throughout the 1980s have included the incorporation of circumstances making it difficult for Member States to meet payments, the differing effects of price changes on exchange rates, and the use of alternate measures and variables giving a different perspective on the capacity to pay such as net worth, wealth, health, nutrition, education, conditions of work and housing, and social security. In all cases lack of conceptual agreement, non-availability of data, and controversiality of data where it existed were sufficient to cause the committee to concentrate its efforts on revising the currently used methodology in accordance with expressed concerns. An attempt as been made to factor the special economic and financial problems of developing countries into the methodology by means of repeated changes in floor levels and in the parameters of the low per capita national income allowance formula. Since 1983 there has been a freeze on the rates of assessment of the least developed countries.

Provision within the methodology for reducing the assessments of countries with low per capita incomes has been existent since the first assessment scale was created. In the absence of statistical information it was implemented through a case-by-case examination and decisionmaking process. Since 1948 a formula has been in use,

> ...which is based on an upper per capita income limit for concession of relief and a maximum percentage allowance...The two parameters were initially set at $1,000 and 40 percent, and the allowance is calculated as follows the difference between a country's per capita national income and $1,000 is expressed as a percentage, and 40 percent of that percentage is deducted from the country's national income. The lower the per capita national income, the closer the percentage deduction approaches 40 percent... (p. 8).

---

[1]See United Nations General Assembly [1989] for the complete document which the authors have summarized here.

Since the initial time of implementation, the method used has not changed. The parameters, however, have slid successively higher such that the 1989-1991 scale was prepared with parameters of $2,200 and 85 percent.

It is noteworthy that at the inception of the UN when initial membership was comparatively small, the ceiling set on percent of total assessments which any one country could pay was 40%. Since membership has grown and the need for funds has been increasingly taken up by newly participating countries, this ceiling has shrunk to 25%. Likewise the initial floor rate was set at .04 in 1946 and there remained until 1973 when it was changed to .01 where it remains at the present.

In view of unfruitful efforts to incorporate the ability of Member States to secure foreign currency into the assessment procedure, the committee turned its attention to external debt payments as a surrogate. This was accomplished in an ad hoc manner until 1985 when the committee "...made adjustments to national income on the basis of a ranking of countries by combined ratios of debt-to-export earnings and debt-to-national income and ad hoc decisions on a cut-off point for relief and the size of the relief deduction..." (p. 9) Provision for payments in currencies other than in United States dollars has been made as well. At present, however, the need for further refinement of the current methodology is still felt.

Wide changes resulted in Member State's assessments from scale to scale due to changes in the methodology as well as to variations in the data. Two formal changes have been integrated into the existing scale methodology in order to avoid excessive variations. ***First of all***, a theoretical limit of 10% on both positive and negative changes between successive scales was adopted. This limit has not proved practicable, however, and thus further changes have been proposed. ***Second***,during the period 1947-1977, the statistical base year was increased from one to seven, and again increased to 10 in 1981 in order to "smooth" changes in assessments due to variations in the data on which they are based.

After the preparation of an assessment scale the committee has the discretionary powers necessary to make final adjustments dependent upon representations made by Member States, upon the Committee's own perception of a certain Member State's ability to pay, or upon extenuating circumstances such as disruptions to economies due to wars, catastrophes, statistical data problems, or inconsistencies. Whereas the point adjustments of the early assessments were of a small magnitude (2 or 3 percentage points), they increased during the mid-seventies to 50 and to 77 by 1988. Thus the so-called mitigation process continues to be scrutinized and criticized on the basis of its "...lackof transparency, the volume of points shifted, the size of individual adjustments and on the resulting distortion of the capacity to pay..."(p. 15).

In summary, the methodology currently in use which has evolved over four decades of debate and revision is as follows:

(i) Gross Domestic Product (of market economies) and Net Material Product (of centrally planned economies) are transformed into "National Income" in United States dollars.

(ii) The National Incomes of those countries needing adjustments for debt relief are reduced by the agreed upon percentages.

(iii) Then national income figures are further adjusted for per capita incomes which are less than the threshold level.

(iv) Then each countries share of the total assessments is calculated.

(v) Finally all countries' assessments are adjusted in an interactive process until ceiling and floor standards are met, and until constraints on limits and total assessments to be collected are met.

II. Summary
Methodology Recommended by the Montreal Protocol for Financing of the Multilateral Fund

The mandate for the Interim Financial Mechanism until such time as the permanent Financial Mechanism is established, is given in paragraph 6 of decision II/8 from "Draft Decisions Approved by the Open-Ended Working Group of the Parties to the Montreal Protocol at Its Fourth Meeting for Consideration by the Second Meeting of the Parties." It is given that, in addition to contributions and outside cooperation, the Multilateral Fund shall be financed "...inconvertible currency or, in certain circumstances, in kind and/or in national currency, on the basis of the United Nations scale of assessments..." (p. 4) The scale of contributions to this Fund are reproduced from Appendix III and given in the following table. It appears that for this interim mechanism, the UN scale has been directly adopted.

Appendix Table A:
Relative Contributions to the Montreal Protocol Fund with no country paying more than 25 percent

Party	UN Scale of Contribution (%)	Montreal Protocol Percentages
Developing countries exempt from contribution until 1999		
Brazil	1.45	0.00
Burkina Faso	0.01	0.00
Cameroon	0.01	0.00
Chile	0.08	0.00
Ecuador	0.03	0.00
Egypt	0.07	0.00
Fiji	0.01	0.00
Ghana	0.01	0.00
Guatemala	0.02	0.00
Jordan	0.01	0.00
Kenya	0.01	0.00
Malaysia	0.11	0.00
Maldives	0.01	0.00
Mexico	0.94	0.00
Nigeria	0.20	0.00
Sri Lanka	0.01	0.00
Syrian Arab Republic	0.04	0.00
Thailand	0.10	0.00
Trinidad and Tobago	0.05	0.00
Tunisia	0.03	0.00
Uganda	0.01	0.00
Venezuela	0.57	0.00
Zambia	0.01	0.00
Developing countries not exempt from contribution at present		
Bahrain	0.02	0.02
Malta	0.01	0.01
Panama	0.02	0.02
Singapore	0.11	0.13
United Arab Emirates	0.19	0.22
Developed Countries		
Australia	1.57	1.85
Austria	0.74	0.87
Byelorussian SSR	0.33	0.39
Canada	3.09	3.64
Finland	0.51	0.60
German Democratic Republic	1.28	1.51
Hungary	0.21	0.25
Iceland	0.03	0.04
Japan	11.38	13.39
Liechtenstein	0.01	0.01

(continued)

Appendix Table A (continued)

Party	UN Scale of Contribution (%)	Montreal Protocol Percentages
Developed Countries (Continuation)		
New Zealand	0.24	0.28
Norway	0.55	0.65
South Africa	0.45	0.53
Sweden	1.21	1.42
Switzerland	1.08	1.27
Ukranian SSR	1.25	1.47
USSR	9.99	11.76
USA	25.00	25.00
European Economic Community (EEC)		
EEC (total for member states)	29.46	34.67
Belgium	1.17	1.38
Denmark	0.69	0.81
France	6.25	7.36
Germany, Federal Republic	8.08	9.51
Greece	0.40	0.47
Ireland	0.18	0.21
Italy	3.99	4.70
Luxembourg	0.06	0.07
Netherlands	1.65	1.94
Portugal	0.18	0.21
Spain	1.95	2.29
United Kingdom	4.86	5.72
Total	92.52	100.00

Source: Appendix III, from Annex IV, Appendices to Decision II/8 ("Financial Mechanism") adopted by the Second Meeting of the Parties to the Montreal Protocol.

Appendix B: Analytical Indices Related to Greenhouse Gas Issues

Appendix Table B-1: Natural Debt Indices

Shown here are basic emissions and population data from the 62 most populous nations in the world (approximately 10 million or larger in 1986). In the last two columns, two Natural Debt indices, as discussed in Parts I and III, are shown. The fourth column is determined by dividing the cumulative carbon as fossil fuel (CO_2) released from 1950-1986 by the 1986 populations. For the last column, it is divided by the total person-years over the same period.

	1950-86 Carbon Emissions (Megatons)	1986 Population (millions)	1950-86 Cumulative Capita-year (millions)	1986 Natural Debt (t/cap)	Average Population Debt (t/cap-y)
USA	37284	240	7360	155.000	5.070
Germany, United	9123	78	2784	117.000	3.280
Canada	2911	26	751	112.000	3.880
Czechoslovakia	1764	16	526	110.000	3.350
Belgium	1081	10	349	108.000	3.100
United Kingdom	5922	57	2018	104.000	2.930
Australia	1360	16	447	85.000	3.040
Poland	2921	37	1177	78.900	2.480
USSR	22039	281	8667	78.400	2.540
Netherlands	1040	15	466	69.300	2.230
Bulgaria	618	9	306	68.700	2.020
France	3646	55	1820	66.300	2.000
Egypt	2801	48	1194	58.400	2.350
Japan	6924	121	3929	57.200	1.760
Hungary	594	11	380	54.000	1.560
Romania	1112	23	735	48.300	1.510
South Africa	1456	33	835	44.100	1.740
Italy	2294	57	1955	40.200	1.170
Korea, Dem.	679	21	507	32.300	1.340
Spain	1116	39	1229	28.600	0.910
Yugoslavia	632	23	739	27.500	0.860
Greece	268	10	324	26.800	0.830
Venezuela	459	18	389	25.500	1.180
Argentina	698	31	874	22.500	0.800
Saudi Arabia	268	12	230	22.300	1.170
Portugal	156	10	339	15.600	0.460
Mexico	1207	81	1862	14.900	0.648
Chile	174	12	336	14.500	0.518
Korea, Rep.	584	42	1126	13.900	0.519
Iran	534	46	1030	11.600	0.518
Malaysia	176	16	310	11.000	0.568
Turkey	467	50	1271	9.340	0.367
Colombia	262	29	734	9.030	0.357
Iraq	144	17	351	8.470	0.410
Syria	91	11	234	8.270	0.389
China	8448	1052	29132	8.030	0.290
Algeria	160	22	518	7.270	0.309
Peru	141	20	480	7.050	0.294
Brazil	950	139	3427	6.830	0.277
Morocco	84	22	550	3.820	0.153
Philippines	207	56	1343	3.700	0.154

(continued)

Appendix Table B-1 (Continued)

	1950-86 Carbon Emissions (Megatons)	1986 Population (millions)	1950-86 Cumulative Capita-year (millions)	1986 Natural Debt (t/cap)	Average Population Debt (t/cap-y)
Thailand	183	52	1296	3.520	0.141
India	2184	772	20080	2.830	0.109
Indonesia	419	171	4394	2.450	0.095
Vietnam	131	61	1619	2.150	0.081
Cote d'Ivoire	21	10	210	2.100	0.100
Pakistan	192	103	2544	1.860	0.075
Sri Lanka	29	17	442	1.710	0.066
Kenya	34	21	428	1.620	0.079
Cameroon	16	10	249	1.600	0.064
Mozambique	22	15	322	1.470	0.068
Ghana	19	14	317	1.360	0.060
Nigeria	132	99	2141	1.330	0.062
Sudan	28	22	525	1.270	0.053
Zaire	30	31	733	0.968	0.041
Burma	34	38	987	0.895	0.034
Madagascar	7	10	248	0.700	0.028
Tanzania	15	23	511	0.665	0.030
Uganda	7	16	348	0.438	0.020
Bangladesh	44	103	2632	0.424	0.017
Ethiopia	10	44	1135	0.227	0.009
Nepal	3	16	434	0.188	0.007
Total	126355	4560	124629	Mean 27.700	Mean 1.010

Source: Authors. Data mainly from Marland et al. [1989].
Legend: CO_2 = carbon dioxide
t/cap = tons per capita

Appendix Table B-2: Ability to Pay Indices

For the same 62 countries as in Table B-1, Ability to Pay is calculated as discussed in Part III. In the first column, 1986 gross national product (GNP) is used with a $1800 threshold and, in the second, 1980 purchasing power parity (PPP), is used with a $3400 cutoff. The columns have been normalized to 100% so that each nation's value is shown as a percentage of the total for all (62) nations.

	Percentage Ability to Pay	
	1986-GNP $1800	1980-PPP $3400
USA	36.72	40.26
Germany, United	7.58	7.85
Canada	3.05	3.19
Czechoslovakia	1.11	0.92
Belgium	0.71	0.96
United Kingdom	3.88	6.80
Australia	1.57	1.22
Poland	0.11	0.96
USSR	17.93	12.05
Netherlands	1.16	1.33
Bulgaria	0.44	0.22
France	4.79	5.65
Egypt	0.00	0.00
Japan	13.00	9.22
Hungary	0.02	0.38
Romania	0.94	0.20
South Africa	0.00	0.42
Italy	3.74	3.55
Korea, Dem.	0.00	0.00
Spain	1.14	1.71
Yugoslavia	0.12	0.00
Greece	0.18	0.16
Venezuela	0.30	0.00
Argentina	0.17	0.45
Saudi Arabia	0.60	1.19
Portugal	0.05	0.06
Mexico	0.06	1.08
Chile	0.00	0.16
Korea, Rep.	0.22	0.00
Iran	0.02	0.00
Malaysia	0.01	0.00
Turkey	0.00	0.00
Colombia	0.00	0.00
Iraq	0.16	0.00
Syria	0.00	0.00
China	0.00	0.00
Algeria	0.18	0.00
Peru	0.00	0.00
Brazil	0.04	0.00
Morocco	0.00	0.00
Philippines	0.00	0.00
Thailand	0.00	0.00

(continued)

Appendix Table B-2 (Continued)

	Percentage Ability to Pay	
	1986-GNP $1800	1980-PPP $3400
India	0.00	0.00
Indonesia	0.00	0.00
Vietnam	0.00	0.00
Cote d'Ivoire	0.00	0.00
Pakistan	0.00	0.00
Sri Lanka	0.00	0.00
Kenya	0.00	0.00
Cameroon	0.00	0.00
Mozambique	0.00	0.00
Ghana	0.00	0.00
Nigeria	0.00	0.00
Sudan	0.00	0.00
Zaire	0.00	0.00
Burma	0.00	0.00
Madagascar	0.00	0.00
Tanzania	0.00	0.00
Uganda	0.00	0.00
Bangladesh	0.00	0.00
Ethiopia	0.00	0.00
Nepal	0.00	0.00
Total	100.00	100.00

Source: Authors.

Appendix Table B-3: Responsibility Indices

These are responsibility indices calculated as shown in Part III and normalized to 100%. Responsibility has been calculated using three Natural Debt (ND) thresholds, 5, 10, 20 tons/capita.

	Percentage Responsibility Emissions: 1950-86		
	ND threshold 5 tons	ND threshold 10 tons	ND threshold 20 tons
USA	33.31	36.00	39.01
Germany, United	8.06	8.61	9.08
Canada	2.57	2.74	2.87
Czechoslovakia	1.55	1.66	1.73
Belgium	0.95	1.01	1.06
United Kingdom	5.20	5.52	5.74
Australia	1.18	1.24	1.25
Poland	2.53	2.63	2.62
USSR	19.05	19.84	19.72
Netherlands	0.89	0.92	0.89
Bulgaria	0.53	0.54	0.53
France	3.11	3.20	3.06
Egypt	2.36	2.40	2.21
Japan	5.83	5.90	5.41
Hungary	0.50	0.50	0.45
Romania	0.92	0.91	0.78
South Africa	1.19	1.16	0.96
Italy	1.85	1.78	1.39
Korea, Dem.	0.53	0.48	0.31
Spain	0.85	0.75	0.40
Yugoslavia	0.48	0.41	0.21
Greece	0.20	0.17	0.08
Venezuela	0.34	0.29	0.12
Argentina	0.50	0.40	0.09
Saudi Arabia	0.19	0.15	0.03
Portugal	0.10	0.06	0.00
Mexico	0.74	0.41	0.00
Chile	0.11	0.06	0.00
Korea, Rep.	0.35	0.17	0.00
Iran	0.28	0.08	0.00
Malaysia	0.09	0.02	0.00
Turkey	0.20	0.00	0.00
Colombia	0.11	0.00	0.00
Iraq	0.05	0.00	0.00
Syria	0.03	0.00	0.00
China	2.94	0.00	0.00
Algeria	0.05	0.00	0.00
Peru	0.04	0.00	0.00
Brazil	0.24	0.00	0.00
Morocco	0.00	0.00	0.00
Philippines	0.00	0.00	0.00
Thailand	0.00	0.00	0.00
India	0.00	0.00	0.00

(continued)

Appendix Table B-3 (Continued)

	Percentage Responsibility Emissions: 1950-86		
	ND threshold 5 tons	ND threshold 10 tons	ND threshold 20 tons
Indonesia	0.00	0.00	0.00
Vietnam	0.00	0.00	0.00
Cote d'Ivoire	0.00	0.00	0.00
Pakistan	0.00	0.00	0.00
Sri Lanka	0.00	0.00	0.00
Kenya	0.00	0.00	0.00
Cameroon	0.00	0.00	0.00
Mozambique	0.00	0.00	0.00
Ghana	0.00	0.00	0.00
Nigeria	0.00	0.00	0.00
Sudan	0.00	0.00	0.00
Zaire	0.00	0.00	0.00
Burma	0.00	0.00	0.00
Madagascar	0.00	0.00	0.00
Tanzania	0.00	0.00	0.00
Uganda	0.00	0.00	0.00
Bangladesh	0.00	0.00	0.00
Ethiopia	0.00	0.00	0.00
Nepal	0.00	0.00	0.00
Total	100.00	100.00	100.00

Source: Authors.

Appendix Table B-4: Additively Combined Allocation Indices

Shown are four versions of the additive Assigned Allocation (RR) as discussed in Chapter III. As shown, these have been calculated using both gross national product (GNP) (1986) and purchasing power parity (PPP) (1980) for Ability to Pay (ATP) and at two Natural Debt (ND) thresholds (5 and 10 tons/capita) for Responsibility. Equal weighting is given each factor and the values have been normalized to 100%.

	Additively Combined Indices			
	ATP-GNP ND=5 Y-1986	ATP-GNP ND=10 Y-1986	ATP-PPP ND=5 Y-1980	ATP-PPP ND=10 Y-1980
USA	35.02	36.79	36.79	38.13
Germany, United	7.82	7.96	7.96	8.23
Canada	2.81	2.88	2.88	2.97
Czechoslovakia	1.33	1.24	1.24	1.29
Belgium	0.83	0.96	0.96	0.99
United Kingdom	4.54	6.00	6.00	6.16
Australia	1.38	1.20	1.20	1.23
Poland	1.32	1.75	1.75	1.80
USSR	18.49	15.55	15.55	15.95
Netherlands	1.03	1.11	1.11	1.13
Bulgaria	0.49	0.38	0.38	0.38
France	3.95	4.38	4.38	4.43
Egypt	1.18	1.18	1.18	1.20
Japan	9.42	7.53	7.53	7.56
Hungary	0.26	0.44	0.44	0.44
Romania	0.93	0.56	0.56	0.56
South Africa	0.60	0.81	0.81	0.79
Italy	2.80	2.70	2.70	2.67
Korea, Dem.	0.27	0.27	0.27	0.24
Spain	1.00	1.28	1.28	1.23
Yugoslavia	0.30	0.24	0.24	0.21
Greece	0.19	0.18	0.18	0.17
Venezuela	0.32	0.17	0.17	0.15
Argentina	0.34	0.48	0.48	0.43
Saudi Arabia	0.40	0.69	0.69	0.67
Portugal	0.08	0.08	0.08	0.06
Mexico	0.40	0.91	0.91	0.75
Chile	0.06	0.14	0.14	0.11
Korea, Rep.	0.29	0.18	0.18	0.09
Iran	0.15	0.14	0.14	0.04
Malaysia	0.05	0.05	0.05	0.01
Turkey	0.10	0.10	0.10	0.00
Colombia	0.06	0.06	0.06	0.00
Iraq	0.11	0.03	0.03	0.00
Syria	0.02	0.02	0.02	0.00
China	1.47	1.47	1.47	0.00
Algeria	0.12	0.03	0.03	0.00
Peru	0.02	0.02	0.02	0.00
Brazil	0.14	0.12	0.12	0.00
Morocco	0.00	0.00	0.00	0.00
Philippines	0.00	0.00	0.00	0.00

(continued)

Appendix Table B-4 (Continued)

	Additively Combined Indices			
	ATP-GNP ND=5 Y-1986	ATP-GNP ND=10 Y-1986	ATP-PPP ND=5 Y-1980	ATP-PPP ND=10 Y-1980
Thailand	0.00	0.00	0.00	0.00
India	0.00	0.00	0.00	0.00
Indonesia	0.00	0.00	0.00	0.00
Vietnam	0.00	0.00	0.00	0.00
Cote d'Ivoire	0.00	0.00	0.00	0.00
Pakistan	0.00	0.00	0.00	0.00
Sri Lanka	0.00	0.00	0.00	0.00
Kenya	0.00	0.00	0.00	0.00
Cameroon	0.00	0.00	0.00	0.00
Mozambique	0.00	0.00	0.00	0.00
Ghana	0.00	0.00	0.00	0.00
Nigeria	0.00	0.00	0.00	0.00
Sudan	0.00	0.00	0.00	0.00
Zaire	0.00	0.00	0.00	0.00
Burma	0.00	0.00	0.00	0.00
Madagascar	0.00	0.00	0.00	0.00
Tanzania	0.00	0.00	0.00	0.00
Uganda	0.00	0.00	0.00	0.00
Bangladesh	0.00	0.00	0.00	0.00
Ethiopia	0.00	0.00	0.00	0.00
Nepal	0.00	0.00	0.00	0.00
Total	100.00	100.00	100.00	100.00

Source: Authors.

Appendix Table B-5: Multiplicatively Combined Allocation Indices

In a similar way as Table B-4, four multiplicative Allocated Payment indices (RR) are shown with both gross national product (GNP) and purchasing power parity (PPP) and at two Natural Debt (ND) thresholds (5 and 10 tons/capita). Again, equal weighting has been given to both factors and the results are normalized to 100%.

Multiplicatively Combined Indices

	ATP-GNP ND=5 Y-1986	ATP-GNP ND=10 Y-1986	ATP-PPP ND=5 Y-1980	ATP-PPP ND=10 Y-1980
USA	69.51	70.33	75.92	76.61
Germany, United	3.47	3.47	3.58	3.57
Canada	0.45	0.44	0.46	0.46
Czechoslovakia	0.10	0.10	0.08	0.08
Belgium	0.04	0.04	0.05	0.05
United Kingdom	1.15	1.14	2.00	1.98
Australia	0.11	0.10	0.08	0.08
Poland	0.02	0.02	0.14	0.13
USSR	19.41	18.93	12.99	12.64
Netherlands	0.06	0.06	0.07	0.06
Bulgaria	0.01	0.01	0.01	0.01
France	0.85	0.82	0.99	0.96
Egypt	0.00	0.00	0.00	0.00
Japan	4.31	4.08	3.04	2.88
Hungary	0.00	0.00	0.01	0.01
Romania	0.05	0.05	0.01	0.01
South Africa	0.00	0.00	0.03	0.03
Italy	0.39	0.35	0.37	0.33
Korea, Dem.	0.00	0.00	0.00	0.00
Spain	0.06	0.05	0.08	0.07
Yugoslavia	0.00	0.00	0.00	0.00
Greece	0.00	0.00	0.00	0.00
Venezuela	0.01	0.00	0.00	0.00
Argentina	0.00	0.00	0.01	0.01
Saudi Arabia	0.01	0.00	0.01	0.01
Portugal	0.00	0.00	0.00	0.00
Mexico	0.00	0.00	0.05	0.02
Chile	0.00	0.00	0.00	0.00
Korea, Rep.	0.00	0.00	0.00	0.00
Iran	0.00	0.00	0.00	0.00
Malaysia	0.00	0.00	0.00	0.00
Turkey	0.00	0.00	0.00	0.00
Colombia	0.00	0.00	0.00	0.00
Iraq	0.00	0.00	0.00	0.00
Syria	0.00	0.00	0.00	0.00
China	0.00	0.00	0.00	0.00
Algeria	0.00	0.00	0.00	0.00
Peru	0.00	0.00	0.00	0.00
Brazil	0.00	0.00	0.00	0.00
Morocco	0.00	0.00	0.00	0.00
Philippines	0.00	0.00	0.00	0.00

(continued)

Appendix Table B-5 (Continued)

	Multiplicatively Combined Indices			
	ATP-GNP ND=5 Y-1986	ATP-GNP ND=10 Y-1986	ATP-PPP ND=5 Y-1980	ATP-PPP ND=10 Y-1980
Thailand	0.00	0.00	0.00	0.00
India	0.00	0.00	0.00	0.00
Indonesia	0.00	0.00	0.00	0.00
Vietnam	0.00	0.00	0.00	0.00
Cote d'Ivoire	0.00	0.00	0.00	0.00
Pakistan	0.00	0.00	0.00	0.00
Sri Lanka	0.00	0.00	0.00	0.00
Kenya	0.00	0.00	0.00	0.00
Cameroon	0.00	0.00	0.00	0.00
Mozambique	0.00	0.00	0.00	0.00
Ghana	0.00	0.00	0.00	0.00
Nigeria	0.00	0.00	0.00	0.00
Sudan	0.00	0.00	0.00	0.00
Zaire	0.00	0.00	0.00	0.00
Burma	0.00	0.00	0.00	0.00
Madagascar	0.00	0.00	0.00	0.00
Tanzania	0.00	0.00	0.00	0.00
Uganda	0.00	0.00	0.00	0.00
Bangladesh	0.00	0.00	0.00	0.00
Ethiopia	0.00	0.00	0.00	0.00
Nepal	0.00	0.00	0.00	0.00
Total	100.00	100.00	100.00	100.00

Source: Authors.

Appendix Table B-6: Emission Reduction Opportunity Indices

Shown here are the estimated relative carbon-equivalent emissions for the years 2000 and 2020, as discussed in Part IV. The totals are 9 gigatons carbon (GT) and 16 GT, respectively. These values are used to calculate the emission reduction opportunity index for three emissions thresholds (350, 100, and 50 g/$), as discussed in Part IV. Here, because the two Germanies are kept separate, there are 63 nations rather than 62 as in the other tables of Appendix B. Also, in distinction from the others, the columns have been normalized to 1.0.

	Projected Emissions 2000	Projected Emissions 2000	2000 REDX @ emissions threshold = 350 g/$	2020 REDX @ emissions threshold = 350 g/$	2020 REDX @ emissions threshold = 100 g/$	2020 REDX @ emissions threshold = 50 g/$
China	0.13	0.18	0.28	0.35	0.21	0.19
USSR	0.17	0.18	0.08	0.04	0.17	0.18
USA	0.15	0.10	0.00	0.00	0.07	0.09
India	0.04	0.05	0.06	0.10	0.06	0.06
SS Africa	0.04	0.04	0.10	0.08	0.04	0.04
Saudi Arabia	0.01	0.04	0.01	0.03	0.04	0.04
Nigeria	0.01	0.03	0.02	0.06	0.03	0.03
Brazil	0.05	0.04	0.07	0.00	0.03	0.04
Indonesia	0.03	0.03	0.06	0.04	0.03	0.03
Mexico	0.02	0.02	0.03	0.02	0.02	0.02
Algeria	0.01	0.02	0.00	0.03	0.02	0.02
Egypt	0.01	0.02	0.01	0.03	0.02	0.02
Poland	0.02	0.01	0.04	0.03	0.02	0.02
Korea, Rep.	0.01	0.02	0.00	0.00	0.02	0.02
Syria	0.00	0.01	0.01	0.02	0.02	0.01
Turkey	0.01	0.01	0.01	0.02	0.02	0.01
Thailand	0.01	0.01	0.03	0.02	0.01	0.01
Venezuela	0.01	0.01	0.01	0.02	0.01	0.01
Colombia	0.02	0.01	0.04	0.02	0.01	0.01
Australia	0.01	0.01	0.00	0.00	0.01	0.01
Romania	0.01	0.01	0.00	0.00	0.01	0.01
United Kingdom	0.02	0.01	0.00	0.00	0.01	0.01
Korea, Dem.	0.01	0.01	0.02	0.01	0.01	0.01
Germany, Dem.	0.01	0.01	0.01	0.00	0.01	0.01
Iran	0.01	0.01	0.00	0.00	0.01	0.01
Yugoslavia	0.01	0.01	0.01	0.01	0.01	0.01
Malaysia	0.01	0.01	0.01	0.00	0.01	0.01
Czechoslovakia	0.01	0.01	0.01	0.00	0.01	0.01
Spain	0.01	0.01	0.00	0.00	0.01	0.01
Greece	0.00	0.00	0.00	0.01	0.01	0.00
Germany, Rep.	0.02	0.01	0.00	0.00	0.01	0.01
Philippines	0.01	0.00	0.01	0.01	0.00	0.00
Bulgaria	0.01	0.00	0.01	0.00	0.00	0.00
Canada	0.01	0.01	0.00	0.00	0.00	0.01
Netherlands	0.01	0.01	0.00	0.00	0.00	0.01
Burma (Myanmar)	0.01	0.00	0.02	0.01	0.00	0.00
Peru	0.01	0.00	0.01	0.01	0.00	0.00
Bangladesh	0.00	0.00	0.00	0.01	0.00	0.00
Vietnam	0.00	0.00	0.01	0.01	0.00	0.00
Pakistan	0.00	0.00	0.00	0.00	0.00	0.00

(continued)

Appendix Table B-6: Emission Reduction Opportunity Indices (Continued)

	Projected Emissions 2000	Projected Emissions 2000	2000 REDX @ emissions threshold = 350 g/$	2020 REDX @ emissions threshold = 350 g/$	2020 REDX @ emissions threshold = 100 g/$	2020 REDX @ emissions threshold = 50 g/$
Argentina	0.00	0.00	0.00	0.00	0.00	0.00
Hungary	0.00	0.00	0.01	0.00	0.00	0.00
Italy	0.01	0.01	0.00	0.00	0.00	0.01
Portugal	0.00	0.00	0.00	0.00	0.00	0.00
Morocco	0.00	0.00	0.00	0.00	0.00	0.00
Iraq	0.00	0.00	0.00	0.00	0.00	0.00
Nepal	0.00	0.00	0.00	0.00	0.00	0.00
Belgium	0.00	0.00	0.00	0.00	0.00	0.00
Chile	0.00	0.00	0.00	0.00	0.00	0.00
Sri Lanka	0.00	0.00	0.00	0.00	0.00	0.00
France	0.01	0.01	0.00	0.00	0.00	0.00
Japan	0.03	0.02	0.00	0.00	0.00	0.00
Total Reduction (GT Carbon)	----	----	3.23	5.57	12.00	13.30
Remaining Emissions/GNP (g/$)	----	----	259.00	233.00	91.20	49.90

Source: Authors.

About the Authors and Editors

Mr. Dilip R. Ahuja is a Senior Scientist at The Bruce Company, Washington, D.C.

Mr. Dennis Anderson, who received master's degrees in econometrics and engineering from the London School of Economics and the University of Manchester, is currently Principal Economist at the World Bank. He was on the team of the World Bank's 1992 World Development Report which focused on the environment, was Visiting Professor in Environmental Economics at the University College of London in 1989-90, and Senior Associate Member of St. Antony's College, Oxford University. He was also Chief Economist of Shell International from 1987-89. He has published two books related to energy and the environment, as well as numerous other publications in the field.

Professor Wesley K. Foell, who holds a Ph.D. in Mechanical Engineering from the Stanford University, has been Director of the Energy Systems and Policy Research Program at the Energy Research Center of the University of Wisconsin in Madison since 1972 where he has been a faculty member in the Department of Nuclear Engineering since 1967. He is also President of Resource Management Associates of Madison, Inc. Among other positions, he has been Visiting Professor at the Asian Institute of Technology, head of various research groups and programs at the International Institute for Applied Systems Analysis (IIASA), a member of various advisory bodies for the State of Wisconsin and the U.S. Government, and a consultant for the World Bank, the U.S. Agency for International Development, the United Nations Development Program (UNDP), and the Organization for Economic Cooperation and Development (OECD). He has considerable years of experience in energy policy, modelling, and environment in developing countries and numerous publications in the field.

Dr. Collin W. Green is a Research Associate at Resource Management Associates of Madison, Inc.

Ms. Lisa A. Griffin holds a master's degree in education from the University of Massachusetts where she studied multi-cultural curriculum design and teacher training. She received her B.A. in international relations from Tufts University. Ms. Griffin is a Consultant in the Finance, Industry, and Energy Division of the Economic Development Institute (EDI) of the World Bank. Her primary responsibilities have been to edit and oversee the publication of EDI's energy training materials in French and English.

Dr. Mark E. Hanson, who holds a Ph.D. from the University of Wisconsin, is a faculty member of the Institute for Environmental Studies of the University of Wisconsin in Madison, a Scientist at the Energy Research Center of the University of Wisconsin, and Director of Technical Services for Resource Management Associates of Madison, Inc. He has several publications and years of experience in energy and environmental studies in developing countries, including conservation policy work and environmental assessments.

Ms. Rebekah Kanter was a Research Fellow at the Environment and Policy Institute of the East-West Center at the time this volume was written.

Dr. Morris Miller, who holds doctorate and master's degrees from McGill University and the London School of Economics, is currently Executive in Residence/Adjunct Professor at the University of Ottawa's Faculty of Administration. Immediately prior, he was on the Board of the World Bank as Executive Director for Canada and several other countries and Deputy Secretary-General for the UN Conference on New and Renewable Resources. He is the author of many books and articles dealing with the current and global situation, the most recent of which is *Debt and the Environment* [United Nations, 1991].

Dr. Corazón M. Siddayao, who received a Ph.D. and two master's degrees in Economics from the George Washington University, is Senior Energy Economist in charge of the Energy Program at the Economic Development Institute of the World Bank in Washington, D.C. Prior to joining the World Bank, she was Research Project Leader in charge of Energy and Industrialization at the East-West Center in Honolulu from 1978-1986, Senior Research Economist at the Institute of Southeast Asian Studies in Singapore from 1975-78, Expert-Consultant at the U.S. Federal Energy Administration from 1974-75, and consultant for various international organizations and governments. She has been Affiliate Professor in Economics at the University of Hawaii since 1978, holds an appointment as Professor of Economics at the University of the Philippines, was Visiting Fellow at the London School of Economics, and Visiting Professor at the Université de Montpellier I, Faculté de Droit et des Sciences Economiques. She is sole author of three books, two of which on petroleum were published by the Oxford University Press, co-author or editor of 17 others, as well as author of over 100 articles and informal publications in energy, the environment, and other fields. She is annotated in several *Who's Who* publications.

Dr. Kirk R. Smith, who holds three degrees from the University of California (Berkeley), including a Ph.D. in biomedical and environmental health sciences, is Research Associate and Program Coordinator in the Environment and Policy Institute (EAPI) of the East-West Center in Honolulu and is Coordinator of the World Health's Program on Environmental Risk and Development based at the Center. In 1978, he helped found, and led, the Energy Program at the Center. His work has focused principally on environmental risks in the developing countries of Asia. He has published six books and more than 80 articles on environment and energy issues in the Asia-Pacific region, and was elected in 1984 by editors and scientific advisers of the *Science Digest* as "One of America's 100 Brightest Young Scientists."

Dr. Joel Swisher is Professor in the Civil Engineering Department at Stanford University. He is currently at the Department of Environmental and Energy Systems Studies, Lund University, Sweden.

Index

Distributors of World Bank Publications

ARGENTINA
Carlos Hirsch, SRL
Galeria Guemes
Florida 165, 4th Floor-Ofc. 453/465
1333 Buenos Aires

AUSTRALIA, PAPUA NEW GUINEA, FIJI, SOLOMON ISLANDS, VANUATU, AND WESTERN SAMOA
D.A. Books & Journals
648 Whitehorse Road
Mitcham 3132
Victoria

AUSTRIA
Gerold and Co.
Graben 31
A-1011 Wien

BANGLADESH
Micro Industries Development Assistance Society (MIDAS)
House 5, Road 16
Dhanmondi R/Area
Dhaka 1209

Branch offices:
Pine View, 1st Floor
100 Agrabad Commercial Area
Chittagong 4100

76, K.D.A. Avenue
Kulna 9100

BELGIUM
Jean De Lannoy
Av. du Roi 202
1060 Brussels

CANADA
Le Diffuseur
C.P. 85, 1501B rue Ampère
Boucherville, Québec
J4B 5E6

CHILE
Invertec IGT S.A.
Americo Vespucio Norte 1165
Santiago

CHINA
China Financial & Economic Publishing House
8, Da Fo Si Dong Jie
Beijing

COLOMBIA
Infoenlace Ltda.
Apartado Aereo 34270
Bogota D.E.

COTE D'IVOIRE
Centre d'Edition et de Diffusion Africaines (CEDA)
04 B.P. 541
Abidjan 04 Plateau

CYPRUS
Center of Applied Research
Cyprus College
6, Diogenes Street, Engomi
P.O. Box 2006
Nicosia

DENMARK
SamfundsLitteratur
Rosenoerns Allé 11
DK-1970 Frederiksberg C

DOMINICAN REPUBLIC
Editora Taller, C. por A.
Restauración e Isabel la Católica 309
Apartado de Correos 2190 Z-1
Santo Domingo

EGYPT, ARAB REPUBLIC OF
Al Ahram
Al Galaa Street
Cairo

The Middle East Observer
41, Sherif Street
Cairo

FINLAND
Akateeminen Kirjakauppa
P.O. Box 128
SF-00101 Helsinki 10

FRANCE
World Bank Publications
66, avenue d'Iéna
75116 Paris

GERMANY
UNO-Verlag
Poppelsdorfer Allee 55
D-5300 Bonn 1

HONG KONG, MACAO
Asia 2000 Ltd.
46-48 Wyndham Street
Winning Centre
2nd Floor
Central Hong Kong

INDIA
Allied Publishers Private Ltd.
751 Mount Road
Madras - 600 002

Branch offices:
15 J.N. Heredia Marg
Ballard Estate
Bombay - 400 038

13/14 Asaf Ali Road
New Delhi - 110 002

17 Chittaranjan Avenue
Calcutta - 700 072

Jayadeva Hostel Building
5th Main Road, Gandhinagar
Bangalore - 560 009

3-5-1129 Kachiguda Cross Road
Hyderabad - 500 027

Prarthana Flats, 2nd Floor
Near Thakore Baug, Navrangpura
Ahmedabad - 380 009

Patiala House
16-A Ashok Marg
Lucknow - 226 001

Central Bazaar Road
60 Bajaj Nagar
Nagpur 440 010

INDONESIA
Pt. Indira Limited
Jalan Borobudur 20
P.O. Box 181
Jakarta 10320

IRELAND
Government Supplies Agency
4-5 Harcourt Road
Dublin 2

ISRAEL
Yozmot Literature Ltd.
P.O. Box 56055
Tel Aviv 61560

ITALY
Licosa Commissionaria Sansoni SPA
Via Duca Di Calabria, 1/1
Casella Postale 552
50125 Firenze

JAPAN
Eastern Book Service
Hongo 3-Chome, Bunkyo-ku 113
Tokyo

KENYA
Africa Book Service (E.A.) Ltd.
Quaran House, Mfangano Street
P.O. Box 45245
Nairobi

KOREA, REPUBLIC OF
Pan Korea Book Corporation
P.O. Box 101, Kwangwhamun
Seoul

MALAYSIA
University of Malaya Cooperative Bookshop, Limited
P.O. Box 1127, Jalan Pantai Baru
59700 Kuala Lumpur

MEXICO
INFOTEC
Apartado Postal 22-860
14060 Tlalpan, Mexico D.F.

NETHERLANDS
De Lindeboom/InOr-Publikaties
P.O. Box 202
7480 AE Haaksbergen

NEW ZEALAND
EBSCO NZ Ltd.
Private Mail Bag 99914
New Market
Auckland

NIGERIA
University Press Limited
Three Crowns Building Jericho
Private Mail Bag 5095
Ibadan

NORWAY
Narvesen Information Center
Book Department
P.O. Box 6125 Etterstad
N-0602 Oslo 6

PAKISTAN
Mirza Book Agency
65, Shahrah-e-Quaid-e-Azam
P.O. Box No. 729
Lahore 54000

PERU
Editorial Desarrollo SA
Apartado 3824
Lima 1

PHILIPPINES
International Book Center
Suite 1703, Cityland 10
Condominium Tower 1
Ayala Avenue, H.V. dela Costa Extension
Makati, Metro Manila

POLAND
International Publishing Service
Ul. Piekna 31/37
00-677 Warzawa

For subscription orders:
IPS Journals
Ul. Okrezna 3
02-916 Warszawa

PORTUGAL
Livraria Portugal
Rua Do Carmo 70-74
1200 Lisbon

SAUDI ARABIA, QATAR
Jarir Book Store
P.O. Box 3196
Riyadh 11471

SINGAPORE, TAIWAN, MYANMAR, BRUNEI
Information Publications Private, Ltd.
Golden Wheel Building
41, Kallang Pudding, #04-03
Singapore 1334

SOUTH AFRICA, BOTSWANA
For single titles:
Oxford University Press Southern Africa
P.O. Box 1141
Cape Town 8000

For subscription orders:
International Subscription Service
P.O. Box 41095
Craighall
Johannesburg 2024

SPAIN
Mundi-Prensa Libros, S.A.
Castello 37
28001 Madrid

Librería Internacional AEDOS
Consell de Cent, 391
08009 Barcelona

SRI LANKA AND THE MALDIVES
Lake House Bookshop
P.O. Box 244
100, Sir Chittampalam A. Gardiner Mawatha
Colombo 2

SWEDEN
For single titles:
Fritzes Fackboksforetaget
Regeringsgatan 12, Box 16356
S-103 27 Stockholm

For subscription orders:
Wennergren-Williams AB
P. O. Box 1305
S-171 25 Solna

SWITZERLAND
For single titles:
Librairie Payot
Case postale 3212
CH 1002 Lausanne

For subscription orders:
Librairie Payot
Service des Abonnements
Case postale 3312
CH 1002 Lausanne

TANZANIA
Oxford University Press
P.O. Box 5299
Maktaba Road
Dar es Salaam

THAILAND
Central Department Store
306 Silom Road
Bangkok

TRINIDAD & TOBAGO, ANTIGUA BARBUDA, BARBADOS, DOMINICA, GRENADA, GUYANA, JAMAICA, MONTSERRAT, ST. KITTS & NEVIS, ST. LUCIA, ST. VINCENT & GRENADINES
Systematics Studies Unit
#9 Watts Street
Curepe
Trinidad, West Indies

TURKEY
Infotel
Narlabahçe Sok. No. 15
Cagaloglu
Istanbul

UNITED KINGDOM
Microinfo Ltd.
P.O. Box 3
Alton, Hampshire GU34 2PG
England

VENEZUELA
Libreria del Este
Aptdo. 60.337
Caracas 1060-A